# Guidelines for Preparing
# Urban Plans

# Guidelines for Preparing Urban Plans

LARZ T. ANDERSON

**PLANNERS PRESS**

AMERICAN PLANNING ASSOCIATION
Chicago, Illinois    Washington, D.C.

Copyright 1995 by the American Planning Association

122 S. Michigan Ave., Chicago, IL 60603

Paperback edition ISBN 1-884829-06-6

Hardbound edition ISBN 1-884829-07-4

Library of Congress Catalog Card Number 94-77951

Printed in the United States of America

# Contents

# Tables

# Figures

# Acknowledgments

Many thanks to John Blayney, Norman Lind, Ray Mills, and Corwin Mocine for their very helpful suggestions.

# Foreword

The art and science of urban planning, in its many aspects, has been the subject of a series of books issued by the professional societies with headquarters in Chicago. The first of these, *Local Planning Administration*, was published in 1941 by the International City Managers Association. This work, edited by the late Ladislas Segoe, became the accepted authority for city planning in the 1940s. The task begun by the association was later taken over by the American Society of Planning Officials, also based in Chicago. Over the years the society, and its successor, the American Planning Association, produced studies, reports, and books that have been a major force in the evolution of the city planning profession. At the head of this line of influential works stands Larz Anderson's *Guidelines for Preparing Urban Plans*.

A comparison of this new volume with Segoe's 1941 work vividly illustrates the changes that have occurred in the theory and practice of urban planning over the last half-century. In 1941, when Segoe's work was published, what was considered city planning in the great majority of American cities and counties, consisted of the enforcement of zoning ordinances, and the regulation of land subdivision. The plan, in the service of which these regulatory processes allegedly were carried on, very seldom existed as an explicit set of public goals and policies. Often, the plan was implicit only in the regulatory processes themselves.

In the last half-century there has been a steady evolution in public understanding of the value of the city plan as a means of controlling the urban environment, conserving its existing values, and guiding its growth in desired directions. This new reliance on the plan, and the planning process, has produced two significant developments. First, planning has become far more complex, affecting a vastly wider range of issues. Second, new legislation and new public awareness has made the city plan much more powerful—seriously affecting property rights, land values, and the quality of urban life.

Today's set of legal and administrative tools for converting the plan into reality far exceeds the historic zoning and subdivision regulation in sophistication, complexity, and precision. Contemporary planning techniques and regulations now include:

• Analysis of environmental and economic impacts.

• Growth management controls.

• Exactions from land developers of money or land for public purposes.

• Special regulation and restriction in flood zones, seismic zones, coastal zones, agricultural zones, and others.

• Historic district regulations, including controls on building, rebuilding, and demolition.

• Master plan and design review requirements for major projects.

• Requirements for affordable housing in project development.

Each of these techniques places substantial limitations on property rights; each intervenes in the free operation of the market; and each imposes financial burdens on the property owner, the developer, and the community. Each new technique is designed to produce a more efficient, humane, and attractive community, and each derives its rationale from the community's comprehensive plan. Each one, therefore, will achieve its intended result, and justify its private and public costs, only to the extent that the plan is grounded in the community's needs and hopes. An effective plan must reflect an accurate picture of current conditions, present a challenging but achievable pattern for future development, and incorporate a fair and accurate assignment of its costs and benefits.

The procedures prescribed in this book will guide the planner in producing such a plan. From the identification of public needs and desires, the analysis of existing problems and opportunities, to the formulation of the plan and its several elements, each step is clearly and fully discussed. Sources of information and methods of analysis are described. The creative process leading from research and analysis to plan and policy is systematically explained.

Planning for the future is not and cannot be an exact science. However, the planner employing with care and judgment the methods presented in this book can have considerable confidence that his plan will achieve the goals it sets for itself.

Corwin R. Mocine,   AICP
Past President, American Institute of
    Planners and former director of planning
    for the cities of Phoenix, Berkeley, and
    Oakland. Now principal in the consulting
    firm of Williams and Mocine and professor
    emeritus at the University of California, Berkeley.

CHAPTER

# 1

# Introduction

**THE GOALS OF THIS BOOK ARE:**

• To introduce and describe some evolving concepts for the preparation of urban plans.

• To provide professional planners with specific guidelines, procedures, and techniques for preparing urban plans.

• To serve as an instructional guide for students of urban planning.

**The major concepts of this book:**

• This book concentrates on planning practice. The author describes the procedures currently used for preparing urban plans, as well as some of the emerging techniques.

• This book is intended for use in planning cities and counties where urban growth is an important local issue. It does not aspire to solve the problems of communities where social or economic conditions are the clearly dominant issues.

• This book is intended for use in planning medium-sized cities and counties in the United States. The procedures described here are probably too involved and expensive for small jurisdictions, and may not be complete enough or technically advanced enough for large jurisdictions.

• This book accepts, as a starting point, the basic concepts of the urban plan as described by T. J. Kent, Jr., in his book *The Urban General Plan*. That is, urban plans should:
—Be long-range
—Be comprehensive
—Be general
—Focus on physical development
—Be related to the social and economic forces that the plans propose to accommodate
—Be officially adopted by the local legislative body

**THE MAJOR RECOMMENDATIONS OF THIS BOOK:**

• The long-range general plan should consist of:
—A core, which identifies trends, issues, general goals, basic design concepts, major policies, and major plan proposals.
—An element for each major subject area in the plan. Land use and circulation ele-

1

ments, which must be prepared in conjunction with each other, are fundamental. Other elements, locally considered to be appropriate, should also be incorporated.

• Short-range "district plans" should be prepared for selected small areas, in addition to the jurisdiction-wide long-range general plan. These short-range plans should be consistent with the goals and policies of the long-range general plan, and should be adopted by the local legislative body. They should be used as the basis for selected plan-implementing measures, such as zoning ordinances and capital improvement programs.

• "Function plans" should be prepared for selected individual topics, such as mass transit, economic development, historic preservation, etc. These plans may be either long- or short-range. They may be jurisdiction-wide, or for sub-areas of a jurisdiction. A function plan may be adopted as an element of a long-range plan only if it is general in nature. If it is specific, it may be adopted as an element of a district plan, or it may remain as a stand-alone plan.

• Short-range district plans and function plans should identify and describe action programs that are appropriate to implement them.

• Long-range general plans should be general in character, and may be based on relatively generalized data. Short-range plans should be quite specific, and should be based on relatively specific data.

• As a general rule, land use plan diagrams for long-range general plans should not be "parcel-specific," but those for short-range district plans, which may be used as the basis for many plan-implementing programs, usually should.

• Long-range plans, which have a time horizon in the range of 15 to 25 years, should be amended as needed to remain up-to-date and continue to reflect the policies of the local legislative body. This implies an annual review, which may result in amendment, and a comprehensive review every five to seven years.

• Short-range plans, which have a time horizon of five or six years, should be reviewed, and possibly amended, annually. The timing of this review should be integrated into the annual budget preparation cycle of the local jurisdiction.

• The planning process should be considered as a continuous cycle. Preparation of a plan is not an end point; implementing the plan, and monitoring the impacts of implementation programs, are essential parts of the cycle.

• Plans, when published, should be kept separate from the publication of background data, and separate from the specifics of implementation programs (such as zoning ordinances and capital improvement programs).

**The book also contains:**

• "How-to-do-it" guidelines for undertaking many of the Tasks that are included in the planning process. These are intended as suggested planning techniques, not as the only acceptable methods.

• A section describing 31 plan-implementing programs.

• A bibliography of "where-to-turn-first" references.

• Selections from recent city and county plans, chosen to provide examples of good contemporary planning practice.

• An appendix that is a catchall of notes on

planning techniques, drawn from the author's 24 years of planning practice, and 17 years of teaching planning.

### What Kind of Urban Plans Are We Talking About?

The term "urban plan," as used in this text, is:

> A document (or series of documents), usually containing text, graphics, and statistics, which describes desired future conditions within the geographic area being considered.

• The urban plans described here are appropriate for use in small to medium-large cities and counties in the United States with populations from 5,000 to 500,000. The resourceful planner, however, should be able to simplify the planning process described here, so as to make it more affordable for small communities. Planners in large jurisdictions should be able to introduce more sophisticated procedures into the planning process than are included in this text.

• The plans described here are strongly oriented toward physical development, which must be appropriate to the local and social economic setting. There should be a linkage between physical planning, economic planning, and consideration of social factors.

• The planning process and procedures described in this book are not appropriate for regional planning or for state planning State and regional plans should not be "local plans writ large."

• The urban plans described here are those that are generally prepared for and adopted by public jurisdictions, such as cities or counties. They are rarely prepared for private developers or for private nonprofit agencies.

### The Intended Audience

The intended audience for the book includes:

**1.** Beginning professional planners who have not yet had broad experience.
**2.** Specialist planners who wish to relate their area of specialization to a comprehensive plan.
**3.** Experienced professional generalist planners who haven't prepared or updated a comprehensive plan recently.
**4.** Students of city and regional planning.

It is assumed that the reader of this book:

**1.** Is interested in learning about advanced professional practices used to prepare general plans for urban areas.
**2.** Is knowledgeable about urban planning goals and general planning techniques.
**3.** Is familiar with: T. J. Kent's book: *The Urban General Plan*, and So and Getzel's book: *The Practice of Local Government Planning* (Second edition).
**4.** Has ready access to Kaiser, Godschalk, and Chapin's *Urban Land Use Planning* (Fourth edition).

The hypothetical reader of this book is the planning director of a public planning agency, who is responsible for updating an existing plan, or preparing a new one. It is assumed that planning consultants, who have somewhat different responsibilities, can adapt the text to meet their needs. It is expected that staff planners with lesser roles, and specialist planners, will appreciate reading about "the big picture" of the various plans prepared in the planning process.

## This Text is Intended to Describe, Not Proselytize

While the author is a strong believer in the usefulness of urban general plans, this text is not intended to convert non-believers. It is meant for those who already know the values (and the limitations) of the planning process, and know that they need to prepare urban plans.

## This is Not a Book on Planning Theory

The recommendations in this text come from the work of professional planners, and from various writings on the theory of planning. The text does not attempt to trace how planning theory has affected planning practice, however. For those who wish to examine the subject, the following texts should be reviewed:

> Etzioni, Amatai. "Mixed-scanning: A Third Approach to Decision Making." Public Administration Review, December 1967. (This text is included in Faludi's Reader noted below.)
> Faludi, Andreas. *A Reader in Planning Theory.* Oxford, England: Pergamon Press, 1973.
> Meyerson, Martin. "Building the Middle-Range Bridge for Comprehensive Planning." Journal of the American Institute of Planners, Vol. 22, No. 2, 1956. (This text is included in Faludi's Reader.)

For texts on professional practice, the following are the most relevant:

> Kent, T. J., Jr. *The Urban General Plan.* Chicago, IL: American Planning Association, 1990. (A reprint of the 1964 edition.)
> So and Getzels, editors. *The Practice of Local Government Planning,* (Second edition). Chicago, IL: International City Management Association, 1988.

## The Origins of This Book

The material presented in this book is drawn from four major sources. First, some materials were derived from my experience as a professional planner with the City of Berkeley, California; with San Mateo County, California; and with the consulting firm of Spangle Associates, also of California. Second, attending and participating in professional meetings  the American Institute of Planners (AIP) (later, its successor organization, AICP) stimulated a lot of thought, and provided contact with planners who were advancing the state of the art. Third, some materials were derived from the class notes and assignments prepared for courses I taught in graduate planning programs at The Ohio State University, and at Virginia Tech. Fourth, some materials were derived from careful review of plans and reports prepared by public agencies and private planning consultants in many locations in the United States.

## About the Appendices

At the end of the book are a number of short reports on various urban planning topics. While many of these are directly related to the main text (and will be referenced where appropriate), several of them are not. It is hoped that the reader will find them useful and thought provoking.

## How to Use This Book

**1.** Don't apply the plan-making process described here blindly to any and all jurisdictions. Modify both the contents and the sequencing of the process to suit your local needs.

**2.** Remember that this text is intended to be inclusive, and to cover a wide variety of contingencies. Many of the topics and suggested techniques mentioned here may be inappropriate for your community. If they are not needed, don't include them in your planning program.

3. Add new topics to the scope of your plan-making as local circumstances dictate.

4. Prepare a work program to prepare and implement your community's plans. (Work programs are discussed in Task 1.12, and described further in Appendix C.)

Probably no jurisdiction should try to complete a plan-preparation program within a single year. The reports produced, and the number of meetings required, are usually more than the citizens of a community can digest in a short period of time, even if sufficient staff time is available. But, don't prepare a planning program that will drag on year after year without providing useful products at least every three to four months. Local elected officials will tell you that any program that doesn't produce tangible results within a two-year period is irrelevant.

# 2

# The Planning Process

## A GENERAL DEFINITION OF THE PLANNING PROCESS

The term planning when used in a general sense, can be defined as being "goal-directed problem solving activity." Urban planners didn't invent planning; the activity is a product of civilization, and has been used ever since mankind changed from being nomadic to agrarian, and planned ahead for food and shelter needed to survive difficult winters.

Planning is a widely used process, which typically includes problem identification, goal setting, design of alternative solutions, evaluation of potential impacts, decision-making, and implementation. When used in this sense, people in many walks of life, such as corporation officers, engineers, army generals, and taxicab drivers, use the planning process.

## THE PLANNING PROCESS AS USED IN THE FIELD

Urban and regional planners have used one form or another of the planning process since the inception of the planning profession. For example, Patrick Geddes long ago advocated this three step procedure: survey, analysis, plan.

Today, most planners use a planning process known to academicians as the *rational model*. Each planner who describes the process has his or her own version, and may identify from three to a dozen (or more) components in it. While a number of writers have criticized the rational model, it is beyond the scope of this book to comment on those criticisms. The fact remains that this form of the planning process is far and away the most widely used planning procedure.

6

**Table 2-1**
**Typical Form of the Urban Planning Process**

1. Identify issues and options.
2. State goals and objectives; identify priorities.
3. Collect and interpret data.
4. Prepare plans.
5. Draft programs for plan implementation.
6. Evaluate potential impacts of plans and implementing programs, and modify the plans accordingly.
7. Review and adopt plans.
8. Review and adopt implementation programs.
9. Administer plan-implementing programs, monitor their impacts, and amend plans in response to feedback.

Notes

A. Public participation is appropriate in many, but not necessarily all, Phases of the planning process.
B. Some Phases of the planning process can be undertaken concurrently, while others should be done consecutively.
C. There usually should be considerable recycling among the various Phases of the planning process as it proceeds. That is, after an advanced Phase of the process has been completed, it is often appropriate to return to an earlier Phase and revise it.

The steps included in the planning process are given in Table 2-1, and their relationships are illustrated schematically in Figure 2-1.

## APPLICATION OF THE PLANNING PROCESS

Urban and regional planners use the planning process as the core of their professional practice. It is true that many planners devote a considerable amount of their time to one phase of the process or another in their day-to-day activities (e.g., administration of regulatory measures, impact analysis, urban design, budget preparation), but the hallmark of the professional planner is the knowledge of and ability to use the planning process in its entirety as a procedure to resolve a broad range of interrelated issues found in urban areas.

The urban planner may use the planning process when attacking a single subject or *function,* such as off-street parking, housing for the elderly, or library services. When this is done, it should be used in a manner that relates the topic being planned to the larger societal context.

The urban planner also uses the planning process to plan concurrently for a wide range of interrelated topics that are of concern to a particular urban area. This activity is generally known as *comprehensive planning.* Documents that result from this process are called *Comprehensive Plans* or *General Plans.*

Some planners avoid using the terms "comprehensive planning" and "comprehensive plan" because the adjective "comprehensive" may imply to some people an all-inclusive range of topics related to the urban scene. They contend that urban planners should not profess to be knowledgeable about everything that relates to urban life; we have limited knowledge and limited resources, and we therefore cannot be truly comprehensive.

The following pages summarize one version of the planning process. While steps in the procedure are listed in numerical order, two points should be emphasized:

**1.** Some of the steps can and should be undertaken concurrently. (For example, Step 3, Data Collection, will probably start concurrently with Step 2, State Goals, and continue henceforth.)

**2.** The various steps are highly interactive. Planners should expect to use a "cut-and-try" procedure, in which one part of the plan is "cut to fit" a specific situation, and then evaluated to see how well it fits with other parts. If the part doesn't fit harmo-

**Figure 2–1** The Planning Process

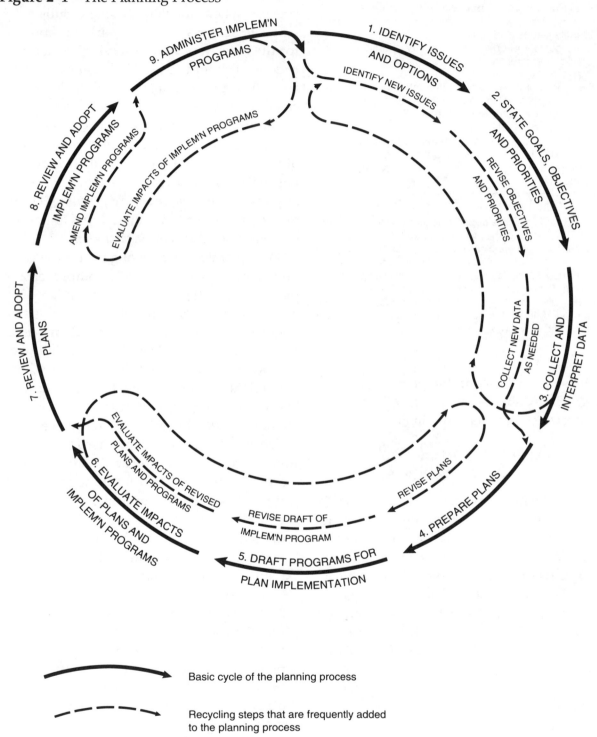

Basic cycle of the planning process

Recycling steps that are frequently added to the planning process

niously, adjustments need to be made to the new part, to the old parts, or to all of them.

## STEPS IN THE PLANNING PROCESS

### Step 1: Identify Issues and Options

To be relevant, the planning process must identify and address not only the contemporary issues of concern to residents, workers, property owners, and business people, but also the emerging issues that will be important in the future. The issues considered should be primarily those that can be affected by local decisions, rather than those that are regional, statewide, or global in scope.

The major development options open to the community should also be identified at this time. What are the choices that the residents must make?

Identification of issues and options requires good communication between the planners and the people who will be affected by the plan. This communication should be established early in the planning process, and continued throughout its course.

### Step 2: State Goals, Objectives, Priorities

Whose goals? Whose objectives? Whose priorities? In a fairly homogeneous society these questions are usually resolved quite quickly. However, in a heterogeneous society, with many minority groups (some advantaged, some disadvantaged) reaching consensus on goals, objectives, and priorities is far more difficult, if not impossible. Sometimes agreement can be reached only on the broadest of goals, and specific objectives and priorities must be worked out on an incremental basis using negotiation and compromise. This step in the planning process requires intensive communication between the planning staff and people who have an interest in the local community.

### Step 3: Collect and Interpret Data

The subject matter and degree of detail of data to be collected and interpreted depends upon which issues are important, what data is readily available, the cost in time and money to collect new data, and the resources available (manpower, time, and money) for data collection. Information is usually needed to describe and analyze the economic, social, and political structure of the planning area, as well as the man-made and natural environment. Table 2-2 presents in summary form a listing of data that is often considered desirable to have when preparing an urban general plan for a community. (In this text the term "data" is considered to be a singular noun, as it frequently is outside of academic circles. Also, "manpower," "mankind," etc. are general terms, intended to include both sexes.)

### Step 4: Prepare Plans

The general plan usually consists of a *core* plus supplemental *elements*. The geographic scope of the plan should include all of the jurisdiction being planned for, plus those adjacent lands that directly impact on it. The subject matter of the plan should include all (or most) of the planning-related topics of greatest concern to the residents of the planning area. Usually the core of the plan should include basic discussion of population, economic activity, land use, and circulation. The elements of the general plan augment the core, and provide more specific consideration of various topics than is possible in the core. Elements may be jurisdiction-wide plans for

**Table 2-2**
**Topics for Which Data is Frequently Gathered During the Preparation of an Urban General Plan**

**Natural Environment**
Slope of terrain
Topographic features
Climate
Vegetation
Fish and wildlife
Geology
Geologic hazards
Mineral resources
Soils and soil capabilities
Water resources
Flood hazards
Noise
Air quality
Water quality

**Built Environment**
Land use
Location and size of employment centers
Visual qualities
Housing (quantity and quality)
Historic sites and buildings
Architecturally significant buildings
Water supply system
Storm drainage systems
Waste water management
Road system
Building permit record

**Government**
Governmental organization
Jurisdictional boundaries
Political conditions
Land development regulations
Zoning
Annexation policies
Assessment practices
Tax rates
Governmental and political issues

**Traffic and Transportation**
Trip generator location
Number of trips generated
Traffic volumes
Road capacities
Transit service
Truck transportation
Air transportation
Rail transportation
Water transportation

**Social and Economic Conditions**
Population size and characteristics
Income characteristics
Retail sales volumes
Labor force characteristics
Social problems
Crime statistics
Cost of living
Agricultural production
Mineral production
Timber production

**Public Services and Facilities**
Fire protection
Police protection
Schools
Libraries
Churches
Parks and recreation
Solid waste management
Health care

**Other**
Land ownership patterns
Location of growth areas
Location of declining areas
Identification of neighborhood characteristics

individual functions, such as rapid transit, fire protection, recreation, or they can be plans for a small segment of the jurisdiction, such as the central business district, the waterfront, or a problem residential area, for which a wide range of topics is considered.

*Elements in General Plans* The land use and the circulation elements usually form a foundation for a general plan. Other elements are added as considered to be appropriate.

A 1992 survey of city and county planning agencies in California (Governor's Office of Planning and Research, "The California Planners' 1993 Book of Lists,") indicated that the following topics were most frequently considered, in addition to the ubiquitous land use and circulation elements:

Community services and facilities;

Parks and recreation;

Utilities;

Housing; and

The natural environment.

Other, but somewhat less popular topics included:

Urban design;

Economic development;

Growth management; and

Historic preservation

*Organization of the General Plan.* Urban general plans are often organized using the outline indicated in Table 2-3. This organization has proved to be easy for the reader to comprehend, and reasonably effective.

## Step 5: Draft Programs for Implementing the Plan

Most people who are concerned with the future of their community want to know what programs will be used to implement a proposed plan, how much the programs will cost, in terms of dollars and restrictions on personal freedom, and whether the programs will achieve the community's goals. Therefore, planners should develop information on these topics before asking that the urban general plan be officially adopted.

The most widely known plan-implementation programs fall into five major categories:

**1.** The enactment and administration of local governmental regulations concerning land use and land development (for example: zoning codes, subdivision codes, building codes, housing codes, grading ordinances, etc.).

**Table 2-3**
**Typical Organization of a Long-Range Urban General Plan**

1. Background
   —Summary of present conditions
   —Assumptions concerning the future
   —Projections of growth or change
   —Current and emerging issues
2. Goals and general policies
3. Overview of major plan proposals
4. Inclusion of Elements, one by one

**Suggested Organization of an Element Within a Long-Range Urban General Plan**

1. Background
   —Summary of present conditions
   —Projections of change or transformation
   —Current and emerging issues
2. Goals and policies
3. Plan recommendations
4. Strategies to implement plan recommendations (sometimes in a "who-does-what" format)

Notes
1. Treatment of the elements in a plan:
   Elements are treated like plans within a plan. That is to say, each element often follows the general outline provided above, but restricts the discussion to the topic of the element.
2. Treatment of appendices:
   The topics included as appendices should be published separately, completely apart from the plan. Subject matter of appendices may include:
   A. Background data
   B. Analysis of the probable impacts of the plan proposals and of the plan-implementation programs
3. Treatment of plan-implementation programs:
   Implementation programs, such as zoning ordinances and capital improvement programs, are not parts of an urban general plan, and should not be published or presented as such.

**2.** Project review (for example: the review of Impact Statements).

**3.** Programs undertaken by local government to provide public services (for example: community recreation programs).

**4.** Construction programs undertaken by local government (for example: construction of a sewage disposal plant).

5. Construction programs undertaken by private individuals or firms (for example: new subdivisions, new employment centers).

Table 2-4 provides a matrix which illustrates methods used to implement urban general plans.

Implementation methods also are discussed in some detail in Chapter 11.

### Step 6: Evaluate Potential Impacts of Plans and Implementing Programs

The impact evaluation Phase of both the plan and of the contemplated implementation programs should include analysis of:

1. Probable environmental impacts.
2. Potential impacts on the local economy (changes in employment, retail sales, etc.).
3. Potential impacts on local government finance (costs of providing services, tax revenues, tax rates, etc.).
4. The social consequences that would probably result.

While the plan is being prepared, its potential impacts should be considered concurrently. If severe adverse impacts are found, planners should modify the plan or the implementing programs to eliminate or substantially mitigate their effects.

**Table 2-4**
**Examples of Methods Used to Implement Urban Plans**

| Activity | Body Taking Action | |
|---|---|---|
| | Public Agencies | Private Individuals, Firms, or Institutions |
| Construction of physical facilities | Public buildings<br>Arterial roads<br>Trunk sewers | Private buildings<br>Subdivision streets<br>Local sewer lines |
| Provision of services | Public schools<br>Transit systems<br>Housing subsidies | Private schools<br>Use of private cars<br>Rental housing |
| Regulation of land use and development | Zoning codes<br>Subdivision codes<br>Housing codes<br>Environmental standards | Deed restrictions |
| Project review | Impact assessments<br>environmental,<br>social, economic,<br>etc.<br>Design review | Design review<br>Feasibility analysis |
| Fiscal policies | Property taxes<br>Exactions and fees<br>Preferential assessment | User charges<br>Homeowners association dues |

### Step 7: Review and Adopt Plans

The urban general plan with all its components, is intended to be adopted as a statement of the policy of the local jurisdiction, and as a commitment to a future course of action.

This step usually includes a broad public information program, followed by official public hearings, and then by official adoption of the plan.

It is essential that those who adopt a plan have a clear understanding of the policies included in the plan, and their implications. Members of a local legislative body should never be asked to adopt a plan they don't understand, or to adopt a plan-implementation program that may result in some unwelcome surprises later.

### Step 8: Review and Adopt Plan-Implementing Programs

This step requires that those who will be affected by the implementation programs be aware of the contents and implications of those programs, before their adoption. Public hearings and official adoption follow.

### Step 9: Administer Implementing Programs; Monitor Their Impacts

The administration of plan-implementation programs is the Phase of the planning process that is most visible to the public eye. It also usually requires the major share of planning staff time and budget. Feedback from those who are affected by the programs to the staff, to the planning commission, and to the legislative body, is an essential part of this process.

### PLANS REQUIRE CONTINUOUS REVIEW AND PERIODIC UPDATING

The planning process is not finished with the completion of the nine steps summarized above. Collecting and analyzing information, and implementing urban general plans is an ongoing process. Policy statements require occasional revision to respond to new conditions; long-range goals need periodic review. As times change, economic conditions change; social values and priorities change.

The effective urban planner uses the planning process as a *continuous* program for keeping the plans of the community current and relevant, and the implementing programs fair and effective. For these reasons it is important to review plans and their implementing programs on a regular basis, and to keep them up-to-date. This usually should be done by:

**1.** Having the planning staff observe, on a continuing basis, notable events and significant trends that are related to the planning program.

**2.** Having the planning commission and the legislative body hold an annual review of the general plan.

**3.** Undertaking a major review and revision program of the general plan every five to seven years.

### References

Kaiser, Godschalk, and Chapin. *Urban Land Use Planning,* 4th ed. Urbana: University of Illinois Press, 1995.

Kent, T. J., Jr. *The Urban General Plan.* Chicago: American Planning Association, 1991 (a reprint of the 1964 edition).

California Office of Planning and Research. *General Plan Guidelines.* Sacramento: Office of Planning and Research, State of California, 1990.

So and Getzels. *The Practice of Local Government Planning,* 2d ed. Washington: International City Management Association, 1988. (See Chapter 3, General Development Plans, and Chapter 4, District Planning.)

CHAPTER

# 3

# Plans

## CHARACTERISTICS OF GENERAL PLANS CONSIDERED HERE

The basic concept of the general plan as described by Hollander, Pollock, Reckinger, and Beal in *The Practice of Local Government Planning* (So and Getzels, editors. *The Practice of Local Government Planning*, 2d ed., Washington: International City Management Association, 1988. See pp. 60-61), accurately reflects good urban planning practice today. They describe the general plan as having these characteristics:

> First, it is a *physical plan*. Although a reflection of social and economic values, the plan is fundamentally a guide to the physical development of the community. It translates values into a scheme that describes how, why, when, and where to build, rebuild, or preserve the community. . . .
>
> A second characteristic of the general plan is that it is *long-range*, covering a time period greater than one year, usually five years or more. . . .
>
> A third characteristic of a general development plan is that it is *comprehensive*. It covers the entire city geographically—not merely one or more sections. It also encompasses all the functions that make a community work, such as transportation, housing, land use, utility systems, and recreation. Moreover, the plan considers the interrelationships of functions. . . .
>
> Finally, a plan is a *guide to decision-making* by the planning commission and the governing board and mayor or manager. . . .

## COMPREHENSIVE PLANNING OR LIMITED PLANNING?

Let us discuss "comprehensive planning" and "limited planning".

*Comprehensive planning* is used here as being:

(a) For a broad range of topics
and (b) For a wide geographic area
and (c) For a long time span

*Limited planning* is used here as being:

(a) For a narrow range of topics
or (b) For a small geographic area
or (c) For a short time span
or (d) For one or more of the above

We need comprehensive planning to:

1. Provide a vision of the long-term future design and character of the community.
2. Show the importance and the interrelatedness of many topics.
3. Show the interdependencies among geographic areas.
4. Show potential long-term impacts.
5. Represent the interests of a broad range of citizens, rather than a few special-interest groups.

We need limited planning to:
1. Recommend solutions to problems centering on individual topics, such as affordable housing.
2. Recommend plans for the future of small distinct geographic areas, such as central business districts.
3. Recommend specific actions to be taken in the near future, such as identifying the projects to be included in the next capital improvement program.
4. Respond to the concerns of specific segments of the general public, such as farmers.

Comprehensive planning, when compared to limited planning, has these advantages:
1. It provides an overall picture of the future of the planning area, and of conditions that will come into being there. This is valuable to those who can comprehend it.
2. It considers the interrelatedness of many topics, and geographic areas.
3. It provides a vehicle for many people, from a broad spectrum of interests, to participate in the planning and decision-making process.
4. The data required can often be collected in a generalized form, rather than a detailed basis.

Comprehensive planning has these disadvantages:
1. It requires a vast amount and a wide variety of data collection and analysis; this is expensive and time consuming.
2. Large groups take longer to reach consensus than do small groups of people who have a common interest.
3. Effective citizen participation in the review of long-range general plans may be difficult to organize. It is usually much harder to get citizens from a broad spectrum of the population to consider a wide range of topics than it is to get special-interest groups to consider a narrow range of topics.
4. Sometimes there is a tendency to recommend actions concerning the distant future, which closes off options better left open.
5. Commitments on long-term projects, in some cases, may bring about changes that are difficult to reverse or modify.
6. Long-range plans are usually not very useful as the basis for compiling short-range capital improvement programs; they tend to contain statements of general policy rather than descriptions of specific projects.
7. Long-range plans are often not well-suited as guides for zoning decisions. This causes problems in those states that require zoning to be consistent with the comprehensive plan.
8. The means of implementing long-range plans are often not apparent, or do not exist, when the plan is being prepared or reviewed. This introduces substantial uncertainty into the planning process.
9. Most lay citizens have difficulty conceptualizing possible conditions in the distant future. With no clear pathway to the future,

they become bewildered when thinking about how we get from where we are today to where we want to be a generation from now.

Limited planning, when compared to comprehensive planning, has these advantages:
**1.** It has limited data requirements.
**2.** Single-topic planning is easier to comprehend than multi-topic planning.
**3.** Short-range projections are more reliable than long-range projections. (The further into the future you project, the greater are the uncertainties, and the greater the chances of error).
**4.** It involves fewer people in the plan-review and the decision-making processes, and is therefore often a much quicker procedure, and one that stirs up less controversy.
**5.** It is a relatively simple procedure, because it reduces the number of combinations and permutations among the factors involved.
**6.** The means of implementing a plan for the near future are usually evident, and their costs, benefits, and impacts can be estimated with considerable certainty.
**7.** It is usually quite easy to get citizen participation in the planning process for small-area or single-topic plans, especially if they are short-range and specific.
**8.** Short-range plans usually can be used as the basis for preparing or reviewing capital improvement programs.
**9.** Short-range plans are far more appropriate for guiding zoning decisions than are long-range plans.
**10.** Making decisions that are limited in geographic area or in the scope of topics makes it possible to observe the effects of

plan-implementing actions. If an action turns out to be unwise, it may be that only a little damage has been done, and corrections may be made quickly.

Limited planning has these disadvantages:
**1.** It often omits consideration of the views and interests of people who are not directly involved with the topic or the area under consideration, although these people may later be affected by secondary or tertiary impacts.
**2.** Single-topic planning usually does not consider the interrelatedness of the many topics found in urban life today.
**3.** Small-area planning sometimes does not consider the relationships of the planning area to surrounding geographic areas.
**4.** Small-area planning sometimes does not consider possible policy precedents being set that will apply to similar areas or similar situations.
**5.** Politically expedient short-term plans often disregard long-term implications.
**6.** The data required for plan preparation, while not for a large area or for a wide range of topics, should be quite detailed and specific.

## COMMENTS ON SOME RECENT GENERAL PLANS

A criticism can be leveled at a number of general plans that have been produced recently: they appear to be excessively long and excessively expensive to prepare. (In 1990 a planning consultant estimated that the minimum fees for preparing an "average general plan" for a "small city" would be about $100,000. In 1994 another consultant offered the rule of thumb that it takes about five planner-years to prepare a general plan for a medium-sized California city or county. A nearby California city, of 100,000 population, in 1991-92 spent about $500,000 to update its general plan.)

Some lengthy plans are incomprehensible when considered as an entity, although each separate "element" in them may be understandable. When this is the case, it is very difficult to grasp "the big picture" of what is planned.

Some plans are very expensive to print and distribute. This means that these plans are not readily accessible to the general public. (For example: one urbanized California county published a general plan in 1986 that came in two volumes, had 1,441 pages, weighed 15 pounds, and had a sale price of $121.)

When plans are expensive to prepare, small jurisdictions cannot afford them, and large jurisdictions are reluctant to revise them, except when fearful of legal action.

Many states have enacted laws requiring cities and counties to prepare general plans, and have mandated what "elements" must be included in these plans. Some of these mandated elements add substantially to the cost of plan preparation. Some of them are not really plans, but are programs to implement plans. Capital improvement programs, zoning ordinances, and housing programs are examples of this practice.

In a review of recent (1988-93) general plans produced by cities and counties, it was found that their contents could be placed in one or more of the following categories:

**1.** Background data—its collection, analysis, and publication for the local jurisdiction and its environs (e.g., population size and characteristics, economic activity, land use, housing inventory, traffic flow, etc.).

**2.** Long-range plans—(i.e., for 15 to 30 years) for the entire jurisdiction, usually organized by subject matter elements. Many of these elements are mandated by state legislation; some are optional.

**3.** Short-range plans—(i.e., for up to five years). These are rarely multi-topic plans for the entire jurisdiction; most often they are for sub-areas (e.g., coastal areas), or for individual topics.

**4.** Implementation programs—(e.g., capital improvement programs, solid waste management programs, housing programs, etc.)

All four of the subject areas are bona fide subjects for planners, and are usually worthwhile doing. However, if two, three or even four of the topics are lumped together in one document, under the heading of "a general plan," they can result in a document that is long, difficult for the layman to understand, in need of frequent amendment, and expensive to produce.

### Recommendations

Some planning practices are in need of reform; plan-preparation programs should include the following five major sections:

**1.** Background data collection, analysis, and publication.

**2.** Long-range general plans, for the entire planning area.

**3.** Short-range district plans, prepared first for fast-changing areas, then for stable areas, as time permits.

**4.** Function plans, for individual topics.

**5.** Plan-implementing programs, usually based on short-range district plans, or function plans, but consistent with the goals and policies of the long-range general plan.

### Background Data

Background data should be collected, analyzed and then published in one or more separate reports, *not* as a part of a general plan. Summaries of relevant data are often appropriate in plans, however. In addition to published data reports, cities and counties should establish data banks. Background data reports be should *not* be "officially adopted" under normal circumstances.

### General Plans

General plans of 15-to-25 year time spans should be prepared for cities and counties. They should be long-range, jurisdiction-wide, general in character, and consider multiple topics. This plan should have many of the characteristics recommended by Kent in his book *The Urban General Plan*. (See T. J. Kent, Jr., op. cit.) This plan should serve as the foundation of the local planning program.

The long-range plan should consider long-range goals, and fundamental urban development policies. It should also contain recommendations for development programs that have long-term implications, such as basic land use patterns, basic circulation patterns, and general growth management policies. It need not always contain discussion of specific implementation measures, because these may not be known when considering conditions 15 to 25 years in the future.

General plans should consist of an overview section plus a number of elements. The geographic area considered should consist of the entire jurisdiction plus surrounding areas of concern. The elements included should be those that are truly long-range in nature, rather than those that address short-term issues that are here and must be resolved soon. They should have the characteristics described by Hollander, Pollock, Reckinger, and Beal, quoted earlier in this chapter. (See So and Getzels, pp. 60-61, op. cit.)

The type of general plan recommended here should not be a replication of the present-day voluminous report; it should be simpler and shorter. It should emphasize concepts, be general in nature, and be policy-oriented.

This is the plan that should be officially adopted as "the general plan" for the community. The long-range general plan should be carefully reviewed every five to seven years, and shortly after any major shifts in the balance of local political power.

### District Plans

District plans should be short-range, for small areas, be specific in character, and consider multiple topics. These plans should have many of the characteristics recommended by Sedway in his chapter, "District Planning" in *The Practice of Local Government Planning*. (See So and Getzels, Chapter 4, op. cit.)

District plans should be prepared first for areas of a jurisdiction where changes are occurring or are anticipated, such as:

1. Areas where many subdivisions are anticipated
2. Central business districts
3. Historic preservation districts
4. Threatened open space preservation areas
5. Redevelopment areas
6. Areas proposed for annexation

District plans for areas where significant change is occurring should be reviewed annually. It is desirable to prepare district plans for all sections of the larger jurisdiction, if time and budget permit. The areas within a jurisdiction where there may be a low priority for the preparation of district plans are those such as: stable residential areas; stable industrial areas; and stable, unthreatened open space areas.

District plans for stable areas should probably be reviewed about every five years. District plans should be consistent with the long-range general plan. (*Consistent:* An action program, or project, is consistent with the general plan if, considering all its aspects, it will further the objectives of the general plan and not obstruct their attainment. Source: California Office of Planning and Research, *General Plan Guidelines,* 1990.) District plans are discussed further in Chapter 9.

### Function Plans

Function plans are plans for a single topic, with tie-ins to related subjects (examples of topics of function plans: mass transit, housing, open space). They may be either short-range or long-range; they may cover an entire planning area, or a sub-section of it.

Long-range jurisdiction-wide function plans that are general in character may be appropriate for inclusion in the general plan as an *element.* Those that are specific in character are not appropriate for inclusion in a general plan, but are better suited as "stand-alone" development plans.

Short-range small-area function plans are often quite specific. Local circumstances will dictate whether they are suitable for inclusion in district plans as "elements," or whether they should be treated as stand-alone plans.

Short-range function plans should be consistent with long-range function plans, if such have been prepared and adopted. Function plans should be consistent with the long-range general plan.

### Plan-Implementing Programs

Plan-implementing programs include such topics as zoning ordinances, subdivision ordinances, capital improvement programs, housing programs, waste management programs, etc. These should be consistent with the short-range plans. Plan implementing programs are discussed in Chapter 11. Implementation programs should, of course, be formally adopted by the local legislative body, but *not* made a part of the general plan, even by reference.

## ADOPTING PLANS

It is desirable (and required by law in many states) to have the planning commission and the legislative body of a local jurisdiction officially adopt the general plan.

A number of states require that certain plan-implementing programs (such as zoning ordinances and capital improvement programs) be consistent with the officially adopted plan. This causes problems when the official plan is long-range, and shows conditions that are appropriate for the distant future (e.g., 20 years from now), while the plan-implementing programs are enacted to reflect current conditions. For example, a long-range plan may indicate that a remote rural area may be transformed into a high density urban area 20 years from now, after roads, utilities, community facilities, etc. are available, and market conditions warrant development. Changing the zoning of the area under the present conditions of the infrastructure and market forces might well encourage the creation of "paper subdivisions" and "leap-frog development."

The use of short-range plans can avoid this problem; they show development that is appropriate for the near future, and can be implemented using existing programs. Some jurisdictions concentrate on short-range planning, and have virtually abandoned long-range planning.

Many planners say that long-range *and* short-range plans are needed; they believe that the abandonment of long-range planning is short-sighted.

If your state's laws require that plan-implementing ordinances be consistent with the general plan of your local government, then perhaps your government can adopt a long-range general plan to serve as a framework for more detailed short-range planning, and adopt a series of short-range district plans as supplements to the long-range plan. The short-range plans should, of course, be consistent with the long-range plan, and the plan-implementing programs should be consistent with the short-range plans.

You should review this possibility with your city attorney or county counsel.

## COMMENTS ON GENERAL PLANS AND DISTRICT PLANS

District plans should represent a bridge between present conditions and the future, which is conceptualized in the long-range general plan. They should emphasize short-term specific objectives rather than long-term general goals. They should contain specific development policies and recommendations. Their time spans should be about five years.

Topics that require resolution in the near future, such as economic development, and housing programs, should be included in district plans. General plans may consider the long-term policies for these topics, but should generally not include the short-term action programs needed for their resolution.

Some aspects of growth (e.g., population, housing demand, employment) projected in the general plan should be quantified in five-year increments. District plans should be oriented toward attaining the first five-year increment of the long-range general plan.

Both general and district plans should be centered on physical development, but neither should be limited to that. The plans should start out by illustrating the agreed-upon concepts of how the physical parts of the planning area should be organized and interrelated (e.g., land use and circulation), and this should serve as a basic framework for other topics.

The general plan should be carefully reviewed about every five to seven years, and shortly after any major shifts in the local balance of political power. Many (but, not necessarily all) district plans and short-range function plans should be reviewed each year, preferably as an early step in the annual capital improvement program process.

### A Cautionary Note

This book identifies and describes many Tasks that can be used to prepare long-range general plans, short-range district plans, and function plans. You may note, after reviewing the scope of the following text, that the amount of work involved, if you were to undertake all the Tasks, would be quite staggering.

Some of the Tasks are probably not appropriate to undertake for your jurisdiction.

This book probably outlines more work than your jurisdiction and your staff can complete within a reasonable period of time. After reviewing the contents of the book, you should decide what type of plan-preparation program is most appropriate for your jurisdiction at this time. Do you need to:

1. Revise your long-range general plan?
2. Prepare some short-range district plans?
3. Prepare some function plans?
4. Revise your plan-implementing programs?
5. All of the above?

Review the Tasks outlined in this book, and then conduct a triage screening process, identifying which ones:

1. Are essential for your jurisdiction.
2. Are desirable.
3. Are not needed.

Prepare a generalized long-term staff work program that shows what planning work you recommend be undertaken, and how it might be scheduled.

### References

Kent, T. J., Jr. *The Urban General Plan*. Chicago: American Planning Association, 1990. (A reprint of the 1964 edition.).

Myerson, Martin. "Building the Middle-Range Bridge of Comprehensive Planning." Originally published in the Spring, 1956 issue of the Journal of the American Institute of Planners Vol. XXII, No. 2. Reprinted in Andreas Faludi's *A Reader in Planning Theory*. (Elmsford, N.Y.: Pergamon Press, 1973).

Perloff, Harvey S. *Planning the Post-Industrial City*. Chicago: American Planning Association, 1980. See Chapter 23, "The Time Horizon in Forecasting."

So and Getzels, editors. *The Practice of Local Government Planning* 2d ed. Washington: International City Management Association, 1988. See Chapter 3, "General development plans," and Chapter 4, "District planning."

# 4

# Introduction To Task Descriptions

## SIX MAJOR PHASES IN THE PLANNING PROCESS

The planning process described here is divided into six major phases:

**Phase I**—Identify the Client and Participants; Draft and Review the Planning Program

**Phase II**—Identify Issues; Collect and Analyze Data

**Phase III**—Prepare, Review, and Adopt the General Plan

**Phase IV**—Implement the General Plan

**Phase V**—Prepare, Review, and Adopt District Plans

**Phase VI**—Implement District Plans

## SEQUENCING OF PHASES OF THE PLANNING PROCESS

The recommended sequencing of the phases of the planning process is illustrated in Figure 4-1. All six Phases of the process should be undertaken in the sequence outlined above.

## SEQUENCING OF TASKS WITHIN THE PHASES

Each of the *phases* of the planning process is divided into a number of specific *tasks*. Each of the Tasks is described in the following pages. The recommended sequencing of these Tasks within each phase is illustrated in a critical path diagram. The diagram should not be interpreted literally. You will find that many of the Tasks can be undertaken concurrently, despite the linear sequence shown in the diagram. You will also discover that you may need to return to an earlier Task and modify it after you have completed a later Task.

A Task description usually contains the following:

**1.** Task number and short title

**Figure 4–1**   Flowchart of Phases in the Planning Process

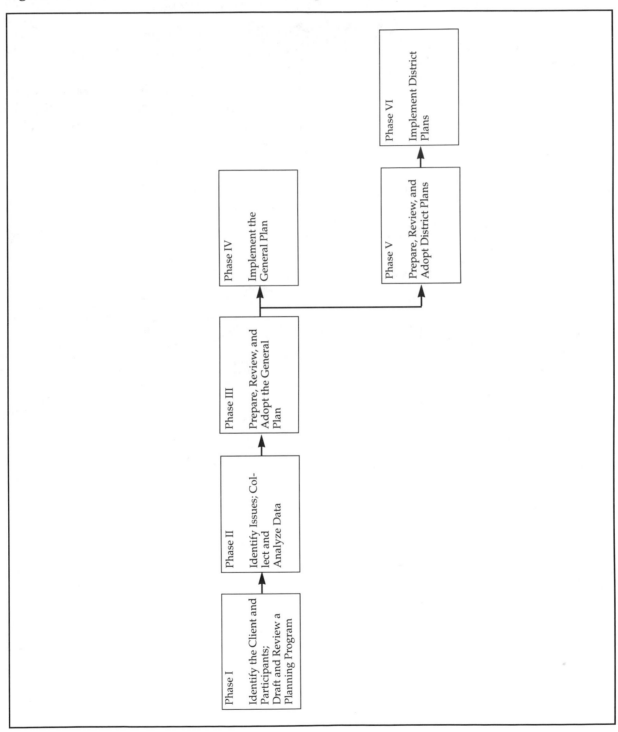

2. A brief discussion of why the Task should be undertaken

3. An outline of the general procedure recommended to be used

4. Identification of specific products, if any, of the Task

5. General discussion

6. Sources of more information

## SOME TASKS MAY NEED TO BE OMITTED OR DEFERRED

The reader is advised that while all of the Tasks are *recommended*, local conditions and circumstances may make some of them unnecessary. It is also highly probable that local resources for planning may be so constrained that some of the Tasks will have to be eliminated, condensed, or combined with other Tasks.

# Phase I
# Identify the Client and Participants; Draft and Review the Planning Program

**Contents**

**Figure 5–1**  Flowchart of Tasks in Phase I

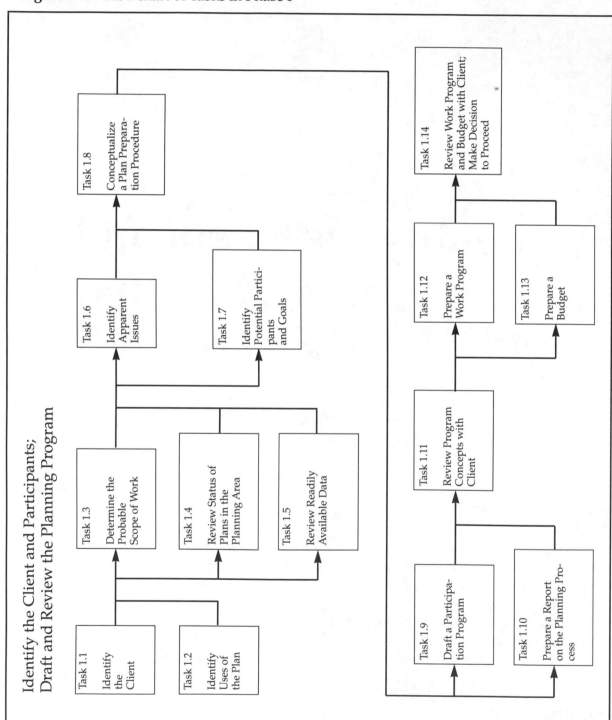

## INTRODUCTION

This phase deals with getting things organized before the planning process starts on substantive work.

The Tasks outlined in the text of Phase I would probably involve a lot of work if you were to start a planning program without any knowledge of the planning area, its residents, government, and local issues. But, how often does this happen? Local governments don't decide to start planning programs without considerable discussion, review of local needs and the budget. If you are the local planning director, you are probably already familiar with the background for local planning, and have just been waiting for someone to give you authorization to proceed. If this is the case, you may have done much of the conceptualization work described in Phase I already, and that is the hardest part.

If you are a planning consultant from outside the area, your job is more difficult. You have to be a "quick study" and learn about local conditions fast. If you can't do this, you may find another line of work more rewarding.

A bit of advice about Phase I: Don't let it drag on too long. If the local legislative body has finally gotten around to asking you to update or prepare a general plan, it will probably want to see progress being made soon. If you can get a work program and a proposed budget to them within a month, you will probably be off to a fine start. If you don't get back to them for three or four months, you're probably off to a poor start.

The text of Phase I applies to the updating or preparation of a long-range general plan. If your assignment is a short-range district plan,

or a function plan, you will have to modify the procedures recommended in this introductory Phase, as well as Phases II and III.

## TASK 1.1 IDENTIFY THE CLIENT

This Task is recommended so that:

**1.** You and your staff will have a clear understanding of who the principal client of the planning process is.

**2.** You will know which other persons, boards, commissions, or agencies should be directly involved in the planning program because of their official status.

**3.** You can identify the appropriate chain of communication between those who are preparing the plan, the principal client, and other people who are involved in the planning process.

### Recommended Procedure

**1.** Identify the principal client.

This is the person or body having the final say concerning the content of the general plan, and the procedures for its preparation. The local legislative body is often considered to be the principal client.

**2.** Identify other officials who have an interest in the general plan.

This should include the planning commission, of course, and may include other boards and commissions (such as a park commission), some administrative officers (such as the city manager, the director of public works, the county counsel, etc.), and state agencies to which the plan must be submitted for review, etc.

**3.** Identify the administrators above you. That is, those people in the chain of command to whom you report on a regular basis.

**4.** Identify the appropriate channels of communication between the staff who will be working in the plan-preparation program and the people and agencies identified above.

Prepare a memorandum for staff information that summarizes your findings.

The product resulting from this Task should be a memorandum, primarily for staff use, which summarizes the information you and your staff developed. You may consider it appropriate to provide a copy of the memorandum to the administrator to whom you are directly responsible.

You are probably already aware of most of the information called for in this procedure.

Concerning the principal client:

T. J. Kent, Jr. argues persuasively that (in cities) the city council should be the principal client of the general plan, and that the plan should be prepared for active use by the council. (Kent, op. cit., p. 23 and Chapter III.) In the majority of American cities and counties the local legislative bodies are the highest authority for most major decisions concerning local affairs. They usually:

**1.** Set formal and informal local policies.

**2.** Speak on behalf of local government, except in those governments where this power is given to a mayor or other administrative officer.

**3.** Adopt budgets, which establish policies concerning what programs are to be emphasized.

Many states require that cities and counties prepare general plans, and that these plans be officially adopted by the local legislative body. (In a survey I made in 1993 of planning legisla-tion enacted by states, I found that of the 28 usable responses received, 19 states required that general plans be adopted by city or county legislative bodies, while 9 states did not.)

For these reasons, it is likely that in many jurisdictions the local legislative body will be considered to be the principal client of the general plan.

In the following text the term "participants in the planning process" and "participants" are used extensively. The participants should certainly include:

**1.** Members of the local legislative body

**2.** The local planning commission

**3.** The chief administrative officer in local government

**4.** Selected citizen participants

**5.** The planning staff

It is impossible to identify just who the selected citizen participants will be because there is so much variation between jurisdictions. In some cases they may be a large committee made up of people who represent a wide variety of interest groups in the planning district. In other cases, they may be a small group of people who have a common interest, and have been hand-picked by the mayor.

**Reference**

Kent, T. J. Jr., The Urban General Plan. Chicago: American Planning Association, 1990.

**TASK 1.2 IDENTIFY USES OF THE PLAN**

Who uses the plan, and how, should strongly influence which topics are included, the time span the plan covers, and its balance between generality/specificity. It should also influence the style of the plan.

## Recommended Procedure

Identify who uses the existing plan. As a starting point, you may wish to consider these people:

- Members of the local legislative body, planning commission, and other local boards and commissions.
- The chief administrative officer in local government.
- Key staff people in local government, such as those working in public works, health, economic development, housing, etc.
- Key people in "outside" governments (e.g., county, state, federal, special district), such as the providers of highways, utilities, housing, environmental protection, social services, etc.
- Key people in civic groups (e.g., taxpayer organizations, homeowner associations, fraternal societies, League of Women Voters, etc.)
- Key people in development-oriented organizations (e.g., real estate groups, bankers, building trades unions, Chambers of Commerce.)
- Key people in conservation-oriented organizations.
- Key people in major local institutions and employers (e.g., universities, hospitals, large corporations).

Identify what these people use the plan for, how often, and which topics in the plan are of special interest to them.

Identify which topics identified by the plan users appear to be well-suited for inclusion in a long-range general plan for the community, and which may be more appropriate for a short-range district plan.

This Task should produce a memorandum for staff use that

**1.** Identifies the users of the existing plan, discusses how they use it, and what they use it for; and

**2.** Discusses which topics appear to be well-suited for inclusion in a long-range general plan, and which are better suited for later inclusion in a district plan.

The information called for in this Task can best be obtained by direct interview.

## References

See Task 1.6, Identify Apparent Issues, and consider combining work in that Task with work in this Task.

Reviewing Chapter 11, Methods Used in Implementing Plans, may bring to mind some of the uses being made of the existing general plan. See especially the section Day-to-day Use of Plans.

If your jurisdiction does not have a general plan at this time, you should probably omit this Task, rather than gather hypothetical material.

## TASK 1.3 DETERMINE THE PROBABLE SCOPE OF WORK

You should start developing a concept of the plan that you will be preparing. You can start on this by identifying the parameters you must work within.

You must know the probable scope of work, so you can make a reasonable estimate of the time and financial resources required to complete it.

The information produced in this Task will be useful to you, your staff, and to the people who will make the decisions about whether a plan is produced.

## Recommended Procedure

**1.** Identify what kind of a plan you are going to prepare or revise, such as:

- A long-range general plan for the entire jurisdiction
- An element of a long-range general plan
- A short-range district plan
- A function plan

**2.** Define the boundaries of the planning area. (A "planning area" usually includes all lands within the local jurisdiction, plus those adjacent lands that clearly influence life or development within the jurisdiction.)

**3.** Identify the topics that should probably be included in the plan; indicate which elements are: essential, or desirable.

**4.** Identify the desirable time scale for the plan.

**5.** Identify state law requirements that will apply to the plan contents, and to its review and adoption procedures.

**6.** Identify time constraints on the planning process. Estimate the earliest possible start time, and latest acceptable finish time.

**7.** Estimate the needed budget. (Note: this cannot be estimated with much accuracy before a work program and budget is prepared, but you (and others) need to know whether you're talking about a $10,000, a $100,000, or a $1,000,000 project).

This Task should produce a memorandum outlining the scope of work that you propose to undertake. While this memorandum is to be written for the information of the local legislative body, it should be reviewed and cleared by your next-step-up administrator and by the planning commission before it reaches them.

All of the information produced in this Task is *preliminary*. It is to be used to shape the directions of the planning program, and to estimate its magnitude and cost. The information developed in this Task will be an important input to the development of your work program and budget.

## TASK 1.4 REVIEW THE STATUS OF PLANS AND PLANNING IN THE AREA

You should consider undertaking this Task so that you can:

**1.** Build on the relevant and substantial plans that are already available; you shouldn't ignore or duplicate them.

**2.** Inform yourself about the general status of planning in the area. You need to know its extent and its degree of sophistication.

You also need to know how well planning is accepted and used in the community. These factors will influence the scope and direction of the planning program you will soon be recommending.

## Recommended Procedure

**1.** Review the existing general plan for your jurisdiction.

**2.** Identify, assemble (if possible), and review any additional plans and relevant reports that have been prepared for the planning area, and for nearby areas. Identify the status of each plan and report (e.g., officially adopted and well-used; adopted and ignored; etc.)

**3.** Critique the plans you review. Which aspects of each plan are good and timely? Which aspects are weak or out-of-date?

**4.** Identify which departments in your city (or county) participate in planning activities—either with their own in-house staff, or in cooperation with the planning department staff.

**5.** Develop information on the status of planning in your jurisdiction. Which local officials take it seriously, and which tend to ignore it?

Are the local legislative body and the local planning commission up-to-speed when it comes to planning, or have they been side-tracked for years with zoning controversies, use permits, and variances?

**6.** Identify the plan-implementation programs, such as zoning, capital improvement programs, growth management programs, etc., that are being used.

Of these programs, which appear to have substantial impact, and which seem to be of marginal effectiveness? Which are being used in a bold manner, and which in a timid manner?

**7.** Identify the plan-implementation programs known to you that are not being used locally.

This Task should result in a memorandum, which is intended for staff use only.

The review of existing plans should help you understand the setting that your planning effort should fit into.

The review of the status of planning activity in the community will tell you whether you will have to devote a great deal of time to explaining concepts and procedures involved in plans and the planning process. If you find that you are working with interested and informed people you can devote more of your staff time to the substantive work of plan preparation.

Use discretion when writing up your find-

ings; if you are a public agency planner what you write becomes a public record, and may be read by anyone who asks to see it.

**Reference**

Review Chapter 11, Methods Used in Implementing Plans.

## TASK 1.5 REVIEW READILY AVAILABLE DATA

You need to know what information is readily available for your use. This will help you make a judgment concerning what new data should be developed in your planning program; this has substantial implications for your work program and budget.

**Recommended Procedure**

Determine what data exists and is reasonably available for your planning area.

While you need not assemble all the available data at this time, you would do well to collect any reports, maps, or files that are free or inexpensive and easy to come by.

The topics for the data you should be reviewing are dependent upon the topics you identified earlier as essential and desirable in Item 3 of Task 1.3.

Be sure to review the availability (and currency) of reproducible base maps and of aerial photographs.

Ask about Geographic Information Systems (GIS) computer files. Does anyone have any? If so, what format are they in? Will they be available to you?

Ask about computer-based transportation planning models. Who has them? Who has the needed data for the region and your planning area?

This Task should result in a memorandum, intended for staff use only.

Don't take any one's word on the existence, quality, or availability of the data. You and your staff should examine it to make sure that it exists, is reasonably complete, is acceptably accurate, and is up-to-date.

This Task provides essential input for your work programming. If the needed data is available in an acceptable form you don't have to budget for it. If the data you want is not readily available, you must budget for its production, use older data, use substitute data, or plan to do without.

### TASK 1.6 IDENTIFY APPARENT ISSUES

The plan you prepare should be responsive to the perceived issues of the day, and to foreseeable issues. In this Task you will make a preliminary identification of those issues, so that you can tailor your planning program to address them.

### Recommended Procedure

**1.** Review the definitions of "issue" provided in Appendix A, "Definitions of Selected Terms Used in Urban General Plans." There are two types of issues:
- Broad issues, such as those relating to society, to the metropolis or the city, to the general economy, etc.
- Specific issues, which are often framed as "problem statements." These may concern local physical development problems, such as traffic in neighborhoods, or economic problems, such as the affordability of local housing.

**2.** Interview a limited number of knowledgeable people and ask them to identify and rank in priority those issues that are important to the planning area now. As a follow-up, ask them to identify future issues.

These interviews may be conducted in conjunction with Task 1.2.

You should consider interviewing all your local legislators, planning commissioners, and chief administrative officer, if feasible. Also interview a few key people in local government whom you believe to be especially well-informed, regardless of their office. This may be the city attorney, or a deputy county clerk. Also interview knowledgeable people outside government, such as newspaper reporters who cover community affairs, religious leaders who have shown concern for what's going on, and community leaders in general.

When writing up your findings, consider reporting:
- Which issues were mentioned most frequently?
- Which issues are considered in need of early resolution?
- Which issues are local in nature?
- Which issues are external in nature (i.e., are not usually affected by local action)?
- Which issues are not yet present, but are thought to be potentially important?

Don't limit your interviews to those people you believe are sympathetic to your point of view.

Try to not let the scope of this Task get out of hand. Remember that this is a first round of issue identification, to be made before the planning program is defined or approved. A second round of issue identification will be made later, which should be more extensive.

This Task should result in a memorandum for staff information identifying local issues, and giving a preliminary indication of what should be considered in the review (or preparation) of the general plan.

This Task has two purposes. The first is substantive. Your interviewees may identify issues you were not aware of, and they may provide you with insight on community priorities. The second purpose is political: Most people like to be asked for their opinions. When you ask people about local issues for the planning program they feel they are "in on the ground floor," and are making an important contribution.

### References

See Appendix A, Definitions of Selected Terms Used in Urban General Plans.

Appendix B, Checklist of Topics for Possible Inclusion in Local Plans or Metropolitan Plans. This checklist provides topics that might be germane in your planning. This checklist is too long and too structured for you use in this Task, but you may wish to use it later on. Reading through the checklist of topics at this time, however, may give you some ideas for topics to ask your interviewees about.

See Task 2.2, Identify Issues and Priorities (Second Round).

### TASK 1.7 IDENTIFY POTENTIAL PARTICIPANTS AND THEIR GOALS

To prepare a relevant plan you must know at the outset who has an interest or concern in what the plan says; this is a very large audience. Not everyone in that audience is going to be able to participate in the plan preparation and review process; only a carefully se-

lected group will be able to do this. These people are "participants."

After you have identified who may be asked to participate, you will structure a "planning-participation program" (see Task 1.9) in which you establish a procedure whereby you can learn from the participants, and they can learn from you, and from each other.

It is a generally accepted planning principle that an urban general plan should reflect a consensus of the goals of the community, as represented by those who participate in the planning process. Therefore the second part of this Task is to make a first approximation of the goals of the community. You will note that in Task 3.2 you will be assigned the job of drafting a statement of goals and policies to be used in the preparation of a general plan.

### Recommended Procedure

**1.** Review the list of the probable users of the plan you identified in Task 1.2. For each user group try to identify a spokesperson. You may wish to add some of the following to the groups you have already identified:

- Major local land owners
- Spokesmen for disadvantaged minorities (e.g., ethnic groups, low-income groups)
- Groups concerned with specific aspects of the quality of life in the community (e.g., housing, law enforcement, education, health services, recreation)
- Representatives from professional groups (e.g., planners, architects, engineers, geologists, landscape architects)
- Media representatives (e.g., local newspapers, radio, television)

**2.** For each of the groups or individuals identified above, make your best-guess of what their goals probably are. (See Appendix A for a definition of "goals.")

This Task should produce a memorandum for staff use that identifies potential participants in the planning process, and records your preliminary assumptions concerning their goals.

This Task should be done quickly; don't make a major project of it. Consider the information developed in this Task to be preliminary, and subject to change as the planning process continues.

In this Task you are identifying potential participants for the information of your client. The client, or a representative of the client, will make the final selection of participants. The criteria your client will use to select participants is hard to predict. In some cases the client will want to get a broad representation from the entire community. The client may select a group of people who can be expected to work in harmony, without "troublemakers" raising unpopular views. People may be selected because they are known to reflect the client's views and priorities; and so on.

The goals that you identify in a preliminary manner in this Task will be subject to a thorough review in the Goals Program.

### Reference

Perloff. Planning the Post-Industrial City. Chicago: American Planning Association, 1980. See pp. 215-232.

### TASK 1.8 CONCEPTUALIZE A PLAN-PREPARATION PROGRAM

This is your opportunity to think through what you're going to do, and how you're going to do it. The concepts you develop here will serve as the basis for the remainder of your plan-making program. What you want to do in this Task is write down your concepts, so that you can review them for logic, consistency, and completeness.

You will use these concepts later as the basis for your Report on the Planning Process Task, and for preparing your work program and budget.

### Recommended Procedure

**1.** Review the issues that appear to face your community (see Task 1.6).

**2.** Review your thinking about who is going to use the plan, how they are going to use it, and what form of a plan appears to be most useful (see Task 1.2).

**3.** Review the outlines of Phases I, II, III, and V of this text. Make a note of which Tasks appear to be especially important, and which should be omitted.

**4.** Prepare flow diagrams of each of the Phases that you are considering including, using a format similar to that used in this text (i.e., a Critical Path Diagram). Show each Task to be included.

**5.** Think about your in-house staff who will be available to work on the planning program. What skills do they have? Are they likely to be able to learn new skills quickly? How much time will each of them be able to devote to the planning program?

**6.** Make a preliminary "best-guess" estimate of how much staff time will be required for each Task. Identify which Tasks can be done in-house, and which require outside help.

**7.** Make a preliminary "best-guess" estimate of the probable elapsed time for all the Tasks that involve citizen participation.

Remember that it takes considerable time for citizen groups to get organized, and time for group members to get to know each other well enough to communicate freely (unless, heaven forbid, you want the citizen committees to just rubber-stamp staff recommendations).

**8.** Add up your estimates of time required for the planning program.

**9.** Write a short report that describes your proposed planning program, and the general plan document that would be produced by it. The primary audience for the report is you. It is intended to record your present concepts of a planning program; you need to have these down on paper. The secondary audience for the report is your staff.

This Task should produce a short report describing the proposed planning program and the resulting plan document. The report should include preliminary estimates of required in-house staff time, outside staff assistance requirements, and total elapsed time needed to complete the planning program.

The report generated in this Task is to serve as the primary source of information for Task 1.9, Draft a Planning-participation Program, and Task 1.10, Prepare a Report on the Planning Program.

A significant difference between this Task and Task 1.10 is that the report produced here is for in-house use by you and your staff, while the report produced in Task 1.10 is intended for public review. That means that while the basic recommendations made in the two reports should be the same, the style, the format, and the amount of detail in the two reports probably should be quite different.

## TASK 1.9 DRAFT A PLANNING PARTICIPATION PROGRAM

You know that plans prepared with substantial local input usually reflect local values and goals far better than do plans prepared by an "outside expert."

You also know that people have far greater loyalty and support for plans they had a hand in preparing. "Our Plan" is often better accepted and more frequently used than "The Expert's Plan."

You need to devise a program that will use local knowledge to good advantage, and will get enthusiastic participation by local people.

This Task is intended to help you identify who should be invited to participate in the planning program, and to describe how these people can participate effectively and constructively.

### Recommended Procedure

**1.** Think about the general procedures you want to recommend. What balance do you think will be desirable between staff and citizen input during the planning process?

You may wish to consider these major options:

- Professional planners study data about the area; come up with basic concepts for community development; outline major patterns of land use, circulation, housing, etc., and then run these by a group of lay citizens to get their reactions and approval. Or,

- Staff "facilitators" organize a series of forums in which local citizens meet and state their goals for the community. The staff role is to stimulate discussions, provide refreshments, and record the ideas that are developed.

You probably realize the first option is technocratic, and as a result, the process probably will neither benefit from the good ideas of local citizens, nor receive much public support.

The second option has several possible outcomes, none very desirable. One is that a vague set of goals will be developed, which is acceptable because it offends no one. Another possible outcome is that the group will develop a number of conflicting factions (e.g., homeowners vs. business interests vs. environmentalists vs. improve-our-streets people, etc.). While each faction may come up with some bold and good ideas, no consensus within the group is developed.

Your challenge is to develop a planning-participation program that avoids the weaknesses of the options outlined above, but:

- Stimulates local people to come up with good, workable ideas
- Develops a broad consensus
- Uses, to good advantage, the professional skills of the local planning staff, or consultants

2. Identify people who should be considered as possible participants. If you are not thoroughly familiar with the community, get help from someone who knows who's who.

Refer back to Task 1.7, Identify Potential Participants and Their Goals.

Consider the following general categories of people:

- Staff services—Chief administrative officer in local government; selected depart-ment heads in local government; planning department staff members from other departments in local government, such as traffic engineering, public health, urban renewal, housing, etc.; staff members from regional and state agencies; and consultant services.
- Appointed or elected officials of local government—Legislative body; planning commission; and other boards and commissions.
- Representatives of the public—Designated representatives of business or civic organizations; and selected citizens who are thought to represent the viewpoints of non-organized sub-groups of the local population.

3. Determine how the people or groups you identified in the preceding lists might be best used in the local planning process.

Consider the following general roles:

- Spokesman for the values, goals, or specific recommendations of a special interest group representing: a geographic area; a sub-group of the local population; or a special interest group representing a local business, profession, or other activity.
- Source of specific information (e.g., history, statistics, etc.)
- Member of a technical advisory committee.
- Qualified spokesman for local governmental policies.
- Possible source of professional staff workers.
- Possible source of volunteer workers.

4. Outline a planning-participation program, which may include:

- Informational meetings for the general public, scheduled for a number of key points in the planning process.
- Citizen's Advisory Committee meetings, in which selected participants: identify current issues; discuss community goals; discuss basic design concepts for the community; recommend priorities; and review, discuss, and comment on staff reports on various topics.
- Technical Advisory Committee meetings, for various subject areas.
- Opportunities for lay citizens to provide volunteer services, such as collecting data or conducting surveys.
- A strong role for planning staff members, to include: writing committee assignments; scheduling committee meetings; providing technical data and reports for committee review; keeping all participants informed about the progress of the planning program; and writing up meeting notes or minutes, and distributing them

**5.** Review the planned participation program with your next-step-up administrator, and, if appropriate, the client.

This Task should produce a report which indicates who you recommend be invited to participate in the planning program, and how you think they might be expected to participate. In some parts of the report you may be able to give the names of specific people; in other cases you may have to use the term "a representative from." This report should not be considered final. It will probably be necessary to make additions and deletions as the planning program progresses. The audience

for this report is your next-step-up administrators, your staff, and any member of the general public who shows an interest.

The preparation of this report is one of the "gearing-up" operations that you need to do before launching your planning program in the community. You will want to include the program you develop in this Task in your work program, which will be prepared in Task 1.12.

In this Task you identify potential participants; you don't invite them. The invitations should be issued later by a leading political figure who is interested in the planning program, such as the mayor, or the chairman of the board of supervisors.

### References

Dandekar, H. C., editor. *The Planner's Use of Information.* Chicago: American Planning Association, 1988. See Chapter 6, "Public Involvement as Planning Communication," by Katharine P. Warner.

See the Citizen Participation in Planning section of the Bibliography.

During 1992-1994 a number of communities had their citizens participate in "visioning" exercises, to identify the type of community they desire, and to draft community goals. As of this writing, there does not appear to be very much written material on the process. Perhaps by the time you read this text there will be more information available.

### TASK 1.10 PREPARE A REPORT ON THE PLANNING PROCESS

You need to provide non-planners with a description of what you propose to do, and what the results of your labors will be. They need to be informed about:

- What the planning process is.
- What a general plan is and how it is used.
- What topics will be considered.
- Who will be invited to participate in the planning process.
- Whose views the plan will represent.
- Who will do the technical work.
- How long the planning program will take.
- How much the program will cost.

## Recommended Procedure

**1.** Identify your audience. Your primary audience is:
- The local legislative body
- The local planning commission
- The administrator to whom you report
  After these people have had a chance to digest and comment on the contents of your report it should be distributed to:
- The proposed participants in the planning program
- People or agencies who were identified as users of the general plan
- The news media, if they were not provided copies concurrently with the primary audiences noted above.

**2.** Outline and write your report based on this suggested outline:

### General introduction
- What the planning process is.
- What a general plan is.
- How a general plan is used in local government.
- How a general plan may be used by people outside of local government.
- Why it is important to update the general plan at this time (or to prepare a plan).

- Which local issues will be considered in the general plan.
- Which local issues, while important, are beyond the scope of the general plan.

### Specific proposal
- Proposed procedure to be used to prepare the general plan.
- Which geographic areas will be considered in the plan.
- Proposed table of contents of the general plan (if known).
- Who will be invited to participate in the plan-preparation process, and how their skills may be used (see Task 1.9).

### Budget matters
- Preliminary time schedule.
- Preliminary budget.
- Identification of proposed sources of funding.

This Task should produce a report following the outline. It is recommended that the report contain a diagram of some sort that shows the proposed schedule of the work to be done.

This is an important report.

In those communities where urban planning is already known, understood, and accepted, it may be inappropriate to dwell at length on some of the elementary topics included in the outline above for the general introduction.

If you already have assurances that the planning program is funded and will proceed, this report will be most useful to all the participants in the planning process. If the planning program is not yet assured, this report may be used as a "selling piece."

While people usually need to know how much the planning program will cost and how long it will take, you can't give them reliable estimates until you have prepared a work program and a budget. You can't prepare a work program and a budget until you and your clients have reached agreement on the scope and contents of the proposed plan. So, give the audience for this report your best "ballpark" estimates of cost and time, based on the scope and contents you have outlined to date, but warn them that these figures are subject to change.

## TASK 1.11 REVIEW PLANNING PROGRAM CONCEPTS WITH CLIENT

Now that you have conceptualized and described a planning program, you must review it with your client. The primary purposes of this review are to make sure that you and the client are in agreement on what the program should contain, and to get clearance to proceed. During the conduct of this Task you get an opportunity to tell your client what you think should be in the program, and the client has an opportunity to tell you what should be added or deleted.

### Recommended Procedure

Review with your client the Tasks that you have completed earlier, namely:

1. Task 1.3, Determine the Probable Scope of Work
2. Task 1.6, Identify Apparent Issues
3. Task 1.8, Conceptualize a Plan-Preparation Program
4. Task 1.9, Draft a Planning-Participation Program
5. Task 1.10, Prepare a Report on the Planning Process

The product resulting from this review should be a memorandum which summarizes the conclusions concerning the planning program that you and your client mutually agree upon.

The term "client" should probably be broadened here to include not only the "principal client" identified in Task 1.1, but also important advisers to that principal client. For example, if you identified the principal client as being the city council, it would be appropriate to review the planning program concepts with the city manager and the planning commission before taking it to the council.

You will have to use your judgment on when and how to review the materials identified above. You don't want to overload the client with copious reports, but you don't want to withhold information that will help the client understand the project.

You should prepare executive summaries of the reports you wish to discuss, and attach those to the complete reports.

### TASK 1.12 PREPARE A WORK PROGRAM

It is essential that you specify what work you and your staff are going to do, when it will be done, and what resources you will need before you make a commitment on a project. Your client will want to review this information before agreeing to fund the project. Work programs, and budgets based on work programs, provide this information.

### Recommended Procedure

The following outline presents the sequence of steps that are often used in the preparation of a work program. It describes a process that is perhaps too demanding for a simple job, but not detailed enough for a complex job. The degree of detail in the work-programming process should, of course, be adapted to suit the characteristics of each job.

**1.** Review thoroughly the scope of work to be done.

Be sure you really understand what the purpose of the work is; what issues are to be considered; what work procedures (if any) have been prescribed; what data is available; what specific end-products are required (such as reports, material products, decisions, etc.); and what your deadlines are.

**2.** Write a one-paragraph or one-page description of the project.

This paragraph or page should:

- Assign a short but meaningful title to the project
- Summarize the goals of the project
- Describe the scope of the project (e.g., limits on the subject matter, the geographic area, the time periods to be considered, etc.)
- Identify the general procedures to be used
- Specify the end-products to be produced

**3.** Conceptualize the whole project as a number of individual Tasks which may be undertaken separately.

Each Task should be an entity in itself. Some Tasks may be undertaken concurrently with others; some other Tasks may have to be undertaken in sequence. Be sure you can describe each Task, and know why it is needed to complete the project as a whole. If you have time or budget constraints, avoid those Tasks that are merely fun to do, or produce "nice-to-know" information, but are not essential to the completion of the project.

**4.** Prepare a brief description of each Task.

Give the following information for each Task, using a standardized format, such as:

- Short title and identifying Task Number
- Objectives of the Task
- Brief description of the work procedure to be used
- Input data required
- Output to be produced (report? map? data?)
- Relationship to other Tasks in the work program, relationships of data needs and relative timing
- Estimated man-days or man-hours required to complete the Task
- Built-in delays (e.g., waiting time) in the Task
- Materials required for the Task (printing? transportation?), and cost estimates
- Statement of who is to do the work

Included at the end of this Task description is a form that may be used to compile the required information. This form should be modified to suit the complexity of the work program that you are producing.

**5.** Produce a diagram which shows the sequence of Tasks to be undertaken.

Your diagram should be prepared in draft form as you are initially conceptualizing the work program. It should be revised and refined as you develop individual Task descriptions.

Your diagram should indicate graphically which Tasks can be undertaken concurrently, and which must be done consecutively. Spread the timing of the Tasks to match the manpower you have available. The graphic form you choose will depend upon the degree of sophistication of your analysis, and of your audience. You may find it worthwhile to prepare both an easy-to-understand summary diagram (such as a Gantt chart) and a detailed diagram (such as a critical path diagram). It is desirable to show the starting and completion dates of each Task, and any critical dates, such as presentations to the client, public hearings, etc.

6. Produce a summary table.

Your summary should include the following information for each Task:

- Task number
- Task title
- Man-days or man-hours required
- Cost of labor
- Cost of materials

The table should give project totals for hours, and costs of labor and materials.

There are many good "project management" computer programs that are excellent for work programming and budgeting. (For example: SuperProject, Harvard Project Manager, Microsoft Project, Time Line, etc.) If you enter required information into the computer most of the programs will draw a critical path diagram, draw a Gantt chart, identify "earliest start time" and "latest start time" for individual Tasks, and add up the totals of required manpower, materials, etc.

These programs are useful, but they do require you to develop information on each Task before entering it into the computer.

Computer spreadsheet programs are useful for preparing budget estimates, but they cannot be adapted to show the time relationships among the Tasks in a project.

Some planners say there are so many uncertainties in the planning process that the time schedules produced by the programs are often unreliable and potentially misleading.

You should note that this text provides a head start on the Task descriptions required for programming work for the preparation of an urban general plan. You have to decide which of the Tasks described in this text you are going to include in your planning program, and develop some additional information, but a substantial bit of your work has already been done for you.

This Task should result in a work program that includes: Task descriptions; graphic illustration of the time-relationships among the Tasks; cost estimates for labor, materials, travel, etc.; plus estimates of direct costs for each Task, each Phase and the entire program.

This Task description discusses the techniques used for work programming; it does not identify what work is involved in other Tasks involved with plan making. You will have to transform the concepts of your planning program (see Task 1.8) into a specific proposal, using the work-programming technique.

Preparation of a work program can be time consuming, but it is one of the most important Phases in the planning process. If you do it well (and if luck is with you) your planning program will go smoothly. If your work program is not thought through you may be confronted with surprises, most of which will be embarrassing or expensive.

### Reference

See Appendix C, Notes Preparing Work Programs.

### TASK 1.13 PREPARE A BUDGET

This Task is essential because both you and your client need to know how much the planning program you propose is going to cost, and how it is to be funded.

**Table 5–1**
**Sample Form for Task Descriptions**

1. Task number:

2. Task title:

3. Objectives of the Task:

4. Work procedures to be used:

5. Input data required:

6. Output to be produced:

7. Which Tasks immediately precede?

8. Which Tasks immediately follow?

9. Which other Tasks interact with this Task?

10. Man-days or man-hours required to do the work:

11. Built-in delays (waiting periods, etc.):

12. What specific-date deadlines or reporting dates are there?

13. Cost of supplies, transportation, publications, etc.:

14. Who is to supervise the work?

15. Who is to do the work?

A detailed budget (one that gives cost estimates for each Task) is also useful because it provides you and your client with information that will allow you to judge the relative cost-effectiveness of each Task. When you have this information you may wish to augment some Tasks in the work program and minimize others.

A budget provides a foundation for measuring the progress you are making towards the completion of your planning program. Later on you will want to make regular progress reports on the degree of completion of individual Tasks, compared to the original time and cost estimates. (These are often referred to as "howgozit reports" and are an essential budgeting tool.) In that way you will be able to tell if you are over budget or (rarely) under budget and can take remedial actions if needed.

## Recommended Procedure

1. Correlate your budget preparation with your work program preparation. It is wise to prepare them concurrently.
2. Review the work program. For each Task estimate:
- Labor costs
- Other direct costs
- Indirect costs

(See Appendix M, "Notes on the Use of Planning Consultants," for definitions of these terms.)
3. Provide totals:
- For each Task
- For each major phase of the planning program
- For each major time segment in the program (each month, each quarter) for

which you will wish to prepare a "howgozit" budget analysis
- For the entire program
4. Identify recommended sources of funds for the program.

## References

See Appendix M, Notes on the Use of Planning Consultants.

Slater, David C. *Management of Local Planning.* Washington, DC: International City Management Association, 1984. See pp. 100–120, which deal with the general topic of municipal budget preparation and administration.

So and Getzels. *The Practice of Local Government Planning* (Second Edition). Washington, DC: International City Management Association, 1988. See Chapter 14, "Finance and Budgeting," especially pp. 435–445.

## TASK 1.14 REVIEW WORK PROGRAM AND BUDGET WITH CLIENT; MAKE DECISION TO PROCEED

This Task provides your client and you with an opportunity for a final review of what work is to be done, what the work will produce, how long it will take, and how much it will cost. After this review is satisfactorily completed, you and your client will make a formal commitment to proceed with the planning program.

## Recommended Procedure

Make sure your client has the latest editions of the work program and of the budget, and has had ample time to review them. Review and discuss with your client the work program and the budget that is derived from it. Make any mutually agreed-upon changes that are appropriate.

If the decision being made is based on an agreement between a local legislative body and its staff, then all that is needed is instruction by the legislative body to the staff, recorded in the minutes of the legislative body, and appropriate budget allocations for the anticipated costs. (Usually the adoption of a formal resolution approving this budget allocation is appropriate.)

If the decision to proceed is based on an agreement between a local legislative body and a public or private planning consultant, then a formal contract should be entered into by both parties.

The result of this Task should be agreement between you and your client concerning the content, timing, and cost of the planning program.

CHAPTER

# 6

# Phase II
# Identify Issues; Collect and Analyze Data

Contents

**Figure 6–1**   Flowchart of Tasks in Phase II

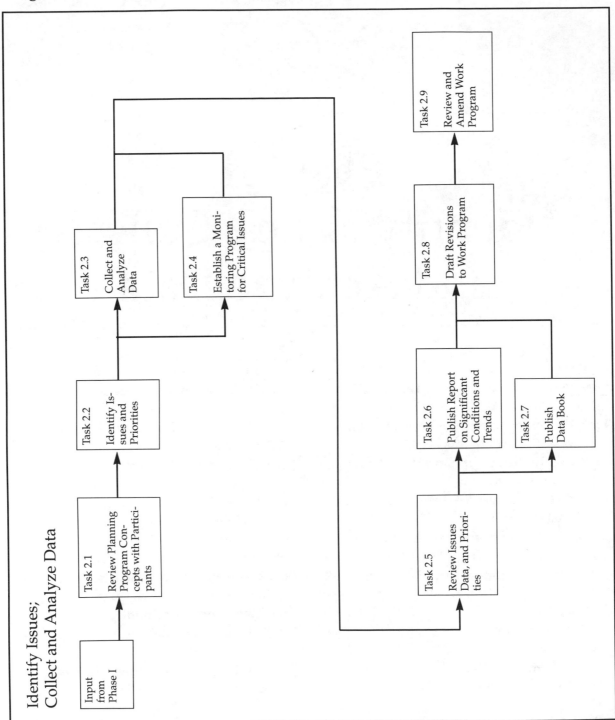

## INTRODUCTION

This Phase of the planning process requires planners to quit musing about what they're going to do, and get to work doing it.

Identifying issues is a very important part of the planning process; collecting and analyzing data is a very important and very expensive part of it.

Identifying issues, at first glance, will seem to be a simple task. But, when you get into it you will be troubled by two questions:

**1.** Have I really identified broadly based community concerns? Are there groups of people I have overlooked? Are there silent issues, for which there are no spokesmen?

**2.** Which of the issues I have identified are truly relevant to the local planning process? Which are so global or national in scale that local government is powerless to influence them? Which are so local or trivial that they concern only a handful of people and are irrelevant to the community as a whole?

Collecting and analyzing data can easily consume 50 percent of a plan-preparation budget, if you let it (in the days of "701 planning" it sometimes sucked up 90 percent of the funds).

Collecting and massaging data is a pleasant pastime; it has a certain mystique, and it is a good excuse to avoid decision making and plan making.

Data collection and analysis require you to do some thinking, in addition to the grunt-work of compiling the stuff. You have to:

**1.** Know for which topics you should collect data. That's why we identify planning issues first.

**2.** Know the difference between data quality and data quantity. A little bit of good data is far more useful than volumes of mediocre data.

**3.** Know when to cut back on data collection (we never completely stop), and get on with other work.

Please refer to Figure 6-2 for commentary on this issue.

So, now on with the job.

## TASK 2.1 REVIEW PLANNING PROGRAM CONCEPTS WITH PARTICIPANTS

This Task will inform participants in the planning program what is involved in the planning process, and what their responsibilities will be.

This Task is really the public kickoff for the planning program. It's an excellent opportunity to generate some enthusiasm in the community for the planning program.

### Recommended Procedure

Before getting too involved in this Task, you and your client should agree on the roles of any committees of participants that may be named. You should probably discuss these questions:

**1.** Is a "citizens planning advisory committee" really needed? Would it be preferable to have no formal committee, but hold a series of communitywide public meetings instead? In this case, the legislative body would serve as hosts, and listen to the views of any and all local citizens. Or would it be preferable to have the planning commission act as the committee on behalf of the community? Or would the legislative body want to serve as the committee itself?

**2.** If a committee is to be named, is it to be strictly advisory? If so, whom are they to advise?

**3.** Will the committee be authorized to determine the content of the plan, which will contain policy statements and community development proposals?

**4.** What procedures are to be established to keep the legislative body informed concerning the directions of the committee, and to provide feedback from the legislators to committee members?

Before the first meeting of any advisory committee is called, the local legislative body must decide on the role and responsibilities of the committee. They may choose to name the members, name the chairman of the committee, set the meeting agenda, chair the meeting, etc.

You and your staff will be expected to take care of the back-room organizational work, but it is the political leaders who must make the decisions and who should have the greatest public exposure.

**Figure 6–2**

*Do You Honestly Believe We Really Have Enough Information to*
*Justify a Decision?*

Reproduced from:
*And on the Eighth Day*
by Richard Hedman and Fred Bair Jr.

Before the first meeting of a planning advisory committee, the planning staff may be expected to:

**1.** Compile mailing lists of proposed participants, of media contacts, etc.

**2.** Mail appropriate materials to participants before the meeting.

**3.** Brief the news media before the meeting.

**4.** Draft an agenda for the meeting, which might include:

- Goals of the planning program
- Procedures to be used in the planning program
- Time schedule for the planning program
- What will be asked of participants
- Question and answer period
- Selection of "citizens' general plan advisory committee" (probably a large group), a "chairman," and a "steering committee" (a small group drawn from the larger advisory committee).
- Request those attending to indicate their areas of interest on a survey form (e.g., goals, housing, the environment, etc.), so they can serve on sub-committees that may be formed.

This Task should result in: direct participation in the planning process by your client; greater community understanding; enthusiasm generated in the minds of the participants; and lists of people who are interested in serving on committees.

The timing of this Task should be considered carefully. You should hold the kick-off when you're ready to start the planning program in high gear; not before, and not much after that time.

Important meetings, such a this, should probably be held after the work program and the budget have been approved. Neither you nor the local legislators want to hold a big public meeting and get everyone full of enthusiasm, and then have them wait for several months while you figure out what you're going to do.

**Reference**

See the section "Citizen Participation in Planning" in the Bibliography.

## TASK 2.2 IDENTIFY ISSUES AND PRIORITIES (SECOND ROUND)

As you will recall from Task 1.6, there are two major types of issues to be considered:

**1.** Broad issues, such as those relating to the form of the city, conflicts between growth and conservation, etc.

**2.** Specific issues, which are often stated in terms of problems, such as traffic flow through residential areas, the lack of affordable housing, etc.

In Task 1.6 you made a preliminary review of what the local issues appear to be, so that you could structure your planning program. Now you should make a more thorough review of issues for three reasons:

**1.** To establish with greater certainty what the current local issues are that should be addressed in the local planning program.

**2.** To have local participants involved in issue identification and ranking, so they become aware of those community issues.

**3.** To provide you and the local participants with information concerning: the relative importance of the issues that are identified, and what priority should be given to their resolution; what the origins or causes of the issues are; and what alternatives appear to be available to resolve the issues.

## Recommended Procedure

**1.** Review the work you did in Task 1.6, Identify Apparent Issues.

**2.** Have an issues committee formed from the participants identified in Tasks 1.9 and 2.1.

**3.** Decide which procedures you will use to accomplish the following:

- Identify issues
- Describe each issue, indicating whether it is a local or national issue (or some of each), and whether it is yesterday's issue, a current issue, or a predictable future issue (or some of each).
- Identify who's affected by the issues
- Rank the relative importance of each issue, and assign a priority for its resolution
- Identify the causes of each issue
- Identify alternative methods available for resolving each issue

**4.** Work with the issues committee in the application of the procedures you select.

**5.** Write a report on local planning issues.

This Task should result in: A greater understanding in your mind and in the minds of the issues committee members of what the local planning issues are; what priorities appear to be appropriate for considering the issues in the planning program; and what reasonable choices are available for the resolution of the issues.

It should also produce a report on issues for the information of all participants in the planning program.

Issues committee members should be truly representative of the entire planning area, not just well-informed, middle-income white males who have some spare time. The scope of information collection and analysis recommended in this Task may overwhelm some members of a citizens' committee if they think they will be asked to do all the work. Professional planners should carefully structure the work of the committee so that its members can contribute what they can, but the staff does most of the summarization and report writing.

## Identification of issues

There are many different ways to identify issues. You may wish to consider using one or a combination of several of the following procedures:

**1.** Develop and use a checklist of issues similar to that presented in Appendix B, Checklist of Topics for Possible Inclusion in Local Plans or Metropolitan Plans. After you put this checklist on a computer spreadsheet you will find it easy to add or delete checkoff columns. At this time you should probably use only Columns 1 and 2 of the checklist. Warning: While you should be able to understand the checklist and its implications, it is quite likely that others cannot. If you choose to use the checklist to survey public views, you should use it as a means of structuring interviews with laymen, and you should do the checking of the boxes in the checklist.

The checklist is a useful introduction to the identification of local issues, but it doesn't do much to tell who's affected by the issues, or how important each issue is. The form of the checklist could be modified, of course. Perhaps Column 3 could be used to record the priority given to each issue, and a Column 4 could be added to identify who's affected by each issue.

**2.** Use the Delphi technique to identify issues and to rank their relative importance. This technique has many forms and variations, some of which have potential for use in the urban planning process. A general description of one procedure for using the Delphi technique is:

- Name a panel of interested, well-informed people, who come from a variety of backgrounds.

- Prepare a list of issues that you think are relevant, and then ask panel members to rank them in order of importance; to rewrite or redefine them as they believe desirable; and to add new issues they believe should be considered. Panel members should do this as individuals, not acting as a discussion group.

- After receiving the responses from the panel members, revise the list of issues to reflect their recommendations. Then resubmit the revised list to the panel members, and ask them to reconsider their previous recommendations, in view of the responses received from the first list of issues. (It is often desirable to have the panel members meet and discuss the issues at the outset of the program, and before making subsequent-round evaluations. Their written responses, however, should be individual reactions, in order to minimize any bandwagon effect).

- Repeat the process as needed, until a consensus is developed concerning issues and their priorities, or until clearly defined conflicting views emerge.

3. Use personal interviews with people selected from a wide range of occupations and interests. Consider having some of the members of the committee doing some of the interviewing.

*Identify who's affected by the issues.* This information should identify both which population groups are affected (e.g., downtown merchants, migrant farm laborers), and the number of people involved. Your estimates will probably have to be approximate here, because of the paucity of data.

*Rank the relative importance of issues, and the priority for their resolution.* This is clearly a job where the views of the local residents must predominate, not those of the professional planner. The procedure for ascertaining how local residents feel about the relative importance of issues is to ask them. Interviewing, followed by using the Delphi process with issues committee members, is the suggested procedure.

*Identify the causes of the issues.* This is a tough job, and it probably can't be done thoroughly without devoting an inordinate amount of time to it. You are interested in identifying the root causes of the issues, not just describing their outward appearance. Remember some issues, such as those that are broad and societal in nature, may not have simple, identifiable, specific causes.

One method for identifying the causes of issues you may wish to consider is to hold a "brainstorming session" among a group of five to 10 knowledgeable people. Then have a small group of two or three well-informed local people review the output from the brainstorming session, discard the ideas that are ridiculous, and develop further the ideas that appear to have merit.

## The Use of Issues

What do you do with issues after you have found them? Issues that have been named and described are useful in several ways. First and foremost, issues identify which topics should be addressed in the plan you are preparing.

The second use of a compilation of issues is more mundane. When you are writing the text of a plan you may choose to link a discussion of some issue with a summary of background data, and use this as an introduction to the goals, objectives, and policies concerning some topic.

### References

Bracken, Ian. *Urban Planning Methods*. New York: Methuen, 1981. (See pp. 37, 92 for a brief discussion of the Delphi process).

Bryson, John M. *Strategic Planning for Public and Nonprofit Organizations*. San Francisco: Jossey-Bass, 1991. (See pp. 245-253).

Perloff, Harvey S. *Planning the Post Industrial City*. Washington: American Planning Association, 1980. (See pp. 195-198 for a brief discussion of the Delphi process).

### TASK 2.3 COLLECT AND ANALYZE DATA

This Task description outlines some general procedures for data collection. It also discusses the need to correlate the characteristics of the data you collect (i.e., topics considered, degree of detail), with the time and geographic scales of the plan you intend to produce.

There are important reasons why data should be collected and analyzed in the planning process. They include:

1. To provide a solid, factual basis for the policies and actions that the plan will recommend.

2. So that you and your staff will know the residents and the area for which you are planning.

3. So that others involved in the planning process (such as legislators, planning commissioners, members of advisory committees, staff members in other departments, etc.) will have information available concerning important local planning issues.

4. So that you will have assembled information which can serve as the basis for establishing a monitoring program for critical issues; and compiling and publishing a data book.

5. So that you and your staff can provide information to those who make occasional inquiries concerning conditions in the planning area (such as news reporters, bankers, real estate agents, etc.)

### Recommended Procedures

1. Identify topics for which data is needed. (These topics were identified in Task 2.2, Identify Issues and Priorities, and are discussed further in the following sub-sections of this Task.)

2. Identify data already on hand or readily available. (See Task 1.5, Review Readily Available Data.)

3. Identify the most promising sources of additional data; collect that additional data, as needed.

4. While you certainly will need jurisdiction-wide totals of data for your planning area, you should try to collect data on a sub-area basis. Census tracts are often satisfactory sub-areas, because lots of data is collected using their boundaries, which are usually clearly recognizable. Traffic Analysis Zones, which are sometimes sub-areas or aggregations of census tracts, may also be useful.

But, the important point is the sub-area boundaries should be used *consistently*, for all types of data, if possible. That is to say, you should use the same sub-area boundaries for population data, economic data, natural resource data, traffic generation data, etc., whenever it is feasible to do so.

**5.** Identify sources of base maps and aerial photographs; collect those maps and photographs that you think will be useful (See Task 2.3.1, Base Maps).

**6.** Always identify the data you collect. Be sure that each piece of data is identified with a title, its source, and its date.

**7.** Recommended time periods for data:

• Go as far back into the past as you plan to project into the future, if this is reasonably easy to do.

• Report data for five-year incremental periods, if it's available. Relate your data increments to the decennial U.S. Census, if possible.

**8.** It is desirable to establish an ongoing (year-in, year-out) data collection program, rather than relying on one-shot crash programs that have to be initiated each time a new project comes along.

**9.** You should identify data topics that can serve as an early warning system to let you know about changing conditions that may affect your community or your planning program. (See Task 2.4, Establish a Monitoring Program for Critical Issues.)

**10.** Organize a data bank. You should have a well-organized collection of data that you and others can easily retrieve and use in your planning efforts. Your usefulness to others will increase if you can provide information.

Your data bank may be in many different forms, such as:

• Tabulations of data in numerical form (e.g., census data)
• Written reports
• Maps
• Photographs
• A computerized geographic information system

You should seriously consider publishing major sections of your data bank in a data book. (See Task 2.7.)

**11.** Consider now the formats you will be using for memoranda, maps, and reports. The formats should be attractive, readable, economical, and standardized. Look ahead to the time you will be publishing your various reports; design a format that can be used consistently. If you are consistent with your formats you will save a lot of staff time, and attain "product recognition." Think ahead to future Tasks, when you will be publishing your Data Book (Task 2.7), a General Plan (Task 3.10), and perhaps several district plans (Task 5.20).

**12.** Remember Spangle's rule: *Don't ever rely on data promised by others until you have it in hand and have examined it for completeness and accuracy.* (William E. Spangle, who enunciated this rule years ago, is an experienced and well-regarded planning consultant in Northern California.)

The time horizon of a plan affects the level of detail that is required in background data. Since the long-range plan is usually more general in nature than is the short-range plan, the data used in its preparation can often be more general. The short-range plan is usually quite specific, and usually requires site-specific data for its preparation.

Geographic scale affects the level of detail

to be recorded in data. Geographic scale affects data collection in two ways. First is the matter of volume of the data. Collecting "fine-grain data" (i.e., many geographic units within your planning area) is often appropriate and manageable for small geographic areas, such as individual sites or neighborhoods. Collecting and filing fine-grain data for larger areas (such as cities, counties, or regions) is time consuming, expensive, and unless you have a sophisticated computer system, unmanageable.

The second effect of geographic scale on data collection concerns *which* data to collect. Traffic data is one example. If you are preparing a short-range plan for a small area you will want to examine data on traffic flows on individual problem streets and at critical intersections. But if you are preparing a long-range plan for a large area you will want to look at present and projected traffic flows through major corridors. You don't need or want detailed small-area data.

Another example: land use data. If you are preparing a short-range plan, especially for a small area, you will need detailed land use data, collected and tabulated on a parcel-by-parcel basis. But if you are preparing a long-range plan, especially for a large area, you will have your needs satisfied by generalized land use data, perhaps collected on a grid-basis, or other "land units" that aggregate parcels of land. (See Appendix D, Four Levels of Land Use Codes.)

For citywide or areawide long-range studies you do not need (and usually cannot use) detailed land use data, such as that prepared using land use codes based on the three-digit or four-digit Standard Industrial Classifica-

tion Code. You will need, for your land use and traffic studies, information on:
1. Residential areas (location and residential densities)
2. Employment areas (location and employment densities)
3. Traffic generators, such as shopping centers, hospitals, universities. etc. (location, number of employees, number of visitors)
4. Open space areas (location)

It is important for you to think through how you are going to use your land use data before you develop a land use code, and before you start the expensive and time-consuming process of collecting the data. Many earlier planning programs devoted as much as 50 percent of the budget to the collection and analysis of land use data. Much of this was not really needed, except in those cases where planners anticipated using the land use data as the basis for making specific zoning recommendations.

In summary, keep in mind the following four points when you are considering collecting and analyzing data for planning purposes:
1. Know how you are going to use your data before you collect it.
2. You should collect and analyze "coarse-grained" (generalized) data if you are going to use it for preparing a long-range plan, or a plan for a large geographic area.
3. You should collect and analyze "fine-grained" (detailed) data if you are going to use it for preparing a short-range plan, or a plan for a small geographic area.
4. The topics of data that are appropriate for small-area planning often differ from those needed for large-area planning.

## References

Kaiser, Godschalk, and Chapin. Urban Land Use Planning 4th ed. Urbana: University of Illinois Press, 1995. See Chapter 4, "Planning Information Systems."

Perloff, Harvey S. *Planning the Post-Industrial City.* See Chapter 19, "Information Needed for Time-Oriented Planning."

Roberts, Margaret. *An Introduction to Town Planning Techniques.* See Chapter 4, "Information."

So and Getzels. *The Practice of Local Government Planning* 2d ed. See Chapter 15, "Information for Planning," by Carl V. Patton.

## TASK 2.3.1 ACQUIRE BASE MAPS AND AERIAL PHOTOGRAPHS

Base maps can be defined as outline maps on which no data has been entered. They usually show political boundaries, road locations, lakes and rivers, railroads, and perhaps major property ownership boundaries. Base maps are often printed in black ink on white paper.

You need base maps so that you can display data on them concerning the topics for which you will be collecting information. You will also use base maps when preparing the graphic representation of the plans you will be producing.

Aerial photographs are very valuable in the planning process because they are perhaps the best source of information concerning physical development of urban and rural areas, as of the date of the photographs.

### Recommended Procedure

Base maps  The preparation of a good base map requires the skills of a person experienced in drafting. If you have such a person on your staff, use his/her talents; if you don't, search for drafting skills in your engineering department, your assessor's department, or from a private engineering firm or drafting service.

The amount of detail appropriate for a base map depends, to a great degree, on the proposed use of the map.

When preparing a base map, you must decide on:

1. The geographic area to be included
2. The scale of the map
3. The sheet size of the map
4. Details to be included, such as:
- Political boundaries
- Water features (rivers, lakes, streams, etc.)
- Major roads only, or all roads
- Property lines
- Topographic contour lines
- Utility line locations
- Location of structures

It is often possible to prepare a family of base maps, starting with a basic parent map that includes few details. Overlays to this parent map may then be prepared, with each overlay adding more details. (One of the overlays should show the contours of the terrain.) This procedure is especially applicable when a computer assisted drafting (CAD) system is used.

The scale of base maps appropriate to your planning area depends upon the size of the area. Table 6-1 summarizes the scales of maps typically used in urban planning studies.

If you are going to be making detailed studies of small areas you will probably want to have a base map that shows individual property lines and the outlines of structures. Maps at a scale of 1"=200' are usually quite satisfactory for this purpose.

**Table 6-1**
*Scales of Maps Typically Used in Urban Planning Studies*

| Type of Planning Area | Map Scale | |
|---|---|---|
| | Representative Fraction | Linear Scale |
| Project planning | 1:600 | 1" = 50' |
| Planning regulations | 1:1,200 | 1" = 100' |
| Sub-area plans | 1:2,400 | 1" = 200' |
| Small cities | 1:6,000 | 1" = 500' |
| | 1:12,000 | 1" = 1,000' |
| Large cities | 1:24,000 | 1" = 2,000' |
| | 1:25,000 | 1" = abt 2,000' |
| Counties | 1:62,500 | 1" = abt 1.0 mi. |
| | 1:100,000 | 1" = abt 1.6 mi. |
| | 1:125,000 | 1" = abt 2.0 mi. |

If you are making generalized studies, or studies of large geographic areas, you will need smaller scale base maps. For some of these studies, maps at a scale of 1"=500', 1"=1,000', or even 1"=2,000' are often suitable.

Be sure to use a map scale that is in widespread use locally, so that your maps are compatible with those of other agencies, unless your agency is the only one doing any mapping, or is so large and dominant that every one else must follow your lead.

It is desirable, although not essential, to have your aerial photographs at the same scale as your base maps.

Recommended sources to check for aerial photographs include:

1. Your engineer's office
2. Your assessor's office
3. Your state department of transportation
4. U.S. Geological Survey
   - EROS Data Center
     Sioux Falls, South Dakota 57198
     (This office maintains an index of aerial photography available in the United States. Send them a precise description of the area you are interested in i.e., latitude and longitude boundaries, and they will tell you what's available.)
   - National Cartographic Information Center
     507 National Center
     Reston, Virginia 22092
     U.S.G.S. publishes many "orthophotos," which are aerial photographs which show the same areas as appear on their "quad maps."
5. SPOT Image Corp.
   1897 Preston White Drive
   Reston, Virginia 22091-1813
   (This company can supply you with satellite images of any location in the world. Their images have a resolution of 10 meters, so they are useful only for showing large objects or areas, rather than small urban features.)

The satellite images available to civilians from U.S. government sources have a resolution of 30 meters. While they are useful for mapping very large rural regions, they are of very little use in urban areas.

**Recommended Products from This Task**

*Base maps.* Have a series of base maps available. Each of the maps in the series should have a different degree of detail. One of the maps in the series should be a topographic map.

The map series should be suitable for the following purposes:

**1.** Recording data (using various graphic techniques, such as showing areas in various colors or patterns, dot maps, pictographs, or written notation).

**2.** Displaying data to an audience, from a distance (such as maps to be taped to a wall, and viewed from a distance of perhaps 20 feet).

**3.** Displaying data in a publication (to be viewed at a distance of perhaps 20 inches).

**4.** Displaying data to an audience using 35mm slides or overhead projector transparencies.

*Aerial photographs.* Have aerial photographs at the scales discussed in the following paragraphs:

**1.** An overview of the entire planning area. These days one satellite image from the SPOT Corporation may be a good solution. Sometimes a photo-mosaic (i.e., many photographs of small areas assembled into a mosaic to form one large image) may be available. Scale may be somewhere between 1:100,000 and 1:24,000.

**2.** "Orthophotos" prepared by the U.S. Geological Survey. These are aerial photographs, corrected for distortion, prepared to exactly match the 1" = 2,000' topographic map quadrangles published by the agency. Unfortunately, orthophotos are not yet available for all urban areas.

**3.** Contact prints of sections of the planning area. These are typically 9"x9" in size. A scale of 1"=1,000' is quite common. These show street patterns and major land uses clearly.

**4.** Enlargements from the contact prints. The preferred scale of these photographs is often 1"=200'. At this scale individual buildings and considerable other "urban development detail" is clearly visible. When more detailed images of small urban areas are needed, images at a scale of 1"=50' are appropriate.

Consider having positive prints on a Mylar base made, so that you can run off copies using a diazo printing process.

Planning agencies often need not be the sole purchasers of aerial photography. In many instances other agencies have already acquired the photography, and will make copies available at a very low cost. Contact the EROS Data Center, identified above, for further information.

If new aerials must be flown, consider a cost-sharing arrangement with other agencies, such as your engineer's office, the assessor's office, or others.

Vertical aerial photography (i.e., photographs taken with the camera pointing straight down) is fundamental, but you should also consider oblique photography (i.e., taken with the camera aimed sideways). Oblique aerials provide images that are more easily recognized by most people than are vertical aerials.

Collecting existing base maps for your planning area, or developing new ones, is an essential step in the planning process.

Granted, to most planners it doesn't seem to be a very socially relevant action. But without good base maps your data collection may develop into a confused mess, defying full and reasonable analysis. Without full and reasonable analysis of your data you won't be prepared to make sound and socially relevant decisions.

Don't overlook the value of up-to-date aerial photographs (and of aerials taken in earlier years). They can tell you a great deal about where urban development has taken place, which land uses existed as of the date of the photograph, and the general characteristics of those land uses. No planning office should be without them.

Many people in local government agencies (especially engineers, assessors, and planners) are now using Computer Aided Drafting (CAD) programs and equipment to produce maps. The advantages include the ability to produce maps in "layers." Each layer contains data on one topic, such as municipal boundaries, property lines, topographic contours, street names, hydrologic features, rail lines, etc. By selecting which layers you wish to have printed out, you can produce a base map with the information you wish to see.

Computer mapping requires:

• A computer with considerable data storage capacity

  • A good CAD program

  • A digitizer, used to input data

  • A plotter, used to print out maps or other graphics

Plotters come in a range of sizes. The small ones are relatively inexpensive, and the large ones are costly. Standard plotter sizes, described by the sheet size of paper or drafting film the plotter can print on, are:

A, which prints on 8 1/2"x11" sheets
B, which prints on 11"x17" sheets
C, which prints on 17"x22" sheets
D, which prints on 22"x36" sheets
E, which prints on 36"x48" sheets

### References

Appendix K, Notes on Maps and Base Maps.

Kaiser, Godschalk, and Chapin. *Urban Land Use Planning* 4th ed. Urbana: University of Illinois Press, 1995. See pp. 98-110.

### TASK 2.3.2 COLLECT AND ANALYZE DATA ON THE NATURAL ENVIRONMENT

This Task consists of gathering and reviewing data on many aspects of the natural environment in your planning area. Just which aspects should be considered depends on which topics are thought to be important locally.

The natural environment is what we start with, and much of it is highly valued by many people. Many aspects of the natural environment are attractive and beneficial, and contribute to our quality of life. Other aspects may be hazardous to our health, life, or property.

This Task identifies which natural features you have in your local planning area, and where they are located. When you know this, you can plan for their preservation, or plan for new development that is reasonably compatible with them, or plan for hazard reduction (or elimination).

Much of the information collected in this Task will be useful later on for planning physical development in your community, and for preparing environmental impact reports.

## Recommended Procedure

Collect data on some (but not all) of the topics listed below. Which topics are relevant depends upon which issues are to be considered in your planning program.

Both the time-scale and the degree of detail required in the data you assemble depends upon whether you are going to prepare a long-range or a short-range plan, the size of your planning area, and your time and budget constraints.

Many of the topics listed will require that some maps be made. When these maps are prepared they should all be at the same scale, if possible. You will find it advantageous to draft the maps on clear Mylar drafting film, so that prints can be made from them, and so that various maps can be overlaid one upon another.

The general categories of data on the natural environment usually include:

1. Topography
2. Slope
3. Slope aspect (i.e., the direction each slope faces)
4. Soils
• Basic soil types
• Soil capabilities for selected uses
5. Basic geology of the planning area
6. Geologic hazards
• Earthquakes
• Landslides
7. Drainage features
• Location of streams, rivers, and lakes
• Drainage basin boundaries
• Flood plain boundaries
8. Fire hazards
9. Vegetation
• General species
• Rare and endangered species

10. Wildlife
• General species
• Rare and endangered species
11. Climate
• General description
• Precipitation
• Temperature patterns
• Wind patterns
12. Environmental quality
• Water quality
• Air quality
• Noise levels
13. Toxic waste sites
14. Water resources
15. Mineral resources
16. Agricultural resources
17. Timber resources

A single report on the natural environment should be produced, with each major topic constituting a separate section. Each section of the report might contain:

1. A definition of the topic, and definitions of related terms
2. A summary of data on the topic, with citations of sources
3. Maps showing where the natural features are found, and which geographic areas they affect
4. Identification of the issues that need to be resolved.
5. A summary of existing local policies concerning natural features
6. An analysis of how the data relates to present and future conditions in the planning area

The primary audience for your report should probably be your local legislators, your planning commissioners, members of your advisory committees, and your staff.

This is one of the more important Tasks in the collection and analysis of background data for rural or urban planning. It should probably be one of the Tasks that you undertake first in your data collection and analysis process.

It will often be found that much of the data identified in this Task has already been developed by others; your job will be to find it, analyze it, and summarize it in a form your audience will understand.

### Reference

Kaiser, Godschalk, and Chapin. *Urban Land Use Planning* 4th ed. Urbana: University of Illinois Press, 1995. See Chapter 7, "Environment."

### TASK 2.3.3 COLLECT AND ANALYZE LAND USE DATA

This Task consists of describing how land is used in your planning area. Your description will be in the form of a map (or series of maps), a numerical tabulation, and a brief written description.

We collect and analyze land use data because existing land uses are the base upon which future of all land uses are built.

### Recommended Procedure

1. Determine the purposes of the study. Define as specifically as you can how the acquired data will be used.

2. Make a visual reconnaissance of the planning area. Spend enough time in the field to get a feel for its general character. Walk through any sub-areas that seem to have unique features or problems. Don't try to collect written or graphic data at this time; just concentrate on recording mental images of the area.

3. Identify the level of detail required in the land use analysis. (See Appendix H, Four Levels of Land Use Codes.) Table 6-2 provides an example of land use categories that may be appropriate for preparing a general plan for a small city. For a long-range general plan for a city or a county, generalized land-use data is often sufficient. However, parcel-by-parcel land-use data is usually required when preparing a short-range district plan that is to be used as the basis for zoning regulations.

4. Acquire a base map, at an appropriate scale, and with an appropriate amount of detail (See Task 2.3.1.) You may choose to have one map of the entire planning area, or a series of maps, which, when assembled, cover the planning area.

5. Identify the major land uses that are expected to be found in the study area.

6. Devise a land use code. Make sure that the code provides you with the information you really need (e.g., residential densities), but will not require the compilation of data you will never use. (Suggestion: Review the land use categories listed in Table 6-2; revise the list as needed; assign coding numbers to the land uses selected.)

7. Make a first draft of a land use survey, using up-to-date aerial photography as your primary data source. Do this in your office, before going out in the field.

8. Field check the work that was done in the office

9. Revise the land use code as required. It is likely that there will be some unanticipated land uses that did not appear in the first land use code you devised.

10. Devise a color code for a land use map. Try to think about the colors you will be

**Table 6-2**
**Example of Land Use Survey Categories for Use in Preparing a General Plan for a Small City**

| | |
|---|---|
| Residential | Institutional, cont. |
|   Very low density |   Government centers |
|   Low density |   Hospitals, health clinics |
|   Medium density |   Cultural activities (libraries, etc.) |
|   High density |   Parks (public and private) |
|   Mobile home parks |   Religious institutions |
|   Group quarters |   Military bases |
| Commercial | Transportation |
|   Central business district |   Freeways |
|   Shopping centers |   Parking lots and garages |
|   Highway commercial |   Railroad yards and rights-of-way |
|   Offices |   Airports |
|   Hotels and motels | Open Lands |
|   Service commercial |   Agricultural lands |
| Industrial |   Forest lands |
|   Intensive industry |   Vacant urban lands |
|   Extensive industry |   Other open lands |
| Institutional |   Rivers, lakes |
|   Schools | |

Notes:
Specify residential density in terms of dwelling units per gross acre of developed land.
Specify industrial density in terms of employees per gross acre of developed land.
Include only major specific transportation uses, such as freeways or rail terminals. Consider local streets as part of the gross area of adjacent land uses

using when preparing the graphics for your sketch plans (Task 3.5), your general plan (Task 3.8), any district plans (Task 5.13). There should be a reasonable degree of correlation of the colors in all of these Tasks. For example, yellows should be used in all of them for low density single family homes; browns for higher density apartments, reds for commercial, etc. (See DeChiara and Koppelman, pp. 115-117.)

**11.** Prepare a land use map. Planners have traditionally prepared large, colored land use maps, which are informative when viewed from a distance of three or four feet. It is extremely expensive to reproduce large multicolored maps such as these.

If you are planning on reproducing a land use map (or a general plan diagram) you may wish to consider making a black-and-white version of it. Printing maps using black ink on white paper is relatively inexpensive. To identify land uses you may use abbreviations (such as OFF for offices, IND for industrial, etc.), or you may use shading films (i.e., sheets of clear plastic which have been printed with patterns of dots or lines).

**12.** Make in-the-field re-checks of those land uses that raised questions in your mind as they were being mapped.

**13.** Measure sub-areas of land uses that were mapped; tabulate them by sub-areas (such as census tracts or traffic zones), and for the total planning area.

**14.** Prepare a report on the findings made from the land use analysis.

**15.** Prepare a map of developed areas for use in Task 2.3.15.

*Document all Your Work.* Keep neat field notes, in which you give the dates of the field inspection, who did the work, and what the notations mean. Put titles, dates, and authors' names on all your work. If your work is in draft form, label it as a draft.

Correlate your land use data collection with the data collection you may need to do in Task 2.3.4, Neighborhoods and Housing, especially if you are going to be making a structure-by-structure survey in that Task.

You may need some land use information as an input to a transportation planning model you may develop later. If so, check now to see what data will be needed, and in what form.

It is sometimes desirable to make an analysis of vacant lands in urban areas, to document how much land is available for in-fill development. If you do this, base it on your land use survey, on a parcel-by-parcel tabulation, with detailed information on parcel characteristics. See Task 2.3.15, Land Availability.

This Task should result in a map (or a set of maps) showing the location of existing land uses in your planning area; a tabulation, by sub-area, of existing land uses; and a written description of what you have found in your analysis of land uses.

Land use mapping and analysis has been a major activity of planners for years. Critics have noted that a substantial portion of this has been wasted effort, because some planners didn't think through how they were going to use the data after it was collected. However, many land use surveys have provided valuable information; data from some of them has been used as the basis for preparing good land use plans, and for drafting reasonable zoning ordinances.

**References**

Appendix E, Notes on Land Use Mapping.
Appendix D, Four Levels of Land Use Codes.
DeChiara and Koppelman. *Urban Planning and Design Criteria* 2d ed. New York: Van Nostrand Reinhold, 1975.
Kaiser, Godschalk, and Chapin. *Urban Land Use Planning* 4th ed. Urbana: University of Illinois Press, 1995. See Chapter 8, "Land Use."
Goodman and Freund. *Principles and Practice of Urban Planning.* See Chapter 5, "Land Use Studies" (pp. 106-136) by Shirley F. Weiss.

### TASK 2.3.4 COLLECT AND ANALYZE INFORMATION ON HOUSING

In this Task you will collect and analyze data concerning:

**1.** The supply of existing housing.
**2.** The condition of existing housing.
**3.** The occupancy of existing housing.
**4.** The affordability of existing housing.
**5.** The location of potential sites for new housing.
**6.** Public and private programs available for the provision of affordable housing.
**7.** Constraints on housing development.

In many communities, housing is an immediate and serious problem. This Task is designed to provide a factual foundation on which housing plans may be built later in the planning process.

In earlier years, considerable attention was focused on the physical condition of housing. "Blight" and "slum clearance" were primary concerns.

Today, attention is on the affordability of housing. Interest rates, land costs, construction costs, "exactions and fees" imposed on builders, and heightened expectations in the minds of many consumers, have combined to substantially increase sales prices and rental rates of housing.

In urban areas that have recently enjoyed the creation of many new jobs, the cost of housing is so high it takes a large share of a worker's income. This has induced many to seek affordable housing in distant suburbs and rural areas. This has further complicated our metropolitan traffic problems.

If you are working in a community that has experienced recent economic decline and population loss, your problems are quite different from those of growing communities. The primary focus in your planning program will probably be on how to improve local economic conditions, as well as how to provide more affordable housing.

**Recommended Procedure**

The work that you do in this Task depends upon what your local problems and issues are, and on the geographic scale of your planning area.

If you are planning for a large area, you should look at aggregated data first, such as that for census tracts. If you are planning for a small area (such as a planning district or a redevelopment area) you will probably need data on blocks, or on individual structures. With that admonition in mind, consider applying some of the following procedures:

**1.** Review the issues that appear to be related to housing. Consider such issues as:

- Is there a housing shortage?

- If there is a housing shortage, does it appear to be caused by:
—A mismatch between the cost of available housing and the ability of local residents to pay for it
—Difficulties local builders have getting financing to build for the lower-income market
—A lack of land available for housing
—Land costs too high for affordable housing
—Financing too expensive for any new construction
—A strong local "not in my back yard" attitude toward new housing construction in the community
—Tough local governmental growth restriction policies, brought on by traffic congestion, threats to the environment, overcrowded schools or utility systems, etc.
—Local fees and exactions (for building permits, utility connection fees, etc.) so high that they substantially raise the cost of new residential construction
- Is there an oversupply of housing?
- If there is an oversupply, does it appear to be caused by:
—A shrinking local economy, with a declining population, and a declining demand for housing
—A large inventory of older housing that has not been well-maintained
—People who can afford good housing choosing to buy or rent outside of your planning area, for various reasons
- Is the physical condition of the local housing stock a problem?
- Are there identifiable population segments that have more serious housing problems than others? If so, which ones are they?

**2.** Review your state's laws concerning the requirements for housing elements of general plans.

**3.** Assemble U.S. Census of Housing reports.

**4.** Compile data on housing in your planning area. Decide if you need aggregated data (e.g., by enumeration district or census tract), or data on individual structures. For aggregated data your primary source will probably be the U.S. Census of Housing. You may be able to update some of the Census data with information from your building inspector's records. For data on small areas you will probably have to make special field surveys.

You should have data on:
- Number of dwelling units, by type and location
- Condition of dwelling units, by type and location
- Market value, or rental rates, by type and location
- Characteristics of occupants (e.g., income, family size, race, age, commuting patterns, etc.) by type and location. Correlate this work with work to be done in Task 2.3.10.
- Identify and describe the special housing needs of the following groups:
—Physically handicapped
—Mentally handicapped
—Elderly
—Large families
—Seasonal agricultural workers
—Households headed by single women
—Homeless

**5.** For small areas, make a field survey of the condition of housing, on a structure-by-structure basis.

**6.** Make an inventory of land available for new housing in your planning area. Map it. Tabulate it by:
- Land area
- Physical characteristics
- Holding capacity, based on current zoning
- Holding capacity, based on current land use plan
- Known development constraints (See Tasks 2.3.15 and 2.3.16)

**7.** Identify public and private housing programs that are available to sponsor or finance housing.

**8.** Identify groups or individuals in the community who are particularly concerned with the various aspects of housing.

**9.** Analyze the data you have collected. Try to identify:
- What are the segments of the local market-demand for housing? What are their characteristics? What are their magnitudes?
- How well are the various market-demand segments, identified above, being served by the market-supply of housing? Which segments are being well-served? Which segments are being poorly served, or ignored?
- What are the unresolved housing issues in your planning area? What actions appear to be necessary to resolve these issues? Who (i.e., agencies or institutions) has the power to take action? What changes in social policy, law, or government programs should be considered? What economic resources appear to be needed? What are the political roadblocks to resolving housing issues?
- What would be the probable effect on the planning area if no new housing actions are taken? (i.e., the "do nothing" option).

Consider a five-year projection, and a 20-year projection.

Two products should result from this Task. The first is a series of well-organized data files. Some of these files may be published later in the data book described in Task 2.7. The second is a report on the findings made from the analysis of the data. The housing subjects discussed above should probably form the core of this report.

This Task should either provide a foundation for the housing element of a long-range general plan, or data and concepts for preparing an action program for a short-range district plan.

If you are preparing a long-range plan, you may wish to concentrate on the policy issues that emerge from the analysis of the data.

If you are preparing a short-range plan, you will want to concentrate on immediate problems, and what can be done about them.

## References

Review general plans from other communities in your area, and, especially the background data reports on housing prepared for those general plans. Gather reports prepared by the best planning departments of local governments in your state.

So and Getzels. *The Practice of Local Government Planning.* See Chapter 12, "Planning for Housing," by Constance Lieder.

Some general references will be found in the Bibliography, under the heading Housing.

## TASK 2.3.5 COLLECT AND ANALYZE INFORMATION ON TRANSPORTATION

This Task involves:

**1.** Identifying which transportation issues have priority for analysis and resolution.

**2.** Collecting and analyzing data on transportation issues and facilities.

**3.** Preparing a report on transportation.

The scope of the study depends on what the local transportation problems are. It may include:

(a) Movement of people in private cars over local streets

or (b) Capacity of the street network

or (c) Parking

or (d) Metropolitan transportation problems

or (e) Public transit (e.g., rail, bus, taxis, etc.)

or (f) Freight movement by various modes (e.g., truck, rail, air, water, pipeline)

or (g) Environmental problems generated by transportation

or (f) Any or all of the above

We need to gather information on transportation because it is closely linked to other aspects of urban planning, including land use planning, economic development, the quality of life, and environmental protection. You can't do adequate urban planning without transportation planning. You can't do adequate transportation planning without good background data. Transportation planning is widely viewed by the public as one of the most important issues in metropolitan America today.

## Recommended Procedure

**1.** Identify the apparent transportation issues in your planning area that appear to merit study. (e.g., traffic congestion, the disruption of residential neighborhoods, parking, commuting times, etc.)

**2.** Work with a professional traffic engineer. You shouldn't abdicate your responsibilities as a professional planner to do this; find someone you can work with on a team. Maintain this working relationship not only in the data collection and analysis phase of the planning process, but also in the plan- preparation phases.

**3.** Consider the formation of a technical advisory committee, composed of interested transportation professionals.

**4.** Determine how traffic will be "modeled" for future land use patterns, and how land use will be related to traffic capacity.

**5.** Consider the formation of a citizens advisory committee.

**6.** Decide which topics merit research and analysis. Review this list with your committees. Your list might include some of the following:

• Local transportation
—Map of the street network
—Capacity of selected streets and intersections in the network
—Traffic volumes observed on selected streets in the network
—"Level of service" (LOS) of selected streets and intersections
—Physical condition of the streets, bridges, tunnels, etc. in the network
—Parking supply and demand
—Accident locations
—Trip generation characteristics of various land uses
—Location, size, and characteristics of major trip generators
—Trip origin-destination data
—Use of local public transit
—Use of ride-sharing and van pools
—Bicycle routes
—Accessibility available to local residents

to employment centers, schools, shopping, recreation, etc.
—Fiscal policies concerning the construction and maintenance of local streets
—Design standards for roads
—Local environmental impacts of transportation
—Ride-sharing programs
—Public attitudes concerning transportation issues

• Metropolitan transportation
—Most of the same topics noted in "Local transportation," but with attention given to metropolitan, rather than local, aspects of transportation facilities, services, etc.

• Inter-city transportation
—passenger movement by:
—Private car
—Bus
—Rail
—Air

• Freight transportation—freight movement by:
—Truck
—Rail
—Water
—Air
—Pipeline

**7.** Conduct research on and analysis of the selected topics.

**8.** Establish priorities for the resolution of identified transportation problems. Try to identify which need immediate attention, and should be considered in short-range planning, and which should be considered in the future and may be appropriate for inclusion in the long-range plan.

**9.** Identify linkages between transportation planning and other topics in planning,

especially land use planning, environmental protection, and economic development.
**10.** Write a report of your findings, and a summary of your basic data.

This Task should result in:
**1.** Data files on selected topics, for in-office use, and for sharing with others who are concerned with transportation. These files may be in the form of text, maps, photographs, tables, computer files, etc. The files should, of course, be "clean," well-organized, and well-documented (i.e., topic, source, date, etc.)
**2.** A written report (including text, tables, and graphics) that includes information on the topics identified above.

Much of the data assembly and analysis indicated here may be included in a local Transportation System Management (TSM) program. See mention of this subject in Chapter 11.

Transportation in urban America appears to be a major unresolved problem. Our reliance on the use of private cars (usually occupied by driver only) for 95 percent of our person-movements results in widespread traffic congestion, high economic cost, environmental degradation, and threatens our quality of life. It also causes serious problems for people who do not drive their own cars, for reasons of physical condition, or limited economic resources.

Our reliance on private automobiles for transportation strongly influences metropolitan land use development patterns; it impels us to develop low-density suburban areas. These suburban areas are of such low population density that the use of public transit is al-

most always impractical, so we can't abandon the use of private cars there even if we wanted to.

As professional planners we should be attacking the urban transportation problem with greater vigor and resources if we are serious about improving the quality of life in urban and suburban America.

If we make good analyses of the transportation issues in our communities it may help us to identify policies that will provide effective means for getting us out of the transportation/land use mess we are in today.

### References

Edwards, John D., editor. *Transportation Planning Handbook.* Englewood Cliffs, NJ: Prentice Hall, 1992. (Published for the Institute of Transportation Engineers.)

Kaiser, Godschalk, and Chapin. *Urban Land Use Planning* 4th ed. Urbana: University of Illinois Press, 1995. See Chapter 9, "Infrastructure and Community Facilities."

So, Frank S. and Judith Getzels, editors. *The Practice of Local Government Planning* 2d ed. Washington: International City Management Association, 1988. (See Chapter 6, "Transportation Planning" by Sandra Rosenblum.)

### TASK 2.3.6 COLLECT AND ANALYZE INFORMATION ON UTILITIES

This Task involves the collection and analysis of several important elements of the physical infrastructure in your planning area. Topics considered may include: water supply, sewage disposal, storm water management, and solid waste management.

In some cases it may also include some the following utilities, which are often privately installed and maintained: electric power systems, natural gas lines, telephone systems, and cable television.

We need information on utilities because:

**1.** Water supply, sewage disposal, and storm water management are important "form-givers" in urban development. That is, the physical and economic constraints related to these topics usually determine which lands will be developed for urban purposes, and at which density. When you plan for the expansion of an urban area you should be aware of the constraints imposed by these utility systems, and of the opportunities for development they offer.

**2.** Most of the utility systems identified above have a long useful life. We usually choose to keep existing utility systems for economic reasons, rather than write them off. This, of course, has a strong influence on patterns of urban development; therefore, information on existing utility systems is usually important to have when you are engaged in urban planning.

**Recommended Procedure**

**1.** Identify what the local issues relating to utilities appear to be.

**2.** Collect and analyze data on some of the following topics:

- Water supply
- Sewage disposal
- Storm water management
- Electricity
- Natural gas, telephone, cable TV, etc.
- Solid waste management

Just which topics should be studied depends upon what the present and emerging issues appear to be.

**3.** For each topic selected consider preparing a report which includes:

- A description of the existing utility network or systems. Include a map of each system showing which areas are served by it. In some cases you may indicate where a map of the system is on file that would be an acceptable substitute.
- Identification of the physical constraints on the expansion of the system (e.g., Which areas cannot be served by gravity-flow sewers? Which areas cannot be provided with water service without the construction of new pumps and storage tanks?).
- An analysis of the existing capacity of the utility system.
- A report on the existing usage of the system. Identify areas of substantial under-usage, and of areas where usage is approaching (or exceeding) its rated capacity.
- A summary of public and private fiscal policies concerning the design and construction of the utility system (optional).
- A summary of public and private fiscal policies concerning fees charged for use of the utility system (optional).

This Task should result in: data files on the selected topics (well-documented with sources, titles, dates, etc., of course); maps of the various utility systems studied; and a written report (or series of reports), with text, maps, tables, etc., that contains information on the utilities you selected for analysis.

The topics discussed under the general heading of "utilities" are not often filled with drama and pathos. They are, however, fundamental, and you must understand your utility system before you can proceed with planning the physical development of your community.

## References

Goodman and Freund. *Principles and Practice of Urban Planning.* See pp. 232-245 in Chapter 8, "Governmental and Community Facilities" by Frank S. So.

Kaiser, Godschalk, and Chapin. *Urban Land Use Planning* 4th ed. Urbana: University of Illinois Press, 1995. See Chapter 9, "Infrastructure and Community Facilities."

Lynch, Kevin. *Site Planning,* 3d ed. See Chapter 8, "Earthwork and Utilities."

Tabors, Richard D., Michael H. Shapiro, and Peter P. Rogers. *Land Use and the Pipe.* Lexington, Mass.: Lexington Books, 1976.

## TASK 2.3.7 COLLECT INFORMATION ON COMMUNITY SERVICES AND FACILITIES

The subject "Community services and facilities" traditionally considers city halls, parks, schools, libraries, fire and police stations, hospitals, etc. This Task is intended to inventory those services and facilities. It is also intended to make a preliminary analysis of how well they are serving the residents of the planning area.

Community services and facilities play an important role in determining quality of life, and they contribute to the determination of urban form.

It is important for professional planners, local policy-formulators, local decision-makers, and the general citizenry to be aware of existing conditions concerning community services and facilities, so that they can make intelligent plans for their future development.

### Recommended Procedure

**1.** Inventory the existing community services and facilities.

For each of the topics considered, various questions might well be examined, such as:

- Where are the physical facilities located? What are their capacities? What are their physical conditions?
- Establish criteria for measuring the quality of service, and then identify which populations are well-served, and which populations are poorly served.
- What is the present public role? What is the present private role? What are the existing public policies concerning these services and facilities?
- What alternative public policies are being advocated by interested parties? (e.g., privatization of selected services).
- Who provides funding for the services and facilities? Who administers them? Who establishes standards for them? Who has a regulatory role?
- What is the dollar cost per person for the services provided (or per unit of some measurable performance standard)?
- Is the funding required directly related to the number of people served (for example, health services), or is one service or facility adequate for the entire community, bearing little relationship to population growth (for example, a sports stadium)?
- Are there apparent trends for citizens using the services and facilities in the future? Does it appear that the demand for them will be greater, remain about the same, or be less?

**2.** The services and facilities to be considered might include the following:

- Administrative centers—city halls, county government centers, district administrative centers , and state and federal administrative offices.

- Education—pre-school, elementary schools, high schools, colleges and universities, and continuing education programs.
- Legal services—courts, district attorneys, and public assistance legal services.
- Cultural facilities—community centers, libraries, auditoriums, concert halls, and museums.
- Religious institutions
- Parks and recreation—park facilities, recreation programs, bicycle trails, spectator sports facilities, and open space preservation programs.
- Health—hospitals, clinics, centers of medical or dental offices, nursing homes, and emergency medical services and paramedical services.
- Public safety—police services and facilities, jails, juvenile halls, fire protection services and facilities, and disaster relief services and facilities.

3. Write a report on the topics you selected for analysis.

This Task should produce data files on community services and facilities and a written report.

When you are reviewing the location of community facilities, you may get information from Task 2.3.3, Land Use.

If you believe this Task is important, a great deal of time can be devoted to it. This may be the case if local issues focus on social or economic problems, or on the quality of life, but the time can be minimized if you are primarily interested in physical design.

## References

Goodman and Freund. *Principles and Practice of Urban Planning* See Chapter 8, "Governmental and Community Facilities," by Frank S. So.

Kaiser, Godschalk, and Chapin. *Urban Land Use Planning* 4th ed. Urbana: University of Illinois Press, 1995. See Chapter 9, "Infrastructure and Community Facilities."

## TASK 2.3.8 COLLECT DATA ON LOCAL HISTORY, ARCHAEOLOGICAL SITES, HISTORIC SITES, ARCHITECTURALLY SIGNIFICANT BUILDINGS AND DISTRICTS

This Task reviews local history and identifies sites, buildings, and districts that are important in the history of the planning area. It is presumed that plans you prepare will make provisions for the preservation of many of these.

Understanding our history is an important part of our culture. Identifying and preserving significant buildings, sites, and districts contributes to that understanding.

**Recommended Procedure**

These five subject areas are considered in this Task:
- Local history
- Archaeological sites
- Historic sites
- Architecturally significant buildings
- Architecturally significant districts

Each of these topics should be investigated and reported on separately. Nevertheless, the general procedures used to gather data is similar, and can be summarized as follows:

1. Review published reports on the subject.
2. Review state and federal registers of historic sites, landmarks, and buildings.
3. Seek out and review unpublished files on the subject. Many of these will be found in university library and departmental

files, in public agency files, and in private organization archives.

**4.** Interview knowledgeable local citizens, and key members of selected private organizations. You may wish to form an advisory committee of these people, so that you can benefit from their knowledge and enthusiastic participation, and so you can keep them informed on what you're doing and what information you're finding.

**5.** Make extensive field investigations; take photographs as needed.

**6.** Prepare a report on the topic. Your report may be in the form of a compilation and re-publication of all the data you have been able to find, accompanied by your notes and interpretations; or an annotated listing of the significant events, sites, buildings, or districts that you have been able to identify; or an annotated report identifying only the sources of data you have found.

Your report should include a map showing the location of the sites, buildings, or districts that have been identified. Note, however, that archaeological sites are usually not mapped in reports intended for general circulation (or are mapped giving only very general locations), so that inquisitive amateurs won't start their own unsupervised archaeological digs.

**7.** Prepare a composite map for use in Task 2.3.15, Lands Available for Development, showing where all sites that should be preserved are located.

This Task should result in a separate report for each of the topics investigated. You may wish to bind these together. You may wish to combine the work in this Task with the preparation of a brief history of your planning area. "Historical Background" is often included in the introductory section of many general plans.

### References

Derry, Anne, et al. *Guidelines for Local Surveys: A Basis for Preservation Planning.* Washington: U.S. Government Printing Office, 1977.
Local historical societies.
Archaeology Departments of major universities.
Architecture Departments of major universities.

### TASK 2.3.9 COLLECT INFORMATION ON VISUAL RESOURCES

If you undertake this Task you can expect to:

• Identify the visual resources of your planning area, and map their locations.

• Prepare a draft statement describing the local sense of values concerning visual resources such as what is locally valued, what is generally accepted as being neither good nor bad, and what is found to be repugnant.

• Prepare a draft statement identifying which features should be encouraged to retain their present visual character (in both developed and undeveloped areas), and what the general character of new urban development should be in specific areas.

We live in the visual environment. It affects our lives for better or worse, although some people seem to be almost oblivious to it.

If we identify and understand our visual resources we may be able to preserve or enhance the quality of our of our environment, and thereby improve the quality of our lives.

### Recommended Procedure

**1.** Review some of the works of Kevin Lynch, including The Image of the City and his chapter in *Principles and Practice of*

*Urban Planning*, "City Design and City Appearance."

**2.** Get to know the structure and spatial organization of your urban area. Know the general location of:

- Residential areas
- Work areas
- Major shopping areas
- Major corridors for traffic passing through the planning area
- Journey-to-work corridors
- Recreation areas (both organized and informal)
- Open space areas
- Centers of educational and other cultural activities
- Landmark features, such as mountains, or major buildings etc.

**3.** Structure a procedure to inventory the visual resources of your planning area.

**4.** Inventory visual resources.

**5.** Prepare a map (or series of maps) of the planning area and its environs, showing:

- Major land uses (generalized, using a "blob technique")
- Activity nodes
- Major land forms, such as rivers, lakes, mountains, etc.
- Vista points of the urban area, and of the nearby open spaces
- Particularly attractive areas (such as open plazas, tree-lined corridors, etc.)
- Particularly attractive individual structures
- Particularly ugly areas
- Visually unique areas that can't be classified as either attractive or ugly (such as a farmers market, a commercial fishing wharf, an automobile row).

Note: This work should be coordinated with Task 2.3.3, Land Use Inventory, and with Task 2.3.8, Local History.

**6.** Analyze the inventory of visual resources. Is there clear evidence of visual resources that are truly valuable? Are there visual elements that most people would regard as eyesores? Do there seem to be development trends that may have a substantial impact on the visual resources in the community?

**7.** Structure a procedure to ascertain the values held by local residents concerning visual features in their environment.

**8.** Undertake and analyze the results of the procedure for ascertaining local values concerning visual resources.

Note: You may have a conflict here. If you have had training in the visual arts, including architecture and landscape architecture, you will probably have developed your own sense of values. Chances are, your values are not shared by the man in the street. So, what are you to do? Will you accept the lowest common denominator of public taste? Will you try to enlighten the plebeians in matters of truth, virtue, and beauty? Or, is there some reasonable middle course?

**9.** Make notes in about what needs to be done concerning the visual quality of your community, such as:

- Design review of new construction
- Historic preservation program
- Open space preservation
- Street-tree planting program
- Billboard regulation
- On-site sign regulation
- Height limits in sensitive areas
- Vista point preservation program

This Task should produce a report which identifies:

**1.** Which values are considered important to residents of the local community concerning their visual resources.

**2.** Specific visual resources in the community that should be preserved. This might be in the form of a list, accompanied by location maps, photographs, and sketches. You may wish to consider making a well-edited videotape to augment your report.

**3.** A preliminary discussion of possible alternative courses of action that might be taken to preserve the positive visual resources of the community, and to ameliorate the negative.

**4.** A preliminary draft of design guidelines for the visual aspects of new development (optional).

Each urban setting has its own visual features; its residents have their own set of values; and the local visual-resource-related issues are unique. It is impossible to prescribe one analysis procedure that will be suitable to all situations.

One technique that was used in an analysis of the visual resources of Blacksburg, Virginia, is summarized in Appendix F.

### References

Appendix F, Summary of Visual Resource Analysis of Blacksburg, Va.

Roberts, Margaret. *Town Planning Techniques*. London: Hutchinson, 1974. See Chapter 17, "Perception" (pp. 395-406).

Goodman and Freund. *Principles and Practice of Urban Planning*. See Chapter 9, "City Design and City Appearance," by Kevin Lynch.

Lynch, Kevin. *The Image of the City*. Cambridge, Mass.: Harvard University Press, 1960.

## TASK 2.3.10 COLLECT AND ANALYZE DATA ON POPULATION AND EMPLOYMENT

Population and employment drive urban development; they have a direct effect on housing, transportation, local commercial activity, etc.

When you understand the patterns, amounts, and causes of past changes in population and employment you will probably have a good understanding of how and why your community developed as it did. And, when you understand the past and the present of your community, you will be in a good position to plan for its future.

### Recommended Procedure

1. Collect data on some of the following topics.

Attempt to get data that reflects conditions over a period of years, so that trends can be identified.

- Population size and characteristics
- Number
- Age distribution
- Sex distribution
- Ethnic composition and distribution
- Income distribution
- Migration data (in-migration, out-migration)
- Vital statistics (number of births, birth rates, number of deaths, death rates)
- Population projections
- Employment
- Size of the labor force
- Employment by industry

- Percent unemployment
(Note: Coordinate with Task 2.3.11)

**2.** Write a report on your findings. Identify trends that you have observed.

While it is essential to analyze population and employment data for urban planning purposes, there are other topics that are also important. If your community has serious social issues it may be appropriate to gather and analyze data on:

- Crime—Incidence of crime (by type and location)
- Health—Quality of public health, infant mortality rate
- Education—Levels of educational attainment

This Task should produce:

**1.** A report that summarizes your data and discusses your findings.

**2.** Well-organized data files. Much of the data you assemble and analyze in this Task is to be published later in Task 2.17, Publish Data Book.

The population and economic data collection and analysis parts of this Task are basic steps in the urban planning process. There are, however, many additional studies that are worthwhile. Just which studies should be made will depend on the local conditions within each community; it is beyond the scope of this book to attempt to discuss them in detail. The additional topics include, among many others: economic base studies; monitoring the quality of life; and analysis of current local social problems.

### References

Kaiser, Godschalk, and Chapin. *Urban Land Use Planning* 4th ed. Urbana: University of Illinois Press, 1995. See Chapter 5, "Population."

Perloff, Harvey S. *Planning the Post-Industrial City.*

So and Getzels. *The Practice of Local Government Planning.* See Chapter 11, "Social Aspects of Physical Planning," by Elizabeth Howe.

### TASK 2.3.11 COLLECT AND ANALYZE DATA ON ECONOMIC CONDITIONS

In this Task you will gather information about local economic conditions, and make some analysis of it. Topics include income, cost of living, retail sales volumes, local employment, housing costs, and natural resource extraction. Your discussion of the topics will relate local conditions to regional, state, and national economic conditions.

The local economy pays the wages that support our citizens, and pays for structures such as housing, stores, factories, roads, and hospitals. We need to know how the local economy works, and what its strengths and weaknesses are, so that we can plan for its continuation and enhancement in future years.

### Recommended Procedure

**1.** Collect data on the following topics. Add to the list if there are additional issues you believe should be considered. Delete those topics which are not locally relevant.

Collect data for a number of years in the past, as well as for the present, so that economic trends can be identified.

- Identify the present and emerging local, regional, state, and national economic issues.
- Discuss the relationships among local, metropolitan, state, and national economic conditions.
- Collect and analyze data on local employment including occupations of the

workers locally employed and wages paid to local employees.

- Cost of living.
- Retail sales volumes by type of retail establishment and by geographic location.
- Discuss the past, present, and emerging role of the central business district.
- Identify and describe major employers in the area. Discuss their present role and their prospects. Discuss how their future is related to the future of the national, regional and local economy.
- Review local housing costs (See Task 2.3.4) including land costs, construction costs, and financing costs.
- Review vacancy rates in housing, in offices, in retailing areas, and in industrial areas.
- Review local transportation costs including cost of commuters' journey to work, cost of inter-city passenger movement, and cost of freight movement by truck, rail, air, and water.
- Discuss data on natural resource extraction including agricultural production, mineral production, and timber production.

**2.** Write a report based on analysis of the data you have collected.

This Task should produce:

**1.** Well-organized data files that can be used in Task 2.7, Publish Data Book.

**2.** A report that summarizes your findings concerning the local economy, and its relationship to the regional, state, and national economies.

If many of the issues in your planning area stem from problems in the economic environment, this Task may be important for your planning program.

### References

Kaiser, Godschalk, and Chapin. *Urban Land Use Planning* 4th ed. Urbana: University of Illinois Press, 1995. See Chapter 6, "The Economy."

Goodman and Freund. *Principles and Practice of Urban Planning.* See Chapter 4, "Economic Studies," by Richard B. Andrews.

### TASK 2.3.12 COLLECT INFORMATION ON GROWTH AREAS

The reasons for undertaking this Task are to identify areas that appear to be growth-prone and growth-resistant, and to quantify the amount of past growth, and the rate of growth. This information should help you quantify future growth rates and amounts.

### Recommended Procedure

**1.** Review records of subdivision map approval. Plot the locations of subdivisions; tabulate their size and characteristics.

**2.** Review records of building permits issued for new construction, for demolitions, and for major remodeling. Make a dot map showing the location of urban growth.

**3.** Compare earlier aerial photographs with recent ones, and identify which sectors of the planning area have changed; describe the nature of that change (optional).

**4.** Tabulate the type and amount of growth, by geographic sub-area, of urban development.

This Task should produce:

**1.** A map showing the location of urban growth. (Preferred alternative: a series of maps, showing the location of growth by five-year periods.)

**2.** Tabulations of data.

**3.** A written analysis of the findings made from the review of maps and statistical data.

This Task, in many circumstances, may be considered one that produces "nice-to-know" information, rather than information that is crucial to the success of your planning program.

This Task should help you in preparing Task 2.4, Establish a Monitoring Program for Critical Issues.

### Reference

Godschalk, Bollens, Hekman, and Miles. *Land Supply Monitoring*. Boston: Oelgeschlager, Gunn, & Hain, 1985.

### TASK 2.3.13 COLLECT INFORMATION ON LAND USE REGULATIONS

Governmental regulations such as zoning codes control how land in specific locations may be used. You will need this information as a background when preparing either short-range or long-range plans.

### Recommended Procedure

**1.** Assemble the regulations concerning land development within your planning area.

Look for the following types of regulations:
- Zoning ordinances
- Subdivision ordinances
- Flood plain regulations
- Airport approach zone regulations
- Historic district regulations
- Locations of designated historic sites or buildings

- Tax abatement programs for agricultural lands (e.g., in California, the Williamson Act lands; in Virginia, the Agricultural and Forestal District lands)
- Transferable development rights programs (currently in New York City and in Maryland)
- Lands that are subject to scenic easements (or dedication of development rights)
- Location of "official plan lines" (or "mapped streets") showing proposed streets
- Growth management programs (e.g., limitations on the number of building permits which may be issued in any one year)
- Areas subject to moratoria on the issuance of building permits (e.g., areas not served by adequate water or sewer lines)
- "Urban service area boundaries," such as those used by California cities to identify the limits of urban expansion.

**2.** Read through the assembled regulations so that you have a general knowledge of how they work, and where they are applied.

**3.** Through interviews with informed people, find out which regulations are being used effectively, and which are not. Identify, if possible, the strengths and weaknesses of each of the programs (optional).

**4.** Write a report on your findings.

This Task should produce a report that summarizes the findings of your assembly and analysis of land use regulations, and one or more maps showing the location of the affected lands.

This Task may be a simple one in a small, unsophisticated community, or it may be a complex one in a community that is experimenting with innovative techniques for land use regulation, open space preservation, or growth management.

The work in this Task should be correlated with Task 2.3.15, Lands Available for Development.

## TASK 2.3.14 MAP CURRENT PROJECTS

This Task is intended to produce a map of land development projects that have been designed and approved, committed, or sanctioned, but not yet built. It illustrates what will probably be built in your planning area in the near future.

There are two reasons why this Task should be undertaken:

**1.** To provide a foundation on which to build short-range or long-range plans. The information included on the map of current projects is a forecast of probable changes in land use.

**2.** To provide a source of up-to-date information to those who wish to know what's going on in your planning area. These people are likely to be local officials (such as legislators or planning commissioners), people who are professionally involved with property development (such as real estate agents, civil engineers, land developers, and bankers), conservation organizations, and local citizens.

### Recommended Procedure

**1.** Define what type of projects you are going to show on your map. These projects should be those that have been approved, but not yet constructed. General categories might include:

- Publicly funded projects, such as capital improvement projects actually budgeted for construction. Typical projects would be trunk sewer line extensions, new schools, etc.
- Privately funded projects that have cleared all administrative hurdles prior to the issuance of a building permit. (You are going to have to decide if those private projects that have not yet received firm financing should be shown.) Typical projects are new subdivisions, new office buildings, new shopping centers, etc.

**2.** Select a base map to use. It is highly desirable to have this at the same scale as the zoning map of your jurisdiction, and of the general plan diagram.

**3.** Devise a mapping notation for showing approved projects.

**4.** Map Current Projects on a Mylar overlay to the base map.

By using the overlay, when you place it on top of your existing land use map you will be able see how planned new projects relate to existing development. When you place the overlay on top of your general plan diagram you will see how proposed new projects relate to the future of your planning area.

**5.** Establish a routine procedure for updating the map of current projects. One person in the office should be assigned the responsibility for entering the changes on a regular basis.

**6.** If staff time permits, prepare a tabulation of current "approved-but-not-yet-built projects," and issue it quarterly.

**7.** Start a new Map of Current Projects at the start of each calendar year.

This Task should produce:

1. An up-to-date map overlay showing the location of projects that will probably be built in the near future.

2. A list, published quarterly, of probable projects, with an indication of what they are, where they will be built, and the name of their sponsor (optional).

This Task will provide information to you and others concerning where new urban development is taking place, and what its characteristics will be.

This Task can be a good source of information if your jurisdiction is monitoring the availability of land for new urban development.

### TASK 2.3.15 LAND AVAILABILITY

If you are going to engage in land use planning you need to have information concerning which lands are potentially available for changes in land use. This Task is intended to develop some indicators of the availability of such lands in your planning area.

**Recommended Procedure**

In this Task, unless lands are not classified as not available, it is assumed that they probably are available for some change in land use.

The basic procedure is to identify what criteria are to be used to identify non-availability of lands, and then apply those criteria to your planning area, as follows:

1. Decide what criteria you will use to determine which lands are probably not available for changes in land use. Consider these questions:

• Should you include only vacant lands, and ignore developed parcels?

• Are you interested in identifying under-developed properties, where the ratio of the value of improvements to the value of land is very low?

• Should you exclude from your inventory vacant lands that have been subdivided into small parcels, and are in areas that are now almost fully developed? There may be a great many of these parcels in your urban area.

• In undeveloped areas, what should be the minimum size of a parcel that you inventory? (5 acres? 10 acres? 40 acres?)

• Are there state or federal lands (such as military bases) whose ownership should be highlighted? These lands are usually "not available," but sometimes this status changes, with potentially strong impacts on future land use patterns.

• Which lands are owned by local or regional public agencies, used for public purposes, and are therefore probably not available? Consider lands such as parks, open space reserves, water supply watersheds, etc.

• Would it be useful to know who owns large tracts of undeveloped land?

2. Apply your screening criteria you decided on to lands in your planning area. This can be done by using a graphic screening procedure, such as plotting the locations of lands you have identified by each criterion on a base map of your planning area. Use a different color for each screening criterion. For example, you might use blue for already-developed lands, green for open space preserves, red for under-developed lands, etc.

Two alternative mapping methods: Instead of using colors on a base map, use shading films like Zipatone on a sheet of clear drafting film such as Mylar. This can be done either on one sheet, or using a separate sheet of drafting film for each criterion used.

Or, use computer mapping. (See Task 2.3.1 for a brief discussion of the subject.) If you have compiled your maps using CAD, you can instruct the computer to plot out the "layers" of data that you have selected, all on one sheet of drafting film.

This Task should produce:

**1.** A map showing lands that are potentially available for development, based on the criteria you selected.

**2.** A map showing ownerships, with various colors or shading patterns. reflecting different categories of ownership, such as private, institutional, federal, state, special district, municipal, etc. (optional).

**3.** A brief report reflecting the findings from the analysis of your data.

### TASK 2.3.16 LAND CAPABILITY

Land capability is defined as a measure of the physical capacity of a specific location to support a specific land use.

This Task describes a procedure for screening out lands in a planning area that do not meet established criteria for supporting specified land uses.

This is an optional Task.

Many times, when planning for future land uses, it is useful to identify areas where land development clearly should not, or cannot be supported. The following procedure illustrates one method of screening out those lands.

**Recommended Procedure**

**1.** Identify the land use for which you wish to find areas that may be appropriate as potential sites.

You may identify a single specific land use, such as a regional shopping center, or a more general category of land uses, such as "low-density suburban subdivision."

**2.** For the land use selected, identify the criteria that must be met if a location is considered to be satisfactory.

For example, we might say that a site for a low-density suburban subdivision must meet these criteria:

- Not in a 100-year flood plain.
- Not in the habitat of rare or endangered species.
- Have a slope of less than 15 percent.
- Not in an area that cannot be economically served by an urban sewer system.

**3.** Prepare data maps on sheets of plastic drafting film; prepare them as overlays to the base map of your planning area. These maps should screen out those areas that do not meet the locational criteria for the land use you are considering.

You should be able to use data that was identified earlier in this Phase of the planning process, such as:

- Areas that are already developed (see Task 2.3.3).
- Lands in flood plains (see Task 2.3.2).
- Areas with geologic hazards (see Task 2.3.2).
- Lands with steeply sloping terrain (see Task 2.3.2).
- Lands protected from urban development because they are in an agricultural preserve (see Task 2.3.13).

- Areas that cannot be served economically by urban utilities (see Task 2.3.6).
- Areas that are the habitat of rare or endangered species (see Task 2.3.2).
- Historic sites and districts (see Task 2.3.8).
- Areas that are inaccessible because of lack of roads (see Task 2.3.5).

**4.** Gather the overlays that mask out the land areas that do not meet the criteria you established and place them over a base map of your planning area.

The areas that remain visible are considered to be not incapable of supporting the land use you defined, according to the criteria you established.

Note: As noted in Task 2.3.15, if you have been doing computer mapping this type of work is greatly simplified. The computer plotter can be instructed to plot out which layers of data you have selected, all on one sheet of drafting film.

This Task should produce a map showing lands that are potentially capable of supporting development, based on the criteria you selected, and a report reflecting findings from the analysis of your data.

The procedure described here is intended to assist you in using the geographically related data that you have assembled up to this time.

If you apply this procedure, you will recognize the need to have your data maps prepared at a standardized scale and with fairly uniform drafting techniques, so that the maps produced can be used in this Task.

### References

Anderson, Larz T. "Seven Methods for Calculating Land Capability/Suitability" Planning Advi-sory Service Report No. 402 Chicago: American Planning Association, 1987 (22 pp.).

If you are interested in establishing a land supply monitoring program in your community you should refer to:

Godschalk, Bollens, Hekman, and Miles. *Land Supply Monitoring.* Boston: Oelgeschlager, Gunn & Hain (in association with the Lincoln Institute of Land Policy), 1985.

### TASK 2.4 ESTABLISH A MONITORING PROGRAM FOR CRITICAL ISSUES

It is important for people working with local government and with urban society in general to be aware of current conditions, and be aware of trends. In this way they may be able to make the most of beneficial trends, and reduce the adverse impacts of detrimental trends.

### Recommended Procedure

Review the data collected in earlier Tasks, especially:

- Task 2.3.5, Transportation
- Task 2.3.10, Population and Employment
- Task 2.3.11, The Economy

From the many topics that you review, select a limited number, perhaps 20 or 30, that you believe are good indicators of the quality of urban life in your community, and whose trends may have important impacts on the future quality of life.

A preliminary list might include:

*Land Use and the Environment*

- The number and value of building permits issued, tabulated by building type
- Percent of residential units vacant
- Percent of office space vacant
- Number of days that the air quality index is in the good range

*Transportation*

- Travel time, during peak hours, on a specific cross-town route, or on a commuter route to a metropolitan employment center
- Traffic volumes at several specific intersections
- Transit patronage

*The Economy*

- Percent of labor force unemployed
- Retail sales per capita
- Total taxable value of real estate
- Average sales price of single family homes

*Social Conditions*

- Birth rate
- Infant mortality rate
- Death rate

Publish your data and its analysis preferably quarterly. Or, if your resources are severely limited, publish annually, timed to precede the start of the annual budget preparation process.

You may want to publish two versions of the report. The first would be a complete report with all of your data, to be given limited distribution. The second would be a two-page summary, intended for widespread distribution.

While this is a desirable Task, it is not really essential to the preparation of an urban general plan. It takes staff time to complete, which may not be available. But, it is work that a good planning office should do anyway, regardless of whether or not it is updating the local plan.

## References

It is recommended that you review recent literature on the subject of social indicators. No specific sources on the subject are suggested at this time.

The Jacksonville Community Council in recent years has published an excellent annual review of local conditions. Their publication might serve as a good example for others to follow. The book: Life in Jacksonville: Quality Indicators for Progress. The council's address: 1001 Kings Ave, Suite 201, Jacksonville, Florida 32207.

## TASK 2.5 REVIEW ISSUES, DATA, AND PRIORITIES

In this Task, think about what you and other participants in the planning process have accomplished. Review the issues you started out to investigate; review the data you have selected to ascertain whether it sheds light on those issues, and whether new issues have become evident. Review priorities; are the priorities you previously established still valid?

This Task will help you to take stock of where you are, so you can make any needed "mid-course corrections" in your planning program.

### Recommended Procedure

**1.** Review the issues you identified in Task 2.2. Are the original issues still important? Which issues, if any, can be dropped? Which issues should be retained? What new issues should be added to your list?

**2.** Review the data you collected in Task 2.3. Does the data appear to be adequate to serve as a basis for making reasonable decisions? What new issues have collection and analysis of the data identified?

**3.** If your review identifies additional data that should be collected and analyzed, this is the time to do it.

**4.** Review the priorities you established in Task 2.2. Are the priorities for issue-resolution you established earlier still valid? Which issues should be given a lower priority? Which a higher priority?

**5.** Write memoranda on conclusions drawn from your analysis.

**6.** Review your memoranda with appropriate committees established to participate in the planning process.

The products from this Task should probably be memoranda, prepared for the information of your staff and appropriate Advisory Committees. The memoranda might consist of:

**1.** A memorandum that updates the identification and description of local planning issues.

**2.** A memorandum that identifies the ordering of priorities you and the Advisory Committee now consider appropriate for the resolution of planning issues.

**3.** A memorandum that identifies what additional data should be collected and analyzed in the near future.

This is an important Task in the planning process, and should be given serious consideration.

While the staff must do most of the routine work in this Task, the subject matter and drafts of your conclusions should be carefully reviewed with appropriate advisory committees.

## TASK 2.6 PUBLISH REPORT ON SIGNIFICANT CONDITIONS AND TRENDS

A report should be published to summarize the present conditions in the planning area, and identify and discus trends to be considered when planning its future.

The report produced in this Task should provide a foundation for discussion with the participants in the planning process, so all of you understand what's going on. It also may serve as one of the early sections of the plan you will be preparing.

**Recommended Procedure**

Review the data collected.

**1.** Consider what should be included in the data book (see Task 2.7), and in what form. Consider which data is significant enough to be included in the report to be produced in this Task.

**2.** Review the data collected and identify recent or emerging trends that appear to be important to consider.

You should distinguish between:

- Trends caused by outside forces such as the national economy, over which citizens have little or no local control.
- Trends that are largely local in their origin, and which citizens may be able to influence.

**3.** Write a report containing:

- A summary of benchmark data
- Identification and discussion of significant trends in the planning area

This Task should produce one report containing a summary of significant data concerning your planning area, and a discussion of locally significant conditions and trends.

The topics to be considered depend on the data you have collected and analyzed. You may wish to consider some of the following topics:

A brief history of the area (Task 2.3.8)

Population characteristics and trends (Task 2.3.10)

Land use trends (Task 2.3.3)

Circulation conditions and trends (Task 2.3.5)

Neighborhood and housing conditions (Task 2.3.4)

Economic conditions and trends (Task 2.3.11)

Environmental conditions and trends (Task 2.3.2)

It is essential that work on this Task be closely related to work on Task 2.7, Publish Data Book.

You may wish to cite in the discussion of each topic the local issues that have been identified (see Tasks 2.2 and 2.5).

Development in urban settlements usually does not follow a smooth statistical curve; the curve is more often "lumpy." A sudden change in national economic conditions may bring about an upward spurt, or a downturn, in local employment, and a boom, or a slump, in local housing construction. Disasters, such as fires, floods, and earthquakes bring catastrophic and rapid changes. Wars can bring about substantial national, regional, and local changes, very suddenly.

Many of these lumps on the curve of time are either entirely unpredictable, or cannot be anticipated more than several months in advance. Sudden changes can play havoc with projections used for short-range plans. When we do long-range planning, we can expect that while these events will take place, their impacts will average out over time.

### TASK 2.7 PUBLISH DATA BOOK

This Task is useful because it can provide all those who are participating in the planning process with relevant information for planning the future of their community.

It can also establish a data bank about the planning area for the use of people who are interested in it, although they may not be directly involved with planning for its future. People such as bankers, members of a Chamber of Commerce, news reporters, real estate agents, etc. may appreciate and profit from having good data readily available.

**Recommended Procedure**

**1.** Assemble and review the data you have. Decide which data should not be reproduced because it is available to the general public in its original format; it is grossly incomplete, of questionable validity, or lacks information on its source and date; it is not germane to your planning area; or it is badly out of date, and is not of historical interest.

**2.** Decide which data to include in the data book. This should be information that is not readily available elsewhere; known by you to be reliable information; germane to your planning area; and within your budget to reproduce.

**3.** Decide early on who your audience will be, how many copies of the text you will reproduce, and how the book will be distributed. These factors will influence not only the style and content of the book, but also the budget.

**4.** Design a uniform format for the presentation of data. This format should usually use a standard paper size (e.g., 8½-by-11-inch); be attractive, perhaps with a distinctive style; be easy to read and comprehend; and be economical to reproduce.

Most of your written materials will probably be reproduced from computer files. Your report format should be established before the data is put into those computer files. Consider using desktop publishing.

**5.** Your data book should be easy to amend. It should be easy to add new pages as better data becomes available, and to delete obsolete data. This suggests a loose-leaf format, with page numbering done by section, rather than consecutively throughout the book.

Each piece of data must have an appropriate title, be dated, and have its source identified.

It is essential to have each page annotated with the date it was compiled, so later you can tell if individual copies of the book contain the most up-to-date pages.

**6.** If you choose to establish a data bank (see Paragraph 10 of the recommended procedures discussed in Task 2.3), or establish a monitoring program for critical issues (see Task 2.4), it is very important that this Task be coordinated with those work projects.

This Task should result in the publication of a data book, as described above.

The work described in this Task is important. Most planning agencies should collect, edit, publish, and distribute data (in various forms), regardless of whether or not they are engaged in updating or preparing an urban plan.

The City of Colorado Springs, Colorado, wrote in its *Comprehensive Plan* (1983 edition):

> The first step in the development of the Comprehensive Plan was the preparation of the Community Profile. In November 1980, the City Planning Department began assembling all available and relevant information needed to understand the physical, social, and economic conditions of the City. The Community Profile was published in September 1981 for general distribution and use by the Task Force and its committees in their discussions of public policy. The data, review of existing conditions, projections and the identification of issues in the Community Profile proved to be an invaluable resource for the planning participants.

### Reference

Dandekar, Hemalata C. *The Planner's Use of Information.* Chicago: American Planning Association, 1988 (a reprint of the 1982 edition).

### TASK 2.8 DRAFT REVISIONS TO WORK PROGRAM

It is important to make desirable changes to the planning program as they come to your attention. You and your client should have an opportunity to improve the work program when agreement can be reached on how this can be done. It would be unfortunate for you and your client to be locked into an inflexible program that you both agree is out of date.

### Recommended Procedure

1. Review the work program agreed to in Task 1.14.

2. Review the work accomplished, and compare it with:
- The content of the work you proposed to complete
- Your original time schedule
- Your original budget
- Current issues and priorities, as described in Task 2.5

3. Prepare a draft revision to the work pro-

gram, recommending any changes in topics, depth of investigation, timing, or budget that you believe to be appropriate.

This Task should produce:
A draft of a revised work program
A draft of a revised budget, if needed
This is a critical Task.

You are probably already behind schedule and over budget. What should you do? You may wish to consider these options:

- Ask for an extension of time
- Ask for an increase in budget
- Cut back on the scope of work
- Find ways to make your staff more productive
- All of the above

### Reference

Refer back to Task 1.14, Review Work Program and Budget with Client, and Task 2.5, Review Issues, Data, and Priorities.

## TASK 2.9 REVIEW AND AMEND THE WORK PROGRAM

It is important that you, your client, and other program participants agree on priorities, and on the scope of future work.

This is the appropriate time to make any changes to the planning program that are needed. These changes may involve program content, timing, budget, or other matters.

It is essential that you and your client are in agreement concerning changes to be made.

### Recommended Procedure

Identify the people or groups it is appropriate to discuss changes with in the planning program. You will probably select your next-step-up administrator, the planning commission, and your local legislative body. In some instances it may be appropriate to discuss these matters with one or more of the citizen committees that have been named to participate in the planning process.

With these people or groups review:
1. The report produced in Task 2.6, Publish Report on Significant Conditions and Trends
2. The issues and priorities that were developed in Task 2.5
3. The recommended changes to the work program, as developed in Task 2.8
4. Any recommended changes to the budget.

This Task should result in a mutual understanding between you, the client, and with other participants, concerning priorities for future work (i.e., which topics are to be considered, when they will be worked on, in what depth, etc.); identification of agreed-upon changes to the planning work program and the budget; and a written record of the items noted above.

# Phase III
# Prepare, Review, and
# Adopt the General Plan

## Contents

**Figure 7.1** Flowchart of Tasks in Phase III

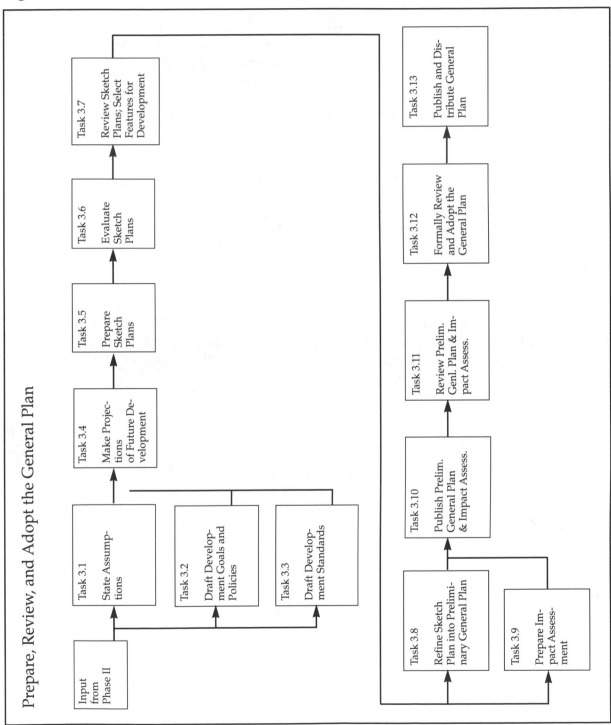

## INTRODUCTION

This phase is the fun part of the planning process. Here you will actually prepare a plan, in cooperation with other participants, of course, and you will tweak it here and there so that it becomes a plan that your local legislative body, your planning commission, and others in the community will endorse and use.

This phase describes how a long-range general plan can be prepared. If your work program doesn't call for a long-range plan, but deals only with a short-range district plan, or a function plan, you should, of course, skip this phase.

Any general plan that is to be officially adopted must be prepared, reviewed, and adopted in accordance with specific state laws and requirements. This usually means including specific topics in the plan, holding official public hearings, and, in several states, preparing and reviewing environmental impact reports. You should review the legal requirements of your state early in the planning process, so you can integrate the required contents and procedures in your work program. It is usually wise to check these out with your city attorney or county counsel early, so there will be no unwelcome surprises for anyone later on.

Before work on this phase begins, the planning staff, the client, and other participants in the planning process should review the work completed in Phase II which dealt with data on the planning area, the analysis of significant conditions and trends, and with the proposed scope of the planning program.

### References

Kaiser, Godschalk, and Chapin. *Urban Land Use Planning* 4th ed. Urbana: University of Illinois Press, 1995. See Part 3, "Advance Planning."

Kent, T. J., Jr. *The Urban General Plan.* Chicago: American Planning Association, 1990.

So and Getzels, editors. *The Practice of Local Government Planning* 2d ed. Washington: International City Management Association, 1988.

### TASK 3.1 STATE ASSUMPTIONS CONCERNING EXTERNAL FORCES

In this Task you prepare statements concerning trends and events caused by external forces that you assume will affect the future physical, social, or economic setting of the area for which you are planning.

Many decisions made in a local community are strongly influenced by events that take place outside the community, and that are largely beyond the control of the local community.

You should know which external trends and events may have a strong influence on local urban planning decisions. You should also know which people, agencies, or fates make decisions which guide these trends and events.

In some cases a local community can change the course or trends of events which originate outside of its borders; in other cases all the community can do is adapt to the inevitable.

### Recommended Procedure

**1.** Decide what time span you are going to consider when making your assumptions. Remember that your projections for the near future will probably be more accurate than those for the distant future.

You may wish to select different time-frames for the different subjects that you discuss.

**2.** Select the topics you wish to consider. Use the topics you included in your report on Significant Conditions and Trends. (See Task 2.6.) Consider only those topics that are substantially influenced by outside forces and that are relevant to the future of your planning area.

**3.** Sit down and think about a subject area. Put down on paper what assumptions need to be made concerning how that subject may affect your planning area. For example, on the subject of employment, you may consider it important to say, for the purposes of planning, that you assume regional employment will increase rapidly in the coming five years (or remain stable, or decrease moderately, etc.).

After you have stated each assumption, make a brief note identifying the person or agency that you believe is responsible for taking actions that will cause the assumption to become a future reality.

After you have finished drafting assumptions concerning one topic, turn to another, and repeat the process.

**4.** Give your estimate of the probability that each of the assumptions you have made will turn out to be valid. While it is usually impossible to develop a reliable statistical probability, you can describe individual assumptions as being very probable, quite probable, or possible, but not probable, or any other set of descriptors you choose (optional).

**5.** Some examples of assumptions you might consider:

- Regional population will continue to increase rapidly for the next 20 years, at an average of 3 percent per year.
- The national economy will improve substantially during the coming five years; inflation will not be a serious problem during that period.
- While there is widespread recognition within the state that unbridled urban growth is causing intolerable traffic congestion, there will be no effective and coordinated regional land use and transportation planning for the coming 10 years.

**6.** The assumptions you draft should not be snatched out of thin air; you will need to have some justification (i.e., reliable sources) for the statements you make. Chances are good you will be questioned or challenged on many of them. Be sure to keep a written record about the sources of and bases for your assumptions.

**7.** Review your draft of assumptions with other participants in the planning process. Try to reach a widely held consensus concerning what assumptions are reasonable to make concerning the future setting of your planning area.

You should produce a fairly brief statement of assumptions that you, and other participants in the planning process, believe are relevant and important.

This Task is a good one to use to start off a citizens advisory committee, if your community is not badly split at the outset of the planning process. Identifying issues and discussing assumptions can often develop good intra-committee communication, which is important.

**Reference**

See also Task 5.9, Draft Statement of Assumptions (for a district plan).

## TASK 3.2 DRAFT DEVELOPMENT GOALS AND POLICIES

In this Task you will work with a goals committee to identify the goals of your community. You will also identify the general policies that your community should follow if it is to attain its stated goals.

*Some definitions.*

*Goal*: A statement that describes, usually in general terms, a desired future condition.

*Objective*: A statement that describes a specific future condition that is to be attained within a stated period of time.

*Policy*: A course of action or rule of conduct to be used to achieve the goals and objectives of the plan.

Before you prepare a plan you should know what the plan is intended to accomplish. This Task is intended to help the residents of your community think about the future of their area, and to reach a consensus on their goals. These goals will then be used in the general plan to guide its recommendations for action.

A pious statement of worthy goals can be a waste of time, however, if those who profess the goals don't know what their implications are. Identify what policies the local community should follow, or what actions it should take, if it is serious about attaining its goals. Matching local policies to local goals is an important part of this Task.

**Recommended Procedure**

**1.** Form an advisory committee (see Task 1.9, Draft a Planning Participation Program).

**2.** Identify the subjects to be considered in the goals and policies. These should be related to the issues that were identified in Task 2.2, Identify Issues and Priorities.

Many communities use general categories such as:
- Basic land use patterns
- Transportation
- Housing
- Economic development
- The environment
- Other topics specifically required by state law

**3.** Draft goals statements in response to the identified issues.

**4.** Draft policy statements in response to identified goals.

**5.** Discuss with the advisory committee:
- The appropriateness of the draft policy statements as responses to the goals
- The probable effectiveness of the draft policies
- The probable beneficial impacts of the draft policies
- The probable adverse impacts of the draft policies

**6.** Revise the goals statements, as appropriate.

**7.** Revise the policies statements, as appropriate.

**8.** Prepare a draft publication of the issues, goals, and policies statements.

**9.** Hold a series of meetings of the advisory committee and interested members of the general public to discuss the draft statements.

**10.** Revise the draft statements as needed.

This Task should produce a report, which is suitable for circulation to interested parties, summarizing the draft of issues that are important to your community, stating the general goals on which consensus has been reached, and setting forth the general policies that local government should follow to attain the goals.

The text should be in a form that can be incorporated, with minimum changes of format, as an integral part of the full general plan that will be prepared at a later date.

Figures 7-2, 7-3, and 7-4, which reproduce the goals and policies sections from the general plans of three cities, provide examples of good practice in general plan writing.

You may want to draft statements of alternative goals and policies in order to resolve identified issues. It is probably worthwhile to do this when there are genuine differences of opinion within the goals committee concerning goals and policies. Statements of alternative goals may point the way to compromise, so that a majority view can be somewhat modified to accommodate a minority view. It is usually a waste of time, however, to draft alternatives just for the sake of having alternatives.

Remember that you are preparing a long-range general plan at this stage. Don't get sidetracked by considering narrowly defined topics. Time for that will come later, when you prepare short-range district plans, or function plans. Don't worry now about formulating detailed and specific policies needed to implement the general goals; time for specific policies will also come later.

The idea of the long-range general plan is to reach agreement on general concepts. After that has been accomplished, you can and should get on with more specific short-range planning (see Phase V).

### References

Kaiser, Godschalk, and Chapin. *Urban Land Use Planning* 4th ed. Urbana: University of Illinois Press, 1995. See pp. 261-277.

San Jose Goals Committee. *Goals for San Jose—Background.* San Jose: San Jose Goals Committee, 1968.

Smith, Frank J., and Randolph T. Hester, Jr. *Community Goal Setting.* New York, Van Nostrand and Reinhold, 1982.

### TASK 3.3 DRAFT DESIRED DEVELOPMENT STANDARDS

In this Task you will define some of the terms you will be using when describing the development you propose in your long-range general plan, and will draft recommended development standards.

When you plan for the future of your community you will have to include consideration of land uses; that is, what activities take place on which lands. When you plan land uses you should think about the populations they will generate, their economic impacts, social implications, trips generated, environmental impacts, services required, and so on. By describing the elements of urban development in specific terms (i.e., identify development standards) you will be able to quantify their impacts later on.

It is essential to define terms so that you, your staff, and other participants in the planning process, will all understand what is meant by the words that describe future development in the community. For example, if you use a term such as "apartments," without indicating what type of structure and density of development you are talking about, you will probably find that each reader will interpret the term differently, and will conjure up

**Figure 7-2** Excerpts from — CITY OF LA VERNE (Calif).
COMPREHENSIVE GENERAL PLAN
(A 20 year plan, adopted 1989)

■ ■ ■

# Goals and Policies.

The following goals and policies address
citywide land use issues.

---

**ISSUE:** Regional pressures to increase
density will place heavy burdens upon
the local and regional circulation system, land fills, sewer and water facilities, impact air and water quality, as
well as city services and facilities.

1. **GOAL:** Density in La Verne will
be limited so that local and regional
facilities are not overburdened.

## POLICIES:

The City shall:

1.1 Require any development that would
put local and regional facilities at or
near capacity to upgrade the affected
facilities.

1.2 Cooperate with regional agencies to
improve regional services and air quality.

1.3 Ensure that the land use policy for the
general plan will provide strict development controls in areas with limited
local services.

1.4 Establish, by 1995, a comprehensive
master capital improvements program
incorporating the following range of
public facilities:

■ Public buildings

■ Water and sewer facilities

■ Street construction and maintenance

■ Parks and recreation facilities

■ Other major capital investments
necessary to sustain the city's development and operations.

1.5 Require a fiscal/service impact analysis on all new residential projects exceeding 10 acres to determine the net
impact on City services including
fire, police, parks, and public works
needs.

1.6 Require a fiscal/service impact analysis on any commercial, industrial,

business park or institutional project
which the community development
department finds may impact the
availability or financing of city utilities and services needed to serve it.

---

**ISSUE: If not property developed, large,
vacant parcels adjacent to La Verne will
adversely affect the quality of life.**

2. **GOAL:** Development of lands adjacent to La Verne will be compatible with development in the city.

## POLICIES:

The City shall:

2.1 Cooperate with other jurisdictions in
developing compatible land uses on
lands adjacent to La Verne.

2.2 Take an assertive posture concerning
developments adjoining the city's
boundaries. This means:

■ Monitoring environmental assessments for these projects.

■ Participating in public hearings.

■ Approving annexations on a
planned rather than piecemeal basis,
by encouraging adjoining properties to
file for annexation at the same time;
and by developing plans to encompass
all annexed properties.

■ Encouraging the Local Agency Formation Commission (LAFCO) to ad-
just sphere of influence lines when
natural landforms make La Verne a
more appropriate provider of public
services. This action should only be
taken when master general plan
amendments, community plans,
specific plans, or zoning have been
adopted for the proposed annexation.

2.3 Discourage annexation which may
imperil the city's long-term ability to
finance, maintain, and operate facilities, seek projects contributing a positive revenue flow.

2.4 Prohibit the extension of water and
sewer facilities to unincorporated
areas unless those parcels annex to
the city.

**Figure 7-2** continued

**2.5** Compute future densities using net rather than gross acreage. For purposes of this general plan, net density refers to that land remaining for development after all development constraints, significant ecological areas, and hazards have been deducted from total acreage. This determination shall be made solely by the City.

---

**ISSUE: Large institutional uses, such as Metropolitan Water District, are outside city policy control. Insensitive development will cause adverse impacts.**

**3. GOAL: To ensure that development of such institutional land uses is compatible with adjacent development, and does not adversely impact city facilities and services.**

## POLICY:

The City shall:

**3.1** Cooperate with owners of institutional uses, and monitor any proposed developments.

**3.2** Require master plans for all institutional development.

**3.3** Require all private enterprises at county-owned facilities to adhere to the La Verne general plan and other related ordinances.

---

**ISSUE: Absent resources to revise the 1974 general plan, the city adopted 17 specific plans. They were substitutes for a comprehensive general plan, filling policy voids. Ranging in size from five to 600 acres, they have resulted in an amalgam of policies, interwoven with other codes and requirements, proving cumbersome to administer and difficult to interpret.**

---

**ISSUE: Absent general plan guidance, the zoning and development codes have lagged behind the needs of the community.**

**4. GOAL: To provide comprehensive, clear development standards and guidelines for all areas of the city.**

## POLICIES:

The City shall:

**4.1** Ensure that all development standards and guidelines are consistent with each other and with the general plan.

**4.2** All development standards and guidelines will address the needs of the community.

**4.3** Ensure that all master plans are consistent with the general plan.

**4.4** Work with adjacent communities to address visual impacts of development in La Verne on these communities.

**5. GOAL: To encourage variety, quality, and innovation in land use practice.**

**5.1** Encourage creative mixed use development through the initiation of zoning and development ordinances which:

- Promote suitable commercial activities in industrial developments;

- Allow for the mixture of residential, commercial, and industrial activities in self-contained neighborhoods which provide basic goods and services within walking distance of homes.

- Develop land use performance criteria that ensure compatibility between uses in mixed use projects.

**Figure 7-3**   Excerpts from — CITY OF HEALDSBURG (CALIF.)
GENERAL PLAN
(A 20 year plan, adopted 1987)

## PART II

### GOALS, POLICIES, AND IMPLEMENTATION PROGRAMS

### SECTION I

### LAND USE

**GOALS AND POLICIES**

**Goal A:   To provide for orderly development within well-defined urban boundaries.**

**Policies:**

1.   Urban development shall be allowed to occur only within the Urban Service Area during the time frame of the General Plan.

2.   City water, sewer, and electrical service shall not be extended to development outside the Urban Service Area.

3.   No development may occur in areas annexed to the City after July 1, 1987, until a specific plan has been prepared and adopted for the area. Such specific plans shall comply with the requirements of State law and address in detail the proposed land use pattern, circulation and other improvements, phasing of development, and financing of infrastructure improvements. Accordingly, specific plans shall be prepared for the unincorporated Fitch Mountain area; the unincorporated Grove Street area; and the northern part of the Urban Service Area. No specific plan shall be required for the unincorporated pockets on the north and south sides of South Fitch Mountain Road and on the south side of Grant Street. No specific plan shall be required for land to be annexed for school purposes.

4.   The City shall not establish annual quantified limits on the rate of growth in Healdsburg, but shall attempt through the specific plans prepared for new development areas to ensure that growth occurs in an orderly fashion and in pace with the expansion of City facilities and services.

5.   The City shall discourage annexations that would result in the creation of unincorporated islands, peninsulas, or other irregular boundaries, provided that such restrictions would not be detrimental to planned growth and development.

6.   The City shall not consider the annexation of the entire unincorporated Fitch Mountain area until the following conditions are met:

   a.   The existing Fitch Mountain Water Company system is upgraded to City standards.

   b.   An assessment district is formed to design and construct a wastewater collection system to City standards with localized treatment facilities or financing of necessary capacity expansion in the City's wastewater treatment system.

94

**Figure 7-3** continued

    c.    County Service Area No. 24 or another public entity initiates and provides financing for the acquisition of Pacific Gas and Electric's electrical distribution facilities in the area and agrees to dedicate such facilities to the City as a condition of annexation.

    d.    An assessment district is formed to design and construct necessary street, drainage, and other improvements to City standards.

    e.    One or more geologic hazard abatement districts are formed and a plan to control and mitigate geologic and soil erosion hazards is implemented.

Notwithstanding this policy, land on the west side and upper slopes of Fitch Mountain may be considered for annexation following the preparation of a specific plan which outlines in detail the configuration of subdivision and development, proposed methods of access, provision of urban services, and mitigation measures for geologic hazards.

**Goal B:** To promote the continuation of land uses outside the Urban Service Area that provide contrast with Healdsburg's urban environment.

**Policies:**

1.    The City shall encourage the County to retain only low-intensity and open-space land use designations outside the Urban Service Area.

2.    The City shall encourage the continuation of agricultural and low-intensity uses adjacent to the Urban Service Area boundary.

3.    The City shall support the deannexation of the incorporated, undeveloped area along Magnolia Drive.

4.    The City shall cooperate with the County in an ongoing effort to assure the achievements of common land use objectives for the unincorporated lands within the Healdsburg Planning Area.

**Goal C:** To provide for a pattern and intensity of land use that reflects historical patterns and at the same time respects natural constraints and conditions.

**Policies:**

1.    Only very low- and low-intensity land uses shall be allowed in areas characterized by steep slopes, environmental hazards, and scenic ridgelines and hillsides.

2.    Intensive urban development shall be allowed only in areas that are relatively free of topographic, geologic, and environmental limitations.

3.    The integrity of distinct and identifiable neighborhoods and districts should be preserved and strengthened.

4.    Clustering of development in the undeveloped Fitch Mountain area and in the northern part of the Urban Service Area shall be encouraged to preserve open space, to meet the policies of the General Plan concerning natural hazards and scenic resources, and to minimize the costs of infrastructure improvements. To this end, density transfers

**Figure 7-3** continued

may be allowed among contiguous parcels pursuant to the provisions of the specific plan prepared for the area.

5. The City may grant a density bonus of up to 25 percent to residential projects that include significant public recreational facilities or other public facilities which benefit the entire community and a density bonus up to 25 percent for residential projects that are deemed by the City to be of superior design. The City shall grant a density bonus of 25 percent to residential projects that reserve at least 25 percent of the units for low and/or moderate income households, 10 percent of the units for lower-income households, or 50 percent of the units for senior citizens. The density bonus shall be calculated based on the maximum density allowable by the base zoning district and any applicable combining districts. In no event shall the total density bonus for any project exceed 25 percent.

6. Development at the interface of different land use designations shall be designed to ensure compatibility between the uses. Residential uses shall be buffered from commercial uses where the two abut at the property lines by ample building setbacks and landscaping on the commercial parcel. Where residential uses of significantly different densities abut, buffering shall be provided on the higher density parcels.

7. The area on the west side of Healdsburg Avenue between Sunnyvale Drive and Chiquita Road designated Mixed Commercial-Industrial shall be developed under strict site development standards for circulation, building setbacks, landscaping, and architectural style, applicable to the entire parcel.

**Goal D: To reinforce the downtown as the commercial and cultural center of Healdsburg.**

**Policies:**

1. The downtown shall be defined by identifiable boundaries. Land use designations shall reinforce the distinction between the downtown and surrounding areas. Landscaping and street trees shall be used to reinforce the distinction between the downtown and adjacent districts.

2. Office uses shall be discouraged on the ground floor of buildings fronting on the Plaza.

**Figure 7-4**   Excerpts from — CITY OF SAN JOSE (Calif).
HORIZON 2000 : GENERAL PLAN
(A 16 year plan, adopted 1984)

## B. Community Development

### 1. Land Use

#### a. Residential Land Use

There are a wide variety of residential neighborhoods in San Jose, each with its own character defined by setting, housing types, densities and, in some cases, cultural heritage. The environment and livability of existing residential neighborhoods are an intangible but important community resource to be preserved. Similarly, these qualities should be fostered in future neighborhoods. To this end, the Residential Land Use goals and policies reflect concerns for the protection of neighborhoods from incompatible land uses, the adequacy of public facilities and services, and protection from hazards.

The Residential Land Use policies also reflect the City's objective to promote higher density residential development in the future than was typical in the past. This objective recognizes that remaining vacant land resources are finite and should be used as efficiently as possible, that the relative affordability of housing is enhanced by higher densities given the rising price of land, and that higher densities make the delivery of public services more cost-effective. A high standard of site planning and architectural design quality can make higher density housing attractive to both the consumer and the neighborhood where it is located.

The Residential Land Use goals and policies are primarily guidelines for the physical development of residential neighborhoods and proximate land uses. The Housing goals and policies, on the other hand, address the maintenance, rehabilitation, improvement and development of housing, particularly relating to affordability.

**Goal:**  Provide a high quality living environment in residential neighborhoods.

**Policies:**

1. Residential development at urban densities should be located only where services and facilities can be provided.

2. Residential neighborhoods should be protected from the encroachment of incompatible activities or land uses which may have a negative impact on the residential living environment.

3. Higher residential densities should be distributed throughout the community. Locations near commercial and financial centers, employment centers, the light rail transit stations and along bus transit routes are preferable for higher density housing.

4. Due to the limited supply of land available for multiple family housing, public/quasi-public uses, such as schools and churches, should be discouraged in areas designated for residential densities exceeding twelve units per acre on the Land Use/Transportation Diagram except in the Downtown Core Area.

5. Residential development should be allowed in areas with identified hazards to human habitation only if these hazards are adequately mitigated.

6. Mobile home parks should be encouraged to locate in various areas of the City rather than concentrating in a few areas.

7. Housing developments designed for senior citizens should be located in neighborhoods that are within reasonable walking distance of health and community facilities and services or accessible by public transportation.

8. Residential social service programs (e.g., board and care facilities) should be equitably distributed throughout the City rather than being concentrated in a few areas. The City should encourage the County and other social service licensing agencies to recognize and implement this policy.

9. When changes in residential densities are proposed, the City should consider such factors as neighborhood character and iden-

**Figure 7-4** continued

tity, compatibility of land uses and impacts on livability, impacts on services and facilities including schools, and impacts on traffic levels on both neighborhood streets and major thoroughfares.

10. In areas designated for residential use, parking facilities to serve adjacent non-residential uses may be allowed if such parking facilities are adequately landscaped and buffered, and if the only permitted access to neighborhood streets is for emergency vehicles.

11. Residential developments should be designed to include adequate open spaces in either private yards or common areas to partially provide for residents' open space and recreation needs.

12. New mobile home parks are not allowed in areas designated for industrial land uses. Existing mobile home parks in industrial areas should, however, be considered permanent rather than interim uses, and should be given the same protection from adjacent incompatible uses as would be afforded any other residential development.

13. In the design of lower density, single-family residential developments, particularly those located in the Rural Residential, Estate Residential and Low Density Residential categories, consideration should be given to the utilization of public improvement standards which promote a rural environment, including such techniques as reduced street right-of-way widths, no sidewalks and private street lighting.

14. Due to the pervasive flooding and geo-technical hazards in the Alviso area, new residential development in Alviso should be allowed only on infill sites within existing neighborhoods.

15. Residential development should be designed with limited access to arterial streets as follows:

- No direct frontage or access on six-lane arterials or within 350 feet of the intersection of two arterials.

- Direct frontage or access elsewhere on four-lane arterials should be strongly discouraged.

The use of frontage roads, corner lots, open-end cul-de-sacs or other street design solutions for access is encouraged.

**b. Commercial Land Use**

The commercial land use policies reflect the need to locate new commercial uses in the community which facilitate convenient shopping and easy access to professional services and which contribute to the economic base of the City. Redevelopment of existing commercial strips and areas and the conversion of existing structures to more appropriate uses should result in the upgrading of these areas.

**Goal:** Provide a pattern of commercial development which best serves community needs through maximum efficiency and accessibility.

**Policies:**

1. Commercial land in San Jose should be distributed in a manner that maximizes community accessibility to a variety of retail commercial outlets and services and minimizes the need for automobile travel.

2. New commercial uses should be located in existing or new shopping centers or in established strip commercial areas. Isolated spot commercial developments and the creation of new strip commercial areas should be discouraged.

3. Any new regional-scale commercial development should be encouraged to locate in the Downtown Core Area rather than in suburban locations.

4. The City should encourage the upgrading, beautifying, and revitalization of existing strip commercial areas and shopping centers.

5. Commercial development should be discouraged from locating or expanding within established residential neighborhoods when such development will have a negative impact on the character and livability of the surrounding residential community.

98

**Figure 7-4** continued

6. New commercial uses or expansion of existing uses within the referral areas of the Airport Land Use Commission should give appropriate consideration to A.L.U.C. policies.

7. New hotel development should be located in the Downtown Area in order to support convention center development and other Downtown revitalization objectives. Hotel/motel development elsewhere in the City may be allowed when it would not interfere with the Downtown revitalization strategy. This policy is effective until the City Council finds that Downtown hotel development objectives are substantially achieved.

8. The City should encourage retail and service establishments to locate in the Downtown Core Area in order to serve residents and employees. In this regard, consideration should be given to providing appropriate assistance to such small businesses.

9. Proposals to convert residential properties along major streets to office or commercial use should be approved only when there is a substantial non-residential character to the area and where satisfactory parking and site design can be demonstrated.

real or imagined social, economic, and environmental impacts, most of which have substantial emotional and therefore political connotations.

**Recommended Procedure**

**1.** Decide what general categories of development you believe will need definition. You may wish to consider:

- Residential areas (e.g., low density, very high density)
- Employment areas (e.g., offices, manufacturing)
- Retail sales areas (e.g., central business district, shopping malls)
- Circulation features (e.g., freeways, arterials, local streets)
- Public services and facilities (e.g., schools, health clinics)
- Non-urban land uses (e.g., agricultural lands)

You should use the same definitions of land uses for planning future development as those you used in your land use survey (see Task 2.3.2) to describe existing development.

**2.** Review the land use, population, and employment data you will need if you are going to use a computer program to project traffic and transit flows. The terminology you use in your general development planning should be compatible with your transportation planning program.

**3.** Review the plans and background data reports of other jurisdictions to see what, if anything, they did to identify and define development standards.

**4.** Expand your list of general topics, identified above, to become a listing of the specific terms you expect to use.

**5.** Provide a definition for each term you have listed. This definition should be descriptive, and, if possible, quantifiable.

For example, you will probably want to define "high density residential areas." What building types do you have in mind? What residential densities? Will you consider a mixture of building types in the areas? What percent of the area will you assume will remain vacant? What type of population (i.e., age, family structure, persons per dwelling unit, etc.) will occupy the housing?

**6.** Identify local examples of each type of development you define, if possible. Describe them; photograph them (often sections of aerial photos are useful here), and quantify their characteristics.

**7.** Compile a report that identifies, defines, quantifies, and illustrates the development standards that you will be using when you prepare the general plan.

**8.** Review the draft of your report with an advisory committee, to make sure everyone understands what is meant by the terms you use.

**9.** Publish a report on development standards.

This Task should produce a report that identifies, defines, quantifies, and illustrates development standards residents of the community want, or will accept, for future development.

Many of the definitions and standards relating to land development in this Task can be derived from your land use survey (see Task 2.3.2). Often, what residents of a community want for the future is closely related to good development they find in their community today.

When you define development standards for land uses you should think about the populations they will generate, their economic, social and environmental impacts, their effect on transportation, etc.

When considering land uses, be sure to differentiate between net densities and gross densities. (See Appendix H for some definitions.)

When considering intensities of land uses, make some allowance for probable vacancy rates in the occupancy of structures. Also make allowance for the percent of land that will probably remain unbuilt.

If you choose to prepare a "built-out" land use plan, in which you assume that all lands will be built on up to their legal limit, and that all structures will be fully occupied, you will be describing a pretty hypothetical situation.

Consider including assumptions on persons per occupied dwelling unit, by dwelling type, and, for large jurisdictions, by geographic area.

In transportation planning, you may need to include assumptions on the number of employees per unit area (e.g., employees per 1,000 square feet of floor area) in employment areas.

### References

See Appendix H, Typical Residential Densities.

Kaiser, Godschalk, and Chapin. *Urban Land Use Planning* 4th ed. Urbana: University of Illinois Press, 1995. See Part 3, "Advance Planning." This section of the text includes consideration of development standards.

Moskowitz and Lindbloom. *The New Illustrated Book of Development Definitions.* Center for Urban Policy Research, Rutgers University: Piscataway: 1992.

(This book is good for definitions of terms, but does not quantify development standards.)

National Recreation and Park Association. *Recreation, Park, and Open Space Standards and Guidelines.* Alexandria, VA: National Recreation and Park Association 1983.

### TASK 3.4 MAKE PROJECTIONS OF FUTURE DEVELOPMENT

In this Task you will look at the data on existing conditions in your planning area, review possible local policies concerning growth, review land development standards, and then make projections of possible future local development.

Make projections of possible future development so that you can:

1. Reflect on the impacts of external forces on local growth (see Task 3.1).

2. Examine the effects of alternative local development policies on local growth (see Task 3.2).

3. Quantify the amount of possible and/or probable future growth.

4. Develop one or more projections for use as the foundation for the sketch planning that you will do in Task 3.6.

**Recommended Procedure**

1. Select the general topics you intend to use for your projections. Recommended ones are:

- Population
- Employment
- Housing
- Land uses

All of these topics are interrelated. Many planners believe that changes in local and regional employment drive population changes, that population changes drive changes in the demand for housing, and that changes in employment and housing drive changes in many types of local land uses. The techniques used for population projection are substantially different from those used with other topics.

2. Use the data you collected and analyzed in previous Tasks as benchmarks upon which projections of future development are based. Remember to look at historical data, as well as data on current conditions.

3. Proceed from large-area to small-area projections, such as: national, statewide, regional, local jurisdiction and sub-areas of the jurisdiction.

You should not attempt to make national, state, or regional projections of land uses.

4. Select a specific time-span for your projections. If you are going to make a long-range plan, you may very well select a 20-year time span. But, you need to start your projections with reliable benchmark data, which means decennial Census data.

5. Specify which alternative rates of development you are going to examine, such as:

- Rapid growth (e.g., averaging 3 percent per year)
- Moderate growth (e.g., averaging 1½ percent per year)
- Slow growth (e.g., averaging ½ percent per year)
- No growth
- Slow decline

The growth rate you select will depend on the assumptions you make concerning the effects of external forces, and on assumed local development policies. See Tasks 3.1 and 3.2.

6. For your local jurisdiction only, identify the urban development policies you would like to consider in your planning. See Task 3.2. Think about applying policies such as:

- There will be a cap on local residential growth, such as 500 housing units per year.
- Local policies will favor economic development above all else.
- Residential growth will occur primarily in low density suburban areas.
- Residential growth will occur primarily in moderate density in-fill development areas.

- The future urban form should be one that relies solely on private automobiles for transportation.
- The future urban form should be one that is served by an effective public transit system.
- Any other patterns of your choice.

7. Get started making projections. Specify which alternative you are going to consider first, and then run the numbers as a test case. Then try another alternative, and see what the results are.

Suggestions:

- Use a cohort-survival computer program for population projections. Be sure to use one that considers in-migration and out-migration.
- Devise computer spreadsheet programs for making projections for topics other than population.
- Use broad categories for your first projections, but subdivide the categories as you want to get a finer-grained analysis.
- First projections of land use should be for total land required for urban development. Subsequent projections might be for major types of land uses.

8. Analyze your projections. Write a brief report that tells what happens when you assume a specific set of development parameters, and what happens when you assume a different set.

This Task should produce a brief report that provides a quantitative analysis of urban growth projections based on the specified assumptions concerning external forces and local development policies. In your report try to identify which alternatives produce results that are highly improbable and clearly undesirable. Also identify which alternatives are clearly possible and probable, regardless of whether they produce desirable results.

Remember that for a long-range (20-30 year) projection, your accuracy is going to be questionable, because there are so many unpredictable factors. Therefore, it is wise to limit your calculations to the effects of major factors, and disregard the minor ones. Don't deceive yourself and your readers by making a fine-grained analysis which is based on very gross assumptions.

Remember that this Phase of the planning process is quantitative only. It isn't intended to say what ought to be done. It doesn't say which land should be developed, or which should be left as open space.

While this Task is a natural for a number-cruncher type of person, physical design-type people should also be involved, because they are the ones who will be applying the results of the analyses later on, and they need to learn about the relationships between assumptions, policies, and space requirements.

### References

Kaiser, Godschalk, and Chapin. *Urban Land Use Planning*, 4th ed. Urbana: University of Illinois Press, 1995. See Part 3, "Advance Planning" (pp. 251–419). This section of the text includes discussion of procedures for making projections of future land development.

Dickey and Watts. *Analytical Techniques in Urban and Regional Planning*. New York: McGraw Hill, 1978.

Goodman and Freund. *Principles and Practice of Urban Planning*. (1968) See Chapter 3, Population Studies, Chapter 4, Economic Studies, Chapter 5, Land Use Studies.

Kreuckeberg and Silvers. *Urban Planning Analysis: Methods and Models*. New York: John Wiley and Sons, 1974.

## TASK 3.5 PREPARE ALTERNATIVE SKETCH PLANS

*Definition.* A sketch plan is a quickly made, preliminary graphic representation of the location of land uses and transportation facilities in a specific geographic setting. Other names for this are: concept plan, preliminary plan, schematic plan, etc.

This Task is intended to allow you to study alternatives concerning which lands are to be developed, the amount of development, and the character of development. The techniques used are primarily graphic. The plans are to be based on the earlier work you did concerning general assumptions, community goals and policies, development standards, projections of growth, etc. The plans you prepare are to be "quick and dirty," in order to portray general impressions of "what would happen if..." You are specifically instructed to avoid making detailed studies in this Task; they would be a waste of time if you made them before basic decisions were reached concerning the desired future form of your community.

Sketch planning allows you to consider alternatives for the future of your planning area, without making a substantial investment of time and money. You should consider formulating alternative scenarios that identify sets of goals, assumptions, and policies; these should describe the major development options that are realistically open to your planning area. For example, Scenario A might assume unfettered rapid growth, no programs for the preservation of open space, low density housing, etc. Scenario B might assume managed growth, and an effective open-space preservation program, high density clustered housing, etc. It is probably a

waste of time to construct scenarios that are clearly improbable.

The work in this Task is primarily land use and transportation planning. After you, your client, and other participants have made fundamental decisions on these topics, you can proceed with planning other elements, such as economic development, housing, environmental protection, etc. But, when doing land use and transportation planning you must concurrently consider their relationship to economic development, housing, environmental quality, etc. You cannot do physical planning in a vacuum. You cannot do other types of planning without being aware of physical development opportunities and constraints.

If you are going to draft a plan, you have to start somewhere. Design studies of land use and transportation alternatives have often proven to be good starting points.

You need to get some "big ideas" down on paper, so you can think about them, develop them further, discuss them with interested parties, and reach agreement on major concepts for community development.

### Recommended Procedure

Sketch planning is the first step in the preparation of a plan diagram, which is usually included in the plan-making phase of the comprehensive planning process. To prepare a meaningful sketch plan the planner must be generally familiar with available data concerning the planning area, with the goals for the planning area, and must have an understanding of the interrelationships of land uses, as well as the relationships between various land uses and transportation facilities.

In preparing a sketch plan, the planner graphically portrays, in a preliminary and tentative manner:

- Locations of the many land uses in the planning area, and their spatial relationships
- The approximate land area required for each of the various land uses, based on previously made land use projections
- Locations of transportation facilities such as roads, transit, rail lines, etc.

With your land use projections as a guide, in conjunction with your assumptions, goals, policies, and development standards, you prepare a schematic plan for proposed land use and transportation facilities for your planning area.

Once you have produced a first draft of your plan, examine it, think about how it could be improved, and then revise it. You repeat this process until you have produced a plan that appears to be worthy of review by others.

Many different sketch planning techniques are available and suitable; there is no single method that is widely recognized as being the best. The technique described below is one that works well for some, so it is recommended that you try it.

First, think about goals for the area. What do the present residents want? What do the property owners want? What does City Hall want? What, in your opinion, would be in the best interests of the present and future society?

Second, review the area you have to work with. Which of the existing land uses do you think should be retained? Which should be replaced by more intensive land uses? Which

by open space? Are there any structures or areas that are so dilapidated they should be removed? What natural or man-made features are so valuable that special efforts should be made to preserve them?

How about the terrain? Which parts have steep slopes, and which are level? Are there any serious natural hazards present?

Where are the major movement corridors? Are there any natural or man-made barriers to movement, such as rivers, railroads, or freeways? Which areas are now served by roads, water, and sewers? Are there some unserved areas today that would be difficult to serve in the future?

Third, identify the major planning options that are open to the community. Which fundamental choices must be made? Examples: Freeway or no freeway? How much multi-family housing? Will a greenbelt around the urban area be preserved?

Fourth, think about basic design concepts. Spread City? Megastructures? Segregation of land uses? Integration of land uses? Sketch the one (or ones) you want to examine, using a schematic format, at a very approximate scale. You may wish to use a plain sheet of paper, rather than a base map, for this sketch. Show the appropriate spatial relationships between major land uses and the major transportation facilities.

Fifth, translate the land uses you have projected into space requirements. (Example: If you have projected a need for 1,000 apartment units, at 25 units to the gross acre, you will need 40 acres for that use. Do this for each of the land uses you plan to include in your study area. You may wish to consider the following land uses:

| Residential uses | Industrial uses |
|---|---|
| Single family homes | Major institutions |
| Townhouses | Parks |
| Low density apartments | Airports |
| High density apartments | Railroads |
| Retail commercial uses | Agricultural areas |
| Offices | Forest areas |
| Mixed use developments | Water areas |

The number of individual land uses to be considered depends upon the scale of your planning, and on the time dimension. For large areas (such as metropolitan regions) you may choose to have just a few land uses such as residential areas, employment areas, major institutions, etc.). For small urban areas, you may wish to plan for most of the land uses identified in the table above.

Sixth, translate your projected space requirements into areas to be shown on your plan, when drawn to scale. For example, if you plan on having 40 acres (gross) of apartments in your planning area, this means they will require 40 acres x 43,560 square feet per acre, which equals 1,742,400 square feet. This can be represented on a map by a rectangular blob measuring about 1,600 feet by 1,100 feet. Draw this blob to scale, at the scale of the base map you will be using. (If your base map is at a scale of 1"=400', then your 40-acre blob will measure 4.0 inches by 2.7 inches.)

Keep in mind that each of your land uses can be kept in a single blob, or can be divided up into a number of smaller blobs, which you can then sprinkle around the planning area.

Seventh, sketch the planned land uses in approximate scale on a sheet of tracing paper over a base map, following one of the design concepts you developed in Step 3. Don't worry about precise scale; think about the spatial relationships among the urban activities you are putting on paper. Include at this time important circulation features, such as freeways, major streets, rail lines, etc.

Make many sketchy designs. Put a fresh sheet of tracing paper on top of your previous effort for each new design, and noodle around, trying to make incremental, or bold, improvements. Try to be imaginative and innovative at this stage, rather than timid and practical. Make lots of preliminary studies on tracing paper. Remember, tracing paper is cheap, but bad design is terribly expensive.

Eighth, integrate a circulation system into the land use pattern. Show freeways and major arterials; disregard local streets for now. Show rail lines, if they are important. Indicate any transit system that should be considered, etc.

Examine your pattern of land uses and your circulation system. Will they work together? Will the circulation system be affordable?

Ninth, when you have developed a design that you would like to draw up and present for review and consideration, take a nice clean base map (or a sheet of tracing paper) and draw up your final version of the sketch plan. It should still be in a sketchy style; it need not be precise, but it should be understandable, legible, and attractive. Use color to show the land uses, using standard notation. Use colored pencils for small areas; use felt-tip marker pens for large areas.

While each sketch plan need not be in a polished form, it should be understandable when viewed by itself. It is recommended that you draft a short narrative that summarizes the concepts of each plan. Or, you may prepare a separate display (using words, numbers, and/or sketches) that summarizes your big ideas, and highlights the features you have incorporated into your sketch plans.

You should produce several alternative sketch plans for your planning area, which consider the major development options realistically still open to your planning area. These are to be primarily in graphic form, and each is to be accompanied by a brief written description of the basic concepts behind the plan.

These sketch plans are to be evaluated (see Task 3.6, following), and one, or features from several of them, will be selected for further development (see Task 3.7).

### Reference

It is strongly recommended that you become familiar with the concepts discussed in Chapter 11, "Overview of the Land Design Process," in Kaiser, Godschalk, and Chapin. *Urban Land Use Planning* 4th ed. Urbana: University of Illinois Press, 1995.

## TASK 3.6 EVALUATE THE SKETCH PLANS

In this Task you prepare first reviews of the potential impacts of each of the sketch plans you prepared in Task 3.5. This evaluation is a rudimentary form of impact assessment. It is not intended to meet any formal legal requirements, but is meant to help you and the participants consider the advantages and disadvantages of each sketch plan. The review of impacts is to consider a broad range of topics, not just the natural environment.

This Task is intended to assist you in:

**1.** Deciding which one of the several sketch plans you have prepared should be selected for further development.

**2.** Identifying desirable plan features which should be included in the first draft of the general plan, and which detrimental features should be excluded.

**3.** Identifying which plan proposals will probably have significant impacts, and should be evaluated thoroughly (and which proposals appear to have little impact and will not require detailed analysis).

The Task also introduces you to the field of impact analysis in a fairly gentle manner. You will find out later that more formal impact analyses can be pretty legalistic, and not as much fun.

### Recommended Procedure

A listing of impact assessment topics follows. These topics identify many (but not all) of the subject areas that urban development often impacts.

You should read through the list, and cross out those topics which are clearly inapplicable to your planning area, and add those topics which you believe are of local concern.

Review the potential impacts of the new development shown in each sketch plan, and mark in the right hand margin of the list a symbol that reflects your belief concerning the impact of new development on the topic under consideration.

Suggested notation

+ +:  strongly beneficial impact

  +:  somewhat beneficial impact

  0:  neutral impact, or no effect

  –:  somewhat detrimental impact

– –:  strongly detrimental impact

  ?:  don't know

topic crossed out:  not applicable

Write a brief report concerning each sketch plan. Describe its basic design concept and its main features. Then go into a more detailed analysis of its apparent strengths and weaknesses.

If you are uncomfortable with the graphic notation suggested above, you can substitute brief written comments for the symbols. Your comments might describe the probable impact, and tell why you think it would come about. Or, you can use some other procedure that you devise. The technique used is not crucial; what is important is that you think about the causes and effects of the probable impacts of development on each of the topics.

If time and staff qualifications permit, you and two or three staff members should make independent impact evaluations of each sketch plan, and then compare the evaluations. If you all agree, this is evidence that the procedure produces consistent, predictable results. If you find a wide variation in impact evaluation, you should determine why. Is the variation due to a confusing procedure, differing analytical skills, or differing personal values?

## Topics Sometimes Considered in Impact Assessments

### Probable Impacts on the Natural Environment

- On the habitat of plants and animals
- On rare or endangered species
- On air quality (caused primarily by changes in the number of vehicle miles traveled)
- On noise levels
- On water quality (caused primarily by surface run-off) Run-off in urban areas is often polluted; run-off from agricultural areas often carries residues of pesticides and fertilizers)
- On open spaces (such as farms, forests, wetlands, mountains, etc.)
- On the general visual attractiveness of the natural environment

### Probable Impacts on the Man-Made Environment

- On historic sites
- On architecturally significant structures
- On archaeological sites
- On the general form of the city
- On the general visual attractiveness of the built environment

### Probable Economic Impacts

- Economic impacts on the following occupational groups:
  —Agriculture, forestry, fisheries, and mining
  —Construction
  —Manufacturing
  —Communications and other utilities
  —Wholesale trade
  —Finance, insurance, and real estate
  —Personal entertainment and recreation services
- On real estate values
  —Within existing developed areas
  —On vacant lands shown for planned development

—On vacant lands shown to remain undeveloped
- On the volume of retail sales in the existing central business district, and in existing shopping centers

*Probable Social Impacts*
- On the distribution of population
  —By income category
  —By age category
  —By ethnic category
- On social problems, such as:
  —Incidence of crime
  —Health care
  —Dependence on welfare payments
  —Quality of education
  —Employment opportunities
  —The homeless
  —Migrant workers and their families
- On "the quality of life" within the com-
munity. (How would you measure this?
What evidence to you need to show the
direction and the amount of change?)
- On the number, type, and burden of new
governmental programs or regulations
needed to implement the plan

*Probable Impacts on Housing*
(List separately for the existing community,
for residential areas to be added, and for
the combined total. Quantify if possible.)
- Number of owner-occupied housing
units
- Number of renter-occupied housing
units
- Percent vacancy (all housing units)
- Median value of housing units
- Median rental rate
- Median household income
- Percent of residents who can afford to
purchase a median priced home

- Percent of residents who can afford the
median rental
- Number of housing units that would be
removed by proposed new construction

*Probable Impacts on Transportation*
- On the number of person trips generated
in 24 hours
- On the number of vehicle trips generated
in 24 hours and during the peak hour
- On the peak hour flow of traffic on the
existing road network
  —Within the existing local community
  —Between the local community and des-
tinations elsewhere in the metropoli-
tan area
- On the length of the average journey to
work
- On the flow of vehicular traffic through
existing residential areas
- On patronage of existing (or proposed)
public transit
- Changes in the Level of Service on roads

*Probable Impacts on Community Facilities*
- On educational facilities and services
- On health facilities and services
- On recreational facilities and services
- On police and fire protection facilities
and services
- On religious institutions

*Probable Impacts on Public Utilities*
- On water supply and distribution facilities
- On sewer lines and sewage disposal facilities
- On storm drainage and flood protection
facilities

*Probable Fiscal Impacts on Local
Government*
- On income from:

—Property taxes
—Sales taxes
—Other taxes
—Subventions and grants
—User fees
—Public utility fees
—Other revenue sources
- On the cost of providing local governmental services for:
—Education
—Public safety
—Welfare
—Public health
—Public utilities
—Streets and highways
—Public transit
—General government
—Capital improvements
—Other governmental expenses
- On tax rates used to levy various taxes

This Task should result in a review of potential impacts on many subjects, either beneficially or adversely, if the sketch plans produced in the preceding Task were to be implemented. One impact analysis should be produced for each of the sketch plans.

This Task is intended to give you a preliminary, but informed judgment concerning the probable impacts of each of your sketch plans. It is not intended to fulfill any legal requirements for impact analysis that are found in state or federal legislation.

### References

Schaenman, Philip S. *Using an Impact Measurement System to Evaluate Land Development.* Washington: The Urban Institute, 1976. (In the author's judgment, this is the definitive work in the field, since

it recommends a number of truly useful means of measuring a wide variety of important impacts.)

Kaiser, Godschalk, and Chapin. *Urban Land Use Planning* 4th ed. Urbana: University of Illinois Press, 1995. See Chapter 17, "Evaluation and Impact Mitigation."

So and Getzels. *The Practice of Local Government Planning* 2d ed., 1988. See Chapter 5, "Environmental Land Use Planning," especially pp. 127-138. (Note that this chapter deals only with environmental impacts, and does not discuss economic, social, or other non-environmental impacts.)

J H K & Associates (principal authors: William R. Riley, James H. Kell, and Iris J. Fullerton). *Design of Urban Streets.* Prepared for the U.S. Department of Transportation, Federal Highway Administration. Washington: Superintendent of Documents, USGPO, Jan. 1980. See Chapter 18 "Social and Economic Impacts of Design" and Chapter 19 "Environmental Factors." While these chapters were primarily written to consider the impacts of streets, they are excellent overviews of impact analysis in general.

### TASK 3.7 REVIEW SKETCH PLANS AND THEIR EVALUATIONS; SELECT FEATURES FOR FURTHER DEVELOPMENT

In this Task you review the sketch plans prepared in Task 3.5, and the evaluations of them prepared in Task 3.6 with the participants in the planning process. You try to reach consensus concerning which plan features are favored, so one plan that incorporates the desirable features can be prepared (see Task 3.8).

This Task should be undertaken so that a meeting of the minds can be arrived at concerning the desired content of the long-range general plan, which is to be prepared in the near future.

It is usually desirable to decide on the major planning options fairly early in the planning process. This can save time that might be wasted while examining clearly unwanted options. It may thereby provide you and other participants more time to consider, refine, and perfect a plan that you agree is the right course for your community.

**Recommended Procedure**

1. Meet with the participants in the planning process, and review the contents and general planning approaches used in each of the sketch plans, and the evaluations of the sketch plans.

2. After discussion, reach consensus, if possible, concerning which of the sketch plans appears to be most appropriate for your jurisdiction, and which features from any of the sketch plans might be included in future plans for the area.

The plan features that are recommended must be in harmony, so that the plan is internally consistent.

The product resulting from this Task should be a memorandum, written for the information of those who participate in this Task, which summarizes the conclusions reached.

## TASK 3.8 REFINE THE SKETCH PLAN TO PRODUCE A PRELIMINARY GENERAL PLAN

We prepare preliminary plans so that we and other people can review and comment on them before they are recommended for formal approval.

**Recommended Procedure**

1. Use the selected sketch plan features (see Task 3.7), and comments you received on them as a starting point for preparing the preliminary general plan.

2. Prepare an outline of topics to be included in the general plan. When doing this, review materials from Task 1.8, Conceptualize a Plan Preparation Procedure, and Task 1.14, Review the Work Program and Budget with Client, to refresh your memory about what you have promised to produce.

While each locality has its own unique needs, you may wish to consider the outline in Table 7-1 as a possible outline for your general plan report.

3. Establish a fundamental urban design philosophy, if you haven't done this in preceding Tasks. Identify the basic urban forms that you believe are appropriate to your planning area. It is conceivable that a planning area may have a different design concept for each of its various parts.

4. Review your previously prepared estimates of growth, especially for population, employment, and housing. Modify them, as needed, based on your impact analysis.

5. Identify the elements that you propose to include in the plan. The Land Use and Transportation elements are essential; they will serve as a foundation for all the other elements.

6. Prepare the Land Use Element, concurrently with the Transportation Element, if possible).

- Quantify the projected growth in the planning area.

**Table 7-1**
**Suggested Outline for a General Plan**

Introduction
- Purpose and nature of the plan
- Role of the planning process in local government
- Relationship of the general plan to district and function plans

Background
- Historical background of development in the community
- Current conditions and trends
  —The built environment
  —The natural environment
  —The economic environment
  —The social environment
- Current and emerging issues that have long-term implications

Assumptions
- Assumed effects of external forces on the future of the local community
  —Physical developments
  —Social developments
  —Economic developments
  —Political developments
- Local policies, values, and actions that will affect development
- Regional issues; regional goals
- Forecasts of regional and local growth

Overview of the plan
- Community goals and policies
- Basic community design concepts
- Major design proposals

Major implementation processes

General plan diagram

Elements
- Land Use
  —Residential areas
  —Working areas (retailing, manufacturing, services, etc.)
  —Other areas
- Circulation
  —Street network
  —Public transit
- Community facilities
- Utilities
- Natural resources, natural hazards, and open space
- Urban design policies
- Growth management policies
- Other elements as needed

—Use a spreadsheet to make your land use projections, using your survey of existing land uses as a starting point.

—The land use categories used in your spreadsheet should be similar to those in the survey of existing land uses (see Task 2.3.2, Collect and Analyze Land Use Data).

—You will usually have to divide the planning area into sub-areas. Depending on the scale of your work, these may be census tracts, traffic analysis zones, blocks, uniform grids, or some other configuration.

—It is often useful to show the projected development using five-year increments, with the first increment representing growth planned in any short-range district plans that are prepared. The sum of all growth increments, when added to the original extent of development, should show the planned development as of the target-year of the plan.

—In many cases the development projected for 20 years will not represent a "build-out" condition. However, if it does, this should be clearly stated, and the reader advised that additional growth cannot be accommodated unless the goals and policies of the plan are changed.

—The spreadsheet should include information that will be needed by the transportation planners on your team.

- Get into physical design. On an overlay to your existing land use map, show where new development might be planned to be located, using your five-year increments.

—Sprinkle the development onto areas that

appear to be suitable and appropriate, drawing on your knowledge acquired in the earlier Tasks of this project, and applying the urban growth policies that have been developed.

—Consider the possibility of redeveloping some areas, if it appears to be appropriate.

—Coordinate the projected growth of land uses with the transportation network needed to serve them, and with the planned availability of infrastructure and community facilities.

7. Prepare a Transportation Element, concurrently with the Land Use Element, if possible.

• Consider only major arterials at this time. Do not get involved with local streets, problem intersections, or off-street parking; these topics are more suitable for short-range planning, which should come later.

• Coordinate your local transportation planning with the work being done by transportation planners in state, regional, county, adjacent county, and adjacent city agencies. Some of them may have a lot of data you can use, and some of them may have computer programs that will run data if you supply it. Their transportation plans may have a strong impact on transportation planning for your area. Some of these impacts may present you with undesirable conditions. If undesirable conditions become evident, negotiations with the neighboring entity should be undertaken.

• You should use a transportation planning model on a computer, rather than a best guess procedure. Your jurisdiction really should be using a model for ana-

lyzing present and future transportation problems, regardless of the status of the local planning program.

• You will need to have data on past, present, and projected land use, housing, population, employment, trip generation centers, and the street network.

• You will need to develop projections of:

—Person-trip movements

—Modal splits

—Vehicle-trip movements

—Level of service on arterial streets

8. Prepare other elements, as considered appropriate. Use information from the Land Use Element and the Transportation Element as a foundation for these.

Table 7-2 provides a suggested outline for a typical element within the general plan. The organization of each element will depend upon the subject matter being treated. For example, an Economic Development Element will probably require an outline that differs substantially from that of a Circulation Element.

9. Draft a general plan diagram. The ideal plan diagram should:

• Contain the basic, essential information about the plan proposals

• Not contain an excess of detail

• Be understandable by citizens who may have borderline skills in map reading

• Be visually attractive

• Be economical to produce and print

(Very few planners have been able to achieve this ideal.)

It is well to remember that the general plan diagram to be prepared at this time should remain general, and is intended to show development in the long-range future. For this reason, the diagram should

**Table 7-2**
**Suggested Outline for a Typical Element in a General Plan**

Note: This outline should be applied to the topic considered in the element, not to a wide range of topics concurrently.
- Historical background (only if particularly relevant)
- Present conditions and trends
- Current and emerging issues
- Assumptions concerning:
  —External forces
  —Local actions and policies
  —Forecasts of demand
- Goals and policies
- Plan proposals (presented in verbal, numerical, and graphic media)
- Actions to be taken to implement the plan (possibly in a who-is-responsible-for-what format)

not be "parcel specific" (i.e., it should not be drafted in a manner that identifies boundaries of individual parcels of property).

For some further comment on general plan diagrams, and some examples, see Appendix I, Notes on General Plan Diagrams.
**10.** Draft the lead-in sections for the general plan, which may include such topics as:

- Introduction
- Background
- Assumptions
- Overview of the plan

The product that results from this Task should be a preliminary long-range general plan.

Topics to be included in the general plan may be limited to those that have long-term impacts, such as physical development that will be on the ground for a long time.

Topics and issues that require immediate attention should be included in short-range plans; perhaps many of them should be excluded from the long-range plan. Topics such as economic development, housing, child care centers, urban renewal, central business dis-

trict revitalization, protecting residential areas from through traffic, etc., usually require immediate attention. For these short-range plans, programs leading directly to implementation are needed. Discussion about them with a 20- to 30-year time horizon tends to be irrelevant.

It would be wise to conceptualize now the format that you wish to use later in the publication of the adopted long-range general plan. Use this format, insofar as possible, for the publication of preliminary drafts, so that there will be a minimum number of changes later on. We will assume that the text of your plan and some of the graphics will be in a computer file, so that you will be able to make changes and corrections easily.

### References

Kaiser, Godschalk, and Chapin. *Urban Land Use Planning* 4th ed. Urbana: University of Illinois Press, 1995. See Chapter 11, "Overview of the Land Design Process," and Chapter 12, "Land Classification Planning."

Kent, T. J. *The Urban General Plan.* (See especially Chapter V, "The General Plan Document.")

So and Getzels. *The Practice of Local Government Planning* 2d ed. (See especially Chapter 3, "General Development Plans," by Hollander, Pollock, Reckinger, and Beal.)

Zucker, Paul C. "Formatting the General Plan" (a 14-page brochure, available from Zucker Systems, 9909 Huennekens St., Suite 120, Sorrento Mesa Design Center, San Diego, CA 92121).

## TASK 3.9 PREPARE IMPACT ASSESSMENT OF THE PRELIMINARY GENERAL PLAN

In this Task you prepare an impact assessment of the preliminary general plan. The topics considered and the degree of specificity to be included will depend upon the legal requirements adopted by your state. This Task is to be undertaken concurrently and interactively with the preparation of the preliminary general plan.

There are two reasons to prepare an impact assessment. The first is to inform yourself and citizens of the jurisdiction you are working with about what the actual impacts of the draft long-range plan would be, if it were to be adopted and implemented. The second reason is a legalistic one. If the preliminary plan is to be adopted as the official plan of your jurisdiction, its contents must comply with your state's legal requirements, and its review and adoption procedure must follow state law. Impact assessment, in some states, is specifically required as a part of the plan review and adoption process.

### Recommended Procedure

**1.** If your state has specific requirements for impact assessments of general plans:

- Review your state's procedural require-

ments for the adoption of a general plan. See your state's planning enabling act.

- Review your state's requirements (if any) concerning impact assessments or reports required at the time of adoption of a general plan. See your state's environmental quality act.
- Follow the procedural requirements of your state's planning enabling act and any requirements you discover concerning impact review of general plans.

**2.** If your state does not have requirements for impact reviews of general plans:

- Review Philip Schaenman's *Using an Impact Measurement System to Evaluate Land Development*, if it is available to you. This report provides a commendable approach to impact review, and identifies a number of ways to measure and quantify various types of impacts. (If the Schaenman text is not available, consult some of the alternatives listed in the References at the end of this Task.)
- Review the impact assessments topics list provided in Task 3.6 and identify which topics appear to be germane to a review of the preliminary general plan.
- Devise a procedure for measuring the probable impacts that would be brought about if the long-range plan were to be implemented. Try to quantify those impacts, rather than just describe them in general terms.
- Review the preliminary general plan, and attempt to quantify its potential impacts.

**3.** Consider the findings of your impact assessment; use them constructively to improve the general plan. If you identified some adverse impacts, can you change some policies or some design features so that their effects can be mitigated?

Think of plan preparation and impact analysis as interactive parts of the planning process, not separate steps to be taken in sequence.

**4.** Write a report identifying the probable impacts of the plan, when it is implemented.

This Task should generate:

**1.** Improvements to the preliminary general plan, brought about by the interaction between the plan-making process and the impact analysis process.

**2.** An impact assessment report on the preliminary general plan. (This report is to be published separately; it is not a part of the plan).

Impact assessments should be used for constructive purposes; they have potential for being more than a legalistic hurdle to be overcome. The work described in this Task is required in some states; it is optional in others. If it is optional, you may choose to restrict your impact assessment to substantial issues, rather than commenting on all the individual topics that you can identify.

It would be well to note that a general plan is intended to be general. The impact assessment of a general plan should therefore also be quite general in character. District plans are usually quite specific. Impact assessments of them should therefore be quite specific.

Experienced planners believe that a separate impact analysis of general plans should not be required. They say that good planners examine the potential impacts of a plan as they are preparing it, and modify the plan in an appropriate manner as needed. When this is done, a separate impact analysis is no more than an expensive, time-consuming formality.

**References**

Refer to the sources cited in Task 3.6

In 1976 The Urban Institute, 2100 M St., NW, Washington, DC, published five excellent reports on impact analysis. They were:

*Social Impacts of Land Development* by Kathleen Christensen

*Land Development and the Natural Environment* by Dale L. Keyes

*Fiscal Impacts of Land Development* by Thomas Muller

*Economic Impacts of Land Development* by Thomas Muller

*Using an Impact Measurement System to Evaluate Land Development* by Philip Schaenman. The fifth report, by Schaenman, gathers information from the other four reports, and recommends a procedure for measuring the probable impacts of land development; this has great potential for use in estimating the probable effects of general plans.

There are many good texts on impact analysis (especially environmental-impact and economic-impact); choose your favorites. These are recommended for consideration.

Burchell, Robert W. *Development Impact Analysis: Feasibility, Design, Traffic, Fiscal, Environment.* Piscataway, NJ: Center for Urban Policy Research, Rutgers University, 1988.

Westman, W. E. *Ecology, Impact Assessment, and Environmental Planning.* New York: Wiley, 1985.

## TASK 3.10 PUBLISH THE PRELIMINARY GENERAL PLAN AND THE IMPACT ASSESSMENT

You publish the preliminary general plan because there is a need for material in a form that is reviewable by all the participants in the planning process.

**Recommended Procedure**

The work involved in this Task is entirely one of preparing materials for publication. This requires some editing, and a lot of work in layout and graphics. This is a good time to bring in an outside editor, and outside graphics people, if you can afford it. See the article on desktop publishing, which is provided in Figure 7-5.

You will probably prepare camera-ready copy in-house, and then have an outside printer run off as many copies as you require.

Upon completion of this Task you should have published:

1. The preliminary general plan.
2. An impact assessment of the preliminary general plan, if such is required by your state.

Preparing text for publication is an art that takes considerable skill. The ability to get a computer to print out text and graphics usually isn't enough to guarantee a readable and attractive publication.

You may wish to consider a format for the plan that will permit insertion of amendments to the plan without requiring republication of the entire text. This can be done using loose-leaf binders, and section-by-section page numbering. There are many good texts on the subject of desktop publishing. Which text you should select depends upon what hardware you have, which word processing program you use, and which presentation graphics software you use.

## TASK 3.11 REVIEW THE PRELIMINARY GENERAL PLAN AND THE IMPACT ASSESSMENT

In this Task you review the contents of the preliminary general plan with your client, and with others who are participating in the planning program. You also review its potential impacts on the community, as described in the impact assessment, if one has been made.

There are three reasons for undertaking this Task. First, you want your client, and others who are participating in the planning process, to really understand what is in the plan, and what its implications are.

Second, there may have been a number of points that you have overlooked that others can bring to your attention.

Third, it is desirable to have an outside, but informed, view about how well-suited the style and tone of your plan-writing is to the local situation, and how understandable the plan is.

**Recommended Procedure**

1. Distribute drafts of the material to those who are appropriate to review it at this time, such as: the legislative body, the planning commission, and other participants in the planning process. This may be done in advance of any meeting, or in a fairly showy presentation meeting.

The materials may be in draft format; you should not spend a lot of time and money publishing a slick edition of material that may require changes.

2. Hold a series of shirt-sleeve work sessions to review the materials. Make note of the comments made. Defend your work when you think it is right; graciously accept constructive suggestions when you think they will strengthen the plan.

This Task should produce memoranda, for staff use, which identify recommended

**Figure 7-5** Desktop Publishing a General Plan

# Desktop Publishing a General Plan

*by Robert S. Cowan, AICP*

The age of information is here and, as we enter the 21st century, our success will depend in large part on how quickly and easily we process data. A city's general plan is nothing more than bits of information gathered together and formatted into a large document, which usually requires subsequent revisions as new data presents itself.

General plans should be complete and up-to-date, internally consistent, in one piece, and easy to comprehend by decisionmakers and lay persons. Although cities and counties have gotten a respite from the onslaught of new general plan requirements promulgated during the 1970s, recent trends dictate a new round of general plan amendments and reformatting efforts to keep plans current, including:

■ Plans must reflect emerging regional policy issues involving solid waste, hazardous materials siting, air quality and congestion management.

■ Plans must be action orientated (i.e., when and how will housing programs be implemented?).

■ For the purposes of internal consistency, an entire document may require a complete revision when one element is amended; one change may ripple through the entire document.

■ Each plan must compete for the reader's attention, so a generous amount of graphics is necessary. Graphics are not only visually appealing, they can also convey a great deal of information concisely.

### Let Your Fingers Do the Walking

A document that depends upon manually inserted graphics into word processing text is not easily amended. However, a key solution to the problem of maintaining a current general plan may already be on our desktops. While most agencies use word processing and various graphics packages to produce charts, tables and graphs, few use a desktop publishing system to create computer-generated maps, illustrations and diagrams and electronically integrate those and other graphics with text to create their general plan.

Prior to 1989, Cupertino's General Plan consisted of approximately 300 pages in a base document, a 100-page document containing a major amend-ment, plus a collection of minor amendments. The base document was typed using a word processing program; however, the illustrations were manually cut and pasted into the document. It was very difficult to reformat the plan to incorporate amendments.

*Cupertino's desktop published general plan.*

### Principles of Change

The city acquired Macintosh computers in 1986 and began to experiment with desktop publishing by reformatting the housing element. In 1989 work began on the reformatting of the entire general plan. The city embarked upon it's desktop reformatting project based upon four guiding principles:

1. The revised plan must be designed to be easily updated. The plan must be photocopied in the office and placed in a 3-ring binder.

2. The document must be richly illustrated to convey ideas using as few words as possible. The reader should be able to glance at illustrations, tables, graphs and highlighted text or carefully read the text to understand the rationale behind policies and programs.

3. The document should provide margin space for cross references to relevant policies in other sections or to external documents such as the zoning code or specific plans.

Since its complete reformatting in 1989, the Cupertino General Plan has undergone three amendments. Depending upon workload, planning staff has been able to forward amendments to subscribers within three weeks after adoption.

### Tips for Desktoppers

The reformatting effort was a major undertaking. The following tips are offered to agencies seeking a desktop publishing approach:

1. Hire a graphics consultant to prepare the final document. Although the city of Cupertino has several staff members who can run Apple computers and desktop publishing software, they are not as quick and competent as a professional.

2. Choose hardware and software packages that are easy to use and popular with graphics and computer consultants. The Mac computer coupled with Microsoft Word, Aldus Pagemaker, Adobe Illustrator, Microsoft Excel and a host of utility programs were all that was required to prepare the Cupertino General Plan.

3. Hire an editor. Cupertino hired an editor who received national recognition for a general plan editing assignment. The initial cost of editing was expensive but justified. The editor was able to determine the significant from the insignificant and eliminate "plannerese," thereby reducing a 350-page document to 115 pages, including generous use of graphics.

4. The electronic file containing the general plan is very valuable. Invest in a high capacity back up system. The Cupertino General Plan is contained in several tape backup cartridges, which are stored in the city clerk's fireproof vault and in an off-site location.

In conclusion, the initial investment for an electronically generated general plan is somewhat expensive but the long-term costs are minimal. The cost of preparing general plans using conventional publication techniques is going to be quite costly given new external forces that will require more frequent general plan updates. Not only does the desktop publishing technology save time and money, it also allows agencies to create a good looking document as well.

*Cowan is director of community development for the city of Cupertino.*

changes to the content, emphasis, or style of the draft materials.

## TASK 3.12 FORMALLY REVIEW AND ADOPT THE GENERAL PLAN

This Task involves formal public hearings and formal adoption of the long-range plan by your local planning commission, and by your local legislative body.

Before a plan is adopted, the adopters must make sure that it reflects a consensus held by the people who have a stake in the planning area. Public hearings are a commonly used method for doing this. Of course, if the public hearings reveal substantial dissatisfaction with the plan as presented at the hearing, serious consideration should be given to revising it before adoption.

The general plan, to be effective, requires official status. It is a statement of the plans and policies that have been carefully considered and specifically endorsed by the local legislative body. The plan is a commitment to a series of actions; it should be made a part of the official record of your local government.

The specific procedures that should be used in this Task depend upon what is required by the laws of your state.

This Task should produce a commitment by the local planning agency and by the local legislative body to the policies and actions stated in the general plan.

### References

Review your state's laws concerning the requirements concerning the adoption of a general plan. Review the required procedures with your city attorney, or your county counsel.

Kent, T. J., Jr. *The Urban General Plan.*

## TASK 3.13 PUBLISH THE ADOPTED GENERAL PLAN

If the plan is to be effective, it must be available to all who are interested in the future of the community, and it should be placed in the hands of those people who should be using it in their deliberations and decision making.

### Recommended Procedure

The publication of the adopted general plan should be a continuation of the process that was initiated with the publication of the preliminary general plan (Task 3.10). In this Task, however, you will publish the plan in its final form, and distribute it.

Carefully consider before publication:
- How many copies of the plan should be printed?
- What will be the production cost per copy?
- What should be the sale price per copy?
- Who is to be sent free copies?
- What program should there be for the sale of the plan?

This Task should produce printed copies of the adopted long-range plan and a program for distributing the plan.

# 8

# Phase IV
# Implement the
# General Plan

## Contents

## INTRODUCTION

Putting a general plan to use is what planning is all about.

This phase of the planning process deals with that topic. It is important for planners to apply a general plan; preparing plans is not an end in itself. While it is true that many planning staffs have some members who specialize in plan preparation, and others in plan implementation, these skills should not be isolated.

This Phase of the planning process discusses some of the principal procedures that are used to put general plans into practice.

## TASK 4.1 REVIEW PLAN-IMPLEMENTING METHODS AVAILABLE

This Task involves reviewing the alternative plan-implementing methods described in the last chapter of this book. After reviewing the optional methods, you should select those you consider to be most appropriate to your local conditions, and then formulate a strategy for putting them into practice.

### Recommended Procedure

1. Review the goals, policies, and recommended actions in the general plan, and identify:

- Which appear to have satisfactory procedures already in place to implement them?
- Which probably cannot be implemented at this time because they are so general in nature that specific measures cannot be tailored to fit them?
- Which probably should not be implemented at this time because existing legislation does not provide a legal procedure, because current economic or political conditions are clearly not suited, or because emerging technologies indicate there will be substantial changes in the future?
- Which appear to require new or revised plan-implementing procedures, that can be adopted in the near future, to implement them?

2. Identify possible additional plan-implementing procedures that you wish to consider. Do this by reviewing the procedures described in the last chapter of this book, and by searching out additional sources.

3. Make a preliminary review of the procedures you have identified. Ask other planners about them. Contact neighboring jurisdictions, and the most successful planning agencies in your state; ask them what works, and what doesn't. If your agency subscribes to American Planning Association's Planning Advisory Service, contact APA and ask for information about new plan-implementing techniques.

4. Identify the procedures that appear to be the most likely to produce desired and effective results in your community.

5. Review your list of potential procedures with others, and discuss informally with them the pros and cons of the various methods. Listen to their feedback. People to be consulted may include:

- Your planning staff, especially those who would be involved in the administration of any new procedures.
- Your next-step-up administrator.
- The planning commission.
- The local legislative body.
- Groups that would be directly affected by some of the procedures, such as land developers, land owners, builders, trans-

portation planners, homeowners groups, conservation organizations, and other civic groups.

**6.** Weed out the procedures you believe would be ineffective, politically unacceptable, too complex, or too costly to institute and administer.

**7.** Prepare an analysis of those procedures left in the running. Make a careful analysis of each, considering:

- What the objectives of the program are.
- How effective the program would be in attaining its objectives.
- Probable staff time required to administer.
- What fees might be charged for staff services.
- Who would be adversely affected by the program.
- What the probable benefits of the program would be.
- What the political fall-out from enacting and administering the program would be.
- What legal steps would be required to enact and administer the program.

**8.** Review your findings from Step 7 with the people you consulted in Step 5.

**9.** Select those procedures you believe are most appropriate for your jurisdiction.

**10.** Tailor a strategy and timetable for the introduction, adoption, and administration of the selected procedures.

The process of reviewing and selecting plan-implementing methods will probably produce memoranda and staff reports. No formal publication is anticipated.

Since long-range general plans are general and not specific, not all plan-implementing programs will be well-suited for them. For example, it is impossible to prescribe with confidence any zoning that should be enacted today that you can be sure will be suitable for the economic, social, and technological conditions 20 years from now. And, preparing a capital improvement program for the coming 20 years is surely bound to be a waste of time. Zoning, capital improvement programming, and many other procedures are not well-suited for implementing long-range plans, although they are suitable for short-range plans. That is why the preparation of short-range district plans for areas where change is anticipated is often a valuable procedure for implementing general plans. These short-range plans show the increment of development that is needed in the first five years if the goals defined in the long-range general plan are to be attained.

A generalized instruction for implementing a general plan is:

**1.** Select and use those plan-implementing measures that are clearly suitable to chart the course of development over a 20-year period.

**2.** Prepare short-range district plans that are specific enough for guiding development for the coming five years (see Phase V).

**3.** Implement the district plans using procedures designed to be suitable for the short-range future (see Phase VI).

**4.** Prepare function plans as needed (see Task 4.4).

**5.** Implement the function plans using appropriate procedures (see Task 4.5).

## TASK 4.2 PREPARE DISTRICT PLANS

District plans are mentioned here because their preparation, adoption, and implementation is an essential part of implementing the long-range jurisdiction-wide general plan.

Procedures for the preparation of district plans will be found in Phase V.

District plans are relatively short-range (five or six years) multitopic plans that consider only a portion of a jurisdiction. They are much more detailed than long-range general plans, and, because of this, they are useful as guides to specific implementing programs, such as zoning ordinances, capital improvement programs, and economic development programs.

District plans must be consistent with the long-range plan.

### TASK 4.3 IMPLEMENT DISTRICT PLANS

Most of the procedures for implementing district plans are similar to those for implementing long-range plans. Planners must, of course, use their judgment concerning which procedures are well-suited for short-range plans, and which are not.

Procedures for implementing district plans will be mentioned in Phase VI.

### TASK 4.4 PREPARE FUNCTION PLANS

Function plans are mentioned at this time because they are potentially useful for implementing general plans. They concern a single topic, and factors closely related to it. Function plans may be prepared for any of a very wide range of topics, such as:

Mass transit
Parks and recreation
Economic development
Utility systems
Timber management
Library systems
Emergency health care services
Geologic hazards
Other topics as needed

Function plans may be for the whole planning area of a jurisdiction, or for a limited section of it. They can be either short-range (five or six years), or long-range (15 to 25 years), or for some other time span.

When function plans are long-range, consider the entire planning area, and general in character, they may be adopted as an element of the long-range general plan. When they are short-range, consider only a section of the local jurisdiction, and general in character, they may be adopted as an element of a district plan.

When function plans are detailed and specific, as they often are, it is not appropriate to adopt them as elements of general plans. It is appropriate to have a general plan include an element that discusses some topic in fairly general terms, but to have a separate function plan prepared on that topic, which discusses it with far greater specificity and detail.

The preparation of function plans is usually optional. There is certainly no need to prepare a separate function plan to augment each element of a long-range general plan or a short-range district plan.

Some local government planning departments, while having staff members who are well-qualified to discuss many topics in general terms, may lack staff qualified to prepare function plans in many of the areas that require specialized professional skills.

Staff planners can certainly contribute to the function-planning process with their knowledge of the planning process in general, their overview of the big picture of the community, and their knowledge of the goals, policies, and development proposals included in the local general plan. However, most public agency staffs will have to call for skilled outside help when detailed function plans are prepared. This outside help may be provided by consultants, or by staff members of line departments within the local government.

Regardless of who prepares a function plan, it must be consistent with the long-range general plan of the jurisdiction.

The general plan of a jurisdiction must have a clearly evident structure, and sufficient detail, to make it possible for those who prepare function plans to make their plans consistent with the general plan.

## TASK 4.5 IMPLEMENT FUNCTION PLANS

Since the subjects, types, and forms of function plans are so varied, it is almost impossible to prescribe a general procedure for implementing them.

Those function plans that are prepared and adopted as elements of a long-range general plan, or of a short-range district plan, may often be implemented by using the generally known plan-implementing procedures augmented by any specific-topic programs that are available.

Function plans that are not a part of a general plan or a district plan usually require implementing programs that are especially tailored to the subject of the function being planned for. See the last chapter in this text, Methods Used in Implementing Plans.

## TASK 4.6 MONITOR FEEDBACK FROM IMPLEMENTING PROGRAMS

Establish an on-going procedure to monitor the effectiveness and progress of the planning program. With information received from this Task the planning staff will be in a position to recommend adjustments that will make good implementing programs better, to recommend that unsuccessful programs be terminated, and to recommend the establishment of new programs to fill gaps in the planning process.

**Recommended Procedure**

The planning staff should be attuned to the impacts of all the plan-implementing programs at all times, and should be encouraged to make constructive suggestions on how to improve them throughout the year. Once a year, before preparing the operating budget of the planning department, a careful analysis of the impacts of plan-implementing programs should be made.

It is recommended that the following procedure be undertaken annually:

**1.** Identify each of the programs that is used to implement the plans of your jurisdiction.

**2.** For each implementing program:

- Identify the objectives of the program. What is it intended to accomplish?
- Identify criteria that can be used to measure to what degree the program is achieving its objectives.
- Apply the criteria.
- Write a report summarizing how successful the program is, what its strengths are, what its weaknesses are, and how it might be improved.
- Make a cost/effectiveness analysis of the program, comparing the cost of administering the program to the benefits received from the program (optional).

**3.** Recommend which programs:

- Should be retained and administered in their present form and present staffing level.

- Should be retained, but strengthened.
- Should be retained, but reduced in scope or diminished in staffing level.
- Should be eliminated.

4. Identify new programs, if any, that should be initiated.

5. Consider whether the plans of your jurisdiction, which are being implemented, might benefit by revision in one way or another. Are the impacts of the plan- implementing programs really building a better community?

An annual report should be produced. In some cases this report may be for staff use only. It would probably be more useful, however, if it is written for the information of the planning commission and the legislative body.

Some of your plan-implementing programs may have only general goals to be attained, rather than specific objectives. Where this is the case, all you can do is make general observations and comments on the programs.

If you initiated a Monitoring Program for Critical Issues, as recommended in Task 2.4, you should review its findings, and see if some of them relate to the plan-implementing programs your jurisdiction is using.

This is an important Task, but perhaps it can be undertaken in a less structured manner than is recommended here. Maybe it can be undertaken occasionally, instead of annually, as a part of the five-year plan review process. Perhaps it might focus on problem programs, instead of all programs.

No matter how you do it, receiving feedback from your implementing programs is important. This Task can be modified, but it should not be ignored.

## TASK 4.7 REVIEW THE GENERAL PLAN EVERY FIVE YEARS; AMEND IT AS NEEDED

Conditions in our cities and counties change, often quite rapidly. These changes may mean that a plan adopted five years ago could use revision. These revisions may involve community goals, policies, allocation of resources, new issues, or other topics in the plan.

Many communities have found that it is more satisfactory to keep general plans up-to-date by regular review and occasional amendment, than it is to allow the plans to decay into obsolescence, and require complete replacement.

### Recommended Procedure

1. Staff reviews and analyzes the present general plan. The review should consider such topics as the strengths and weaknesses of the plan, as evidenced in its application in the recent years.

2. A public meeting should be held, which includes:

- Staff review of:
  —An overview of the planning process
  —What the general plan is trying to accomplish
  —A preliminary evaluation of the apparent strengths and weaknesses of the general plan
- Public testimony concerning:
  —What current issues should be added to and discussed in the plan
  —A review of the major goals of the community
  —A review of the major policies stated in the plan

It may be difficult to get the audience to think in terms of "big picture" concepts for the long-term development of the community. Chances are, they'll complain about street congestion, the homeless problem, etc. Don't ignore the "today's problems" you hear; they may be useful inputs to Task 2.4, Establish a Monitoring Program for Critical Issues, and Task 4.6, Monitor Feedback from Implementing Programs.

3. Prepare a summary of testimony received at the public meeting.

4. Staff should draft suggested amendments to the long-range plan, and review them with the planning commission.

5. Staff should review the draft amendments with interested parties.

6. Official hearings on the proposed plan amendments should be held by the planning commission and by the legislative body; adoption should follow.

7. The amended sections of the general plan should be republished and distributed.

This Task may result in reaffirmation of the general plan, as written, or moderate revisions of selected sections of the general plan, or a decision to undertake a major review and revision of the general plan.

As planners, planning commissioners, and local legislators know, undertaking a thorough remake of a general plan is expensive, harrowing, and time consuming. It should be avoided, if reasonable alternatives are available.

Annual reviews of the general plan, accompanied by minor revisions, may preclude, and be preferable to, major overhauls every five years.

The term "every five years" is arbitrary. Some stable, problem-free jurisdictions may not need to make major reviews of their general plans that often. Some other areas, especially those where significant social, economic, or political changes have occurred recently, may need to revise their general plans before they are five years old.

## TASK 4.8 REVIEW THE PLANNING PROGRAM ANNUALLY

This Task involves a re-evaluation of your jurisdiction's planning program, to make sure that it is heading in the right direction, and is being effective.

Note: This Task is a nonsequitur; it is not really part of the plan-preparation process, but it can make that process substantially more effective.

Conditions change in our cities and counties. Economic conditions, social goals, environmental issues, physical conditions, etc. change over the years. As conditions change, it is quite likely that planning objectives and priorities will also change. This Task is intended to give all those who are involved with planning for the future of a community an opportunity to reflect on the goals, policies, and procedures used in the local planning process.

### Recommended Procedure

It is impossible to prescribe one review procedure that will work for all cities and counties. Each program should be tailored to local conditions. A planning program review should probably include many of the following steps.

1. Review and consider new procedures or techniques that might be incorporated into

the planning program, such as strategic planning, "visioning," geographic information systems, etc.

2. Hold an all-day review session with senior staff members and with your next-step-up administrator, to review the status of the planning program. Daylong retreats, held in informal settings away from office interruptions, are desirable.

Topics for discussion might include:

- What are the goals of the planning program?
- How well do we seem to be meeting our goals?
- Are these the right goals for today?
- If we achieve them, will that solve our planning-related problems?
- What problems or issues have arisen since the present planning program was formulated or last revised?
- What planning-related problems or issues are foreseeable in the coming year? In the coming five years?

Upon review of the planning goals and policies, consider:

- Which new goals or policies should be added?
- What priority should they be given?
- Which of the present goals, objectives, policies, or programs should be dropped?
- Which of the present goals, objectives, policies, or programs should be given more emphasis? Less emphasis?

3. Hold an informal work session involving:

- Senior planning staff
- Next-step-up administrators
- Planning commissioners
- Local legislative body
- Representatives of citizen groups (optional).

The agenda should be review of the findings and recommendations that were developed in the staff retreat.

The desired outcome of the meeting:

- Improved communications among all parties
- Agreement on goals and objectives of the planning program
- General agreement on priorities among planning programs, to be considered during the coming budget year

It is desirable to produce one memorandum summarizing the findings from the staff-level work session, and another memorandum summarizing the findings from the second session.

This Task is time consuming, but potentially very worthwhile. Some jurisdictions may wish to undertake it annually (at least at staff level); some only in times of crisis. If this Task is undertaken, it should be scheduled to precede the preparation of the annual budget for the planning program.

# Phase V
# Prepare, Review, and
# Adopt District Plans

**Contents**

**Figure 9-1**   Flowchart of Tasks in Phase V

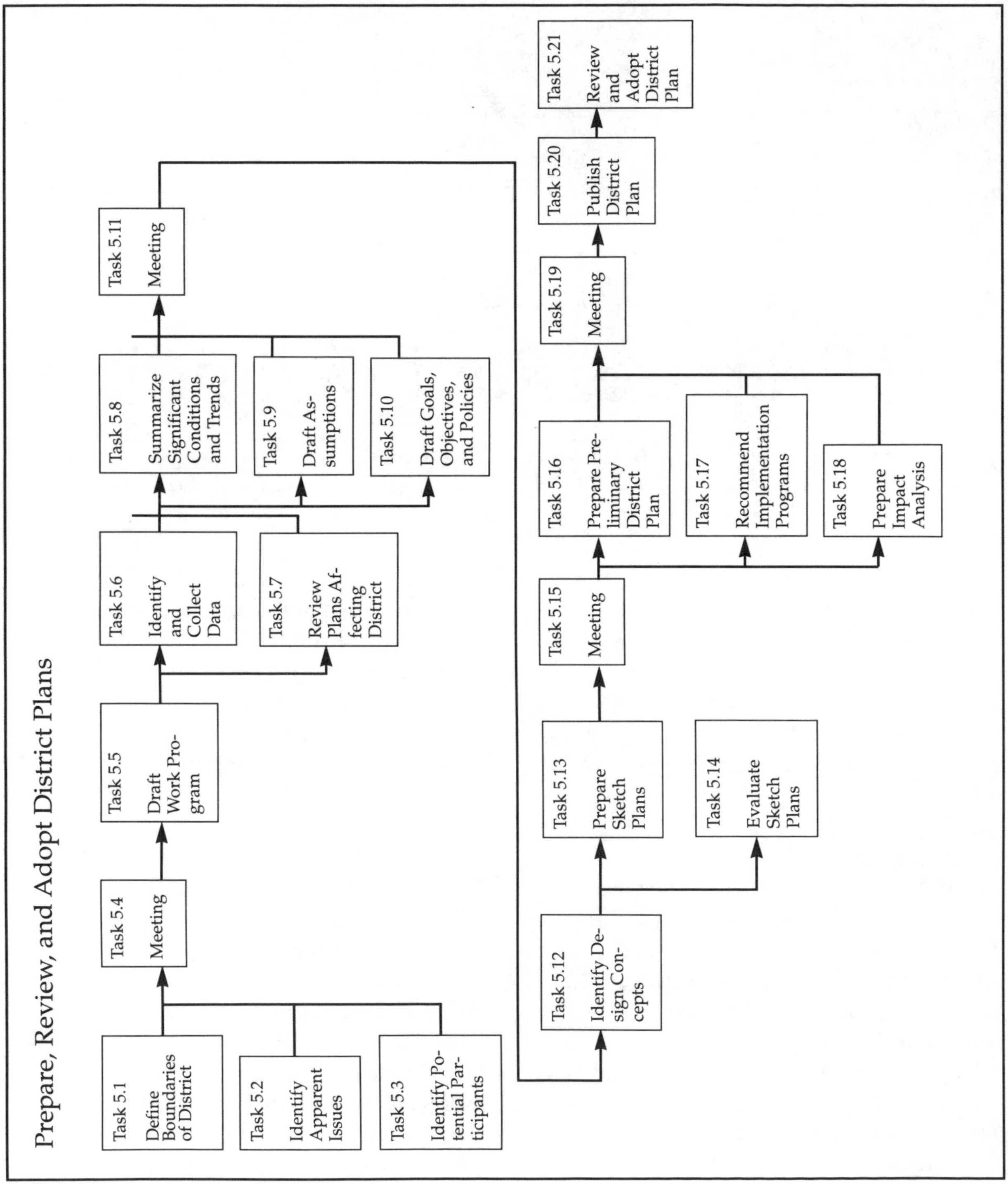

Prepare, Review, and Adopt District Plans

## INTRODUCTION

District plans are short-range multitopic plans for sub-areas of a jurisdiction.

District plans are sometimes prepared for problem areas and for areas where rapid change or development is desired. District plans are also prepared for stable areas, where change is not desired or expected.

District plans are typically prepared for:

- Central business districts
- Large planned unit developments
- Redevelopment areas
- Historic preservation districts
- Stable residential neighborhoods
- Permanent open-space areas

In theory, district plans should cover all parts of a jurisdiction, and be reviewed and updated frequently. In practice, this is difficult to accomplish because it would require a very large staff to do all the work, and the planning commission and the legislative body would probably spend a lot of time in public hearings concerning the district plans. In view of this, some jurisdictions prepare district plans only for "hot spots," pay considerable attention to implementing the plans, and continuously and carefully monitor the results.

Many jurisdictions leave stable areas alone, until they have the staff time to prepare district plans for them; these plans are usually designed to reinforce the stability of the areas.

There are a number of characteristics of district plans that distinguish them from general plans. Some of these are:

- District plans cover only a portion of a jurisdiction; general plans include the entire jurisdiction within their planning area.
- District plans have short-range (five or six year) time horizons; general plans have long-range (15 to 25 year) time horizons.
- District plans indicate considerable specific detail (many of them are "parcel specific"); general plans remain general in character.
- District plans include specific objectives, which indicate what should be done, when it should be accomplished, and sometimes, who is responsible for doing it. General plans include general goals, and only a general description of how they are to be attained.
- District plans usually describe what actions should be taken to implement the near-term recommendations described in the long-range general plan; they are not intended to implement all the recommendations shown in the long-term plan.
- District plans must be consistent with the general plan. That is, they must further the goals and policies of the general plan and not obstruct their attainment.

In the following text the terms "participants in the planning process" and "participants" are used extensively. It is impossible to identify just who these people would be, because there is so much variation among jurisdictions. In some cases the participants may be a large committee representing a wide variety of interest groups in the planning district. In other cases, the participants may be a small group with a common interest, hand-picked by the mayor.

Four meetings of participants are specifically scheduled in the text that follows. This number should be considered a minimum; you will probably see advantages in having much more contact with the participants than is indicated here.

The following discussion of the district planning process omits reference to the relationship between the planners and the client (i.e., the legislative body) and the local planning commission. It is assumed that the planners have a well-established relationship with these bodies, and a well-established chain of communication, via appropriate administrative channels.

### References

An excellent description of district planning, written by Paul H. Sedway, is included as Chapter 4, "District Planning" in So and Getzels' *The Practice of Local Government Planning* 2d ed.

Kaiser, Godschalk and Chapin discuss a form of the district plan in their book, *Urban Land Use Planning* 4th ed. See especially pp. 73-75, which describe "The Development Management Plan."

## TASK 5.1 DEFINE PROPOSED BOUNDARIES OF THE DISTRICT

You should identify the area for which you propose to prepare a plan, and define its boundaries so you can:

- Tell other people, with clarity, what area you are talking about.
- Identify the place of residence or employment of the people you will be working with in the district planning process.
- Identify the general locus of social, economic, and physical development issues that you are concerned about.
- Identify the specific boundaries of the area for which you will be collecting and analyzing data.

### Recommended Procedure

In the urban planning process you are concerned with social and economic activities, and with physical changes. These events all have geographic locations. In this task you attempt to produce a reasonable and logical definition of the boundaries of an area which encompasses these activities; these boundaries will define your planning district.

You probably know, at the outset, the general location of your planning area, but now you must draw lines on a map to show its specific boundaries.

Boundaries of planning areas are often lines that identify barriers to cross-movement. Rivers, for example, are difficult to cross, except where bridges or tunnels are present. Likewise, freeways are impossible to cross, except where over- or under-crossings are present. Mountains often impede cross-movements, as do escarpments. Rail lines often have few locations where crossing is permitted. All of these physical features are occasionally used to define the boundaries of planning areas.

It may be that it would be more appropriate to define boundaries using the edges of social groupings, economic activity areas, political jurisdictions, or census tracts. If so, you should try to identify those edges, and use them to define some or all of the boundaries of your planning area.

The basic procedure for preparing a draft of the boundaries of a planning area is to get a base map of your area and draw lines on the base map to show the boundaries of the planning area, using some of these criteria.

The boundaries of the planning district may need to be adjusted after you review the current issues found in the district (see Task 5.2), and after review of the draft boundaries by the participants of the planning area (see Task 5.5), or after the review of data that you collect (see Task 5.6).

## TASK 5.2 IDENTIFY APPARENT ISSUES IN THE DISTRICT; MAKE PRELIMINARY SELECTION OF TOPICS TO BE INCLUDED IN THE DISTRICT PLAN

You should review issues for three reasons:

**1.** To establish with greater certainty what the current local issues are that should be addressed in the local planning program.

**2.** To have local participants involved in issue identification and ranking, so they become aware of those community issues.

**3.** To provide you and the local participants with information concerning: the relative importance of the issues that are identified, and what priority should be given to their resolution; what the origins or causes of the issues are; and what alternative solutions appear to be available to resolve the issues.

### Recommended Procedure

The procedure recommended in Task 1.6, Identify Apparent Issues, is appropriate for use in this Task.

The procedures discussed in Task 2.2, Identify Issues and Priorities (second round), may be appropriate, but are perhaps more complex than is warranted at this stage for a small planning area.

Remember that this is a preliminary identification of issues, and is subject to change when the participants review your list of issues and priorities in Task 5.4.

This Task should result in a memorandum that identifies local issues, and makes a preliminary ranking of their relative urgency. This memorandum should be written for the participants you will be working with in the district.

In district planning you will have a much closer relationship with participants than you did when preparing the long-range jurisdiction-wide general plan. Because of this relationship it should be relatively easy to identify local issues, and their relative importance. A fairly informal procedure is appropriate for use in this Task.

### Reference

See Task 1.6, Identify Apparent Issues, and Task 2.2, Identify Issues and Priorities (second round), and the sources of information that were identified in them.

## TASK 5.3 IDENTIFY POTENTIAL PARTICIPANTS

Identifying potential participants for planning a district is part of the team-building process. You need to know who has the qualifications, interest, and willingness to serve on the planning team.

### Recommended Procedure

It is recommended that you use the procedure outlined in Task 1.7 for identifying special interest groups or people interested in the planning process. From your list of interest groups, try to identify someone who can speak as a representative of each group.

This Task should not be done by staff acting alone; it needs input from the client, or from someone who speaks for the client.

This Task should result in a list of people who may be nominated to participate in the district planning process. The list you produce may have two parts:

• People who are truly interested in the district, who have the ability to make positive contributions to committee discussions, and who are probably willing to participate in the district planning process.

• People who are interested, and wish to be kept informed, but who do not want to personally in the planning process.

The selection of people to serve on a committee of local government is a political process. While you can suggest candidates, the client will do the actual selecting. The client's criteria for naming citizens to committees, such as a district planning committee, will vary widely from place to place.

### Reference

See Task 1.7, Identify Potential Participants and Their Goals.

### TASK 5.4 MEET WITH PARTICIPANTS; FORM ADVISORY COMMITTEES

This meeting initiates public participation in the district planning process. It gives you an opportunity to explain what the planning process is, and what it is expected to accomplish. It also gives you an opportunity to recruit participants in the district planning process, so the plan that is developed will be their plan, not the staff's plan or a consultant's plan.

### Recommended Procedure:

Meet with people who have been nominated to be participants in the district planning program. In the meeting you should:

1. Review the purposes and procedures of the planning process. Discuss the relationship of the district plan to the jurisdiction-wide general plan. Summarize how district plans are implemented.

2. Review the boundaries of the proposed planning district.

3. Outline the scope of the proposed planning program, identify which topics are suggested for inclusion, and review the proposed time schedule.

4. Outline a proposed participation program, which may include formation of: a committee of the whole, which includes all people who are asked to participate in the planning process; a steering committee, of limited size; and technical advisory committees, of professional specialists.

5. Outline the general responsibilities of the committees.

6. Initiate a process for selecting chairmen of the committees, if they have not already been named.

7. Ask those present to:

• Review and comment on the proposed boundaries of the planning district

• Identify the issues present in the planning district which should be considered in the proposed plan

• Identify general long-range goals for the district

• Identify the specific objectives they wish to see attained in the district in the coming five years

The meeting should produce:

1. Greater understanding by the participants of what can be accomplished by preparing and using a plan for the district.

2. Some enthusiasm among the participants, and a desire to take part in the plan preparation process.

3. Identification of who is interested in serving on which committee.

### References

See Task 1.9, Draft a Planning Participation Program.

See Task 2.1, Review Planning Program Concepts with Participants.

See also the discussion in Task 2.2, Identify Issues and Priorities.

### TASK 5.5 DRAFT WORK PROGRAM

A work program identifies what work is to be accomplished, and when it will be delivered; this is important information for the sponsor of the planning program, and for the citizens who have been asked to participate in it.

A work program also enables the planning staff to predict how long each phase of the planning program will take, and what resources will be needed. It also identifies who will be responsible for completing each Task.

#### Recommended Procedure

Work programs are described in general terms in Task 1.12, and some specific procedures are recommended there.

This Task should produce:

1. A work program that includes
- Task descriptions
- Graphic illustration of the time-relationships among the tasks, and a program completion date.
- Identification of who is to undertake each task, noting which work will be done by volunteers
- Cost estimates for labor, materials, travel, etc.
2. Estimates of direct costs for
- Each task
- Each phase
- The entire program

Preparation of a well-thought-out work program is one of the key elements of good planning practice. A good work program benefits the sponsor, the staff, participating volunteers, and the public.

#### Reference

See Task 1.12, Prepare a Work Program.

### TASK 5.6 IDENTIFY AND COLLECT DATA

Task 2.3 cited reasons for collecting data for planning programs in general. Three of those are appropriate to repeat:

1. To provide a solid, factual basis for the policies and actions the plan will recommend.
2. So you and your staff will know the area for which you are planning, and will know its residents.
3. So that others involved in the planning process, such as legislators, planning commissioners, members of advisory committees, staff members in other departments, etc., will have information available concerning important local planning issues.

#### Recommended Procedure

1. Produce a base map of the district, and assemble aerial photographs.
2. Identify topics for which data is needed.
3. Identify data on hand or readily available. Much of this may have been assembled for use in preparing the general plan.
4. Identify the most promising sources of additional data.
5. Collect the additional data, as needed.

District planning is usually, but not always, a form of physical planning that considers:
- Urban design concepts
- Land use
- Circulation

- Infrastructure (i.e., utilities)
- Community facilities

Other topics, such as economic development, housing, historic preservation, etc., are sometimes included, but they must be integrated into a framework established by the physical design topics identified above.

### Reference

See Task 2.3, Collect and Analyze Data, and its many subdivisions.

### TASK 5.7 REVIEW PLANS AFFECTING THE DISTRICT

Reviewing plans prepared by others often helps you to understand the relationship of the planning district to the surrounding areas. General plans and data reports for nearby areas often provide information that will be useful when preparing your district plan.

### Recommended Procedure

Assemble and review:

1. The current general plan for your jurisdiction.
2. Any function plans that affect the district.
3. All previous plans for the district, regardless of their age and status.
4. Plans of adjacent cities and counties.
5. Plans prepared by metropolitan and state agencies.
6. The map of Current Projects prepared in Task 2.3.14.

This Task should generate a fairly brief memorandum, primarily for staff use, describing the content and status of plans that affect the district.

### References

See Task 1.4, Review the Status of Plans and Planning in the Area.

See Task 2.3.14, Current Projects.

### TASK 5.8 SUMMARIZE SIGNIFICANT CONDITIONS AND TRENDS

A report is needed that summarizes present conditions in the planning district, and identifies trends that should be considered in planning its future.

### Recommended Procedure

1. Review the data collected to date and identify significant present conditions that should be noted, and recent or emerging trends that appear to be important.
2. Write a memorandum, for the information of participants and the staff, containing a summary of benchmark data concerning significant conditions, and identification and discussion of noteworthy trends that will probably affect the future of the planning district.

The conditions and trends considered in this Task should be related to the issues that were identified in Task 5.2.

### References

See Task 2.6, Publish Report on Significant Conditions and Trends.

See Task 5.2, Identify Apparent Issues in the District.

### TASK 5.9 DRAFT STATEMENT OF ASSUMPTIONS

It is important to know what's going on in the outside world that may affect development within your planning district. You and the participants should consider which of these outside forces can be influenced by local action, and which cannot. You and the participants should also consider which forces within the district can be expected to be at work during the coming five years, and what their foreseeable impacts may be.

## Recommended Procedure

**1.** Review issues concerning the planning district (see Task 5.2) to identify which topics should be considered in this Task.

**2.** Identify and describe forces outside the planning district that can be expected to influence its development during the coming five years. Describe the probable effects of these forces.

**3.** Identify and describe forces within the district that can be expected to influence its development, and describe the probable effects of these forces.

**4.** Prepare a memorandum that states what you believe is reasonable to assume concerning development within the district during the coming five years.

You may wish to discuss some of these topics:

- Economic activity (e.g., employment, sales)
- Population trends (e.g., amount, type)
- Housing trends (e.g., amount, type)
- Traffic flows (e.g., location, amount)
- Environmental quality

You may wish to draft your memorandum so it considers these alternatives for the planning district:

- What will probably happen in the planning district if your local government and others do little or nothing to change the predictable course of events.

- What can conceivably happen if your local government and the participants prepare a plan, which includes an effective implementation strategy, and use it effectively.

This Task should produce a memorandum, for the information of staff and participants, that clearly states what events or forces may influence the development of the district during the coming five years. The memorandum produced in this Task should be reviewed by the participants during Task 5.11, and is subject to change.

### Reference

See Task 3.1, State Assumptions Concerning External Forces.

## TASK 5.10 DRAFT STATEMENT OF GOALS, OBJECTIVES, AND POLICIES

You need to write a draft of goals and objectives so they can be reviewed and discussed by participants in the planning process. They need to reach agreement on where they are going before you and they spend a lot of time developing details of the plan.

Identify the policies that your jurisdiction should follow to attain the goals and objectives of the plan. In a sense, goals and objectives describe what a community is buying, and policies represent the price tag.

### Recommended Procedure

**1.** Review:
- The definitions given in Appendix A of goals, objectives, and policies
- The goals stated in the general plan for the jurisdiction
- The development standards used in the general plan

• The issues discussed and found to be important in the recent meeting of the participants (see Task 5.4).

2. Prepare drafts of the general goals for the district. These should probably include:

• Basic concepts of the district. What is its function to be? What is to be its general physical structure?

• The location and character of major land uses

• Basic circulation patterns

• Community facilities to be provided

• Other appropriate topics

This may be in the form of a "vision statement."

Much of this material may be drawn from your jurisdiction's general plan.

3. Prepare drafts of specific objectives for the district, which are to be attained within the short-range future.

You may wish to consider:

• Which existing features of the district should be preserved?

• Which existing features or conditions should be modified or removed?

• What new facilities should be built in the district?

• Which new services should be provided for the district?

4. Prepare a draft of policies that should be followed in the short-range future to attain the specific objectives for the district you have identified.

The most useful policy statements are often in the form of "who should do what, and when it should be done." You probably should not get that specific at this time, but keep the technique in mind for use later in Task 5.17, Recommend Implementation Programs.

Since the district plan probably is being sponsored by the local city or county, and will be adopted by it, most of the policies developed will indicate what actions should be taken by the various public agencies over which the city or county has administrative control.

References to policies that should be adopted by private persons, firms, or agencies are advisory in nature, since cities and counties lack power to require private parties to do very much. Public agencies have lots of power to prevent them from doing bad things, but almost no power to make them do good things.

This Task should produce a memorandum, for review by participants in Task 5.11, which contains drafts of:

• Long-range general goals for the planning district

• Short-range specific objectives for the planning district

• Policies to be adopted and used to achieve the objectives of the district plan

This work should be done in close cooperation with an active committee of participants; it should not be done by staff members working alone.

The work done in this Task should be considered as draft material. One reason for this is that the participants will review it in Task 5.11, and will probably have ideas for additions, changes, and deletions.

A second reason to treat it as draft material is that it contains the essence of the district plan that will be prepared in later Tasks. You cannot (or must not) undertake this Task without thinking about its implications for the design of the district. This Task is described here as a unit only for your convenience. It is intended to illustrate how to prepare a draft of one part of a plan; this part really should not be separated from the whole.

### References

See Task 3.2, Draft Development Goals and Policies, and Task 3.3, Draft Desired Development Standards.

City and County of Denver, Colorado. 1989 Denver Comprehensive Plan. This well-written plan departs from the style of many general plans, and contains a number of interesting features. Of note here is the way that many individual topics are treated. Generally speaking, the discussion of each topic includes:

- A brief background description
- Issues and Opportunities
- Objectives and Concepts
- Policies
- Strategies and Actions

The objectives and concepts, policies, and strategies and actions are usually short-range in nature. The time-frames for completing the strategies and actions are usually specified as "fast track" (two years or less), "short term" (less than five years), or "long term" (five years and beyond). An excerpt from the Urban Design section of the Denver plan is provided in Figure 9-2 as an example of the plan's organization.

### TASK 5.11 MEET WITH PARTICIPANTS

This meeting is intended to bring all participants up-to-date on work that has been done so far, and to get their general ideas and concepts concerning the future of the district. It is intended to be a constructive step toward developing a consensus about the district.

### Recommended Procedure

Hold a meeting of all interested participants, and have them:

**1.** Review the information presented in the Significant Conditions and Trends memorandum produced in Task 5.8.

**2.** Review the draft of the Assumptions, produced in Task 5.9.

**3.** Review the draft of Goals, Objectives, and Policies produced in Task 5.10.

**4.** Discuss major options for development of the district that are to be explored in future studies. Topics may include:

- Basic urban design options
- Major land uses desired
- Major circulation patterns desired
- Desired growth rate, or growth management policies

A written record of the proceedings should be made for the information of any interested participant.

No specific work product should be expected from this Task, but it should result in greater understanding by participants of the issues and opportunities present in the district. Meetings such as this should help in developing a consensus concerning goals, objectives, and policies.

It is difficult to say how many or which participants should be asked to attend this meeting; the decision depends upon your local situation. You and the political leaders of your jurisdiction may find it desirable to have a large, well publicized meeting of everyone who has an interest in the future of the district; you may consider it desirable to have a fairly small meeting of key community leaders; or you may choose some middle course.

### Reference

See Task 2.1, Review Planning Program and Concepts with Participants.

**Figure 9-2**  Excerpt from the 1989 Denver Comprehensive Plan,
City and County of Denver, Colorado

## 3. DESIGN AND PLACEMENT OF INSTITUTIONAL BUILDINGS

Civic buildings originally were designed and incorporated into the park and parkway system. The yard or front lawn for the civic building was the park or parkway, thereby getting double duty out of the open space. This included not only City buildings but also schools. For instance, East High School is linked to City Park; South High is linked to Washington Park; West High is linked to Sunken Gardens and Speer Boulevard. Additionally, buildings were located to provide punctuation at the terminus of arterials. For instance, North High is at the north end of Speer Boulevard.

This setting created an image for civic architecture of grace and beauty. Most buildings were of superior civic design. Civic leaders provided vision for these large scale civic design efforts. The architecture and landscaping made statements about "community" and democratic values.

*ISSUES AND OPPORTUNITIES*

Aesthetics gave way to function and economy. The tradition of prominent location of civic buildings and facilities in park-like settings and graceful and pleasing designs has been lost.

The separation of public functions such as School from City, has made it increasingly difficult to coordinate location and design decisions. But there is a renewed commitment to cooperation particularly in the siting of new schools and parks and in their joint development.

With the City embarking on the construction of many new prominent facilities such as the airport and convention center, it has the opportunity to recapture the design tradition.

*OBJECTIVES AND CONCEPTS*

Achieving the highest standards of design and location of civic buildings and facilities will once again be a City objective.

Major civic buildings, buildings which house special functions or have important symbolic significance, including schools, will face on special streets and open spaces so they may be seen prominently from several directions.

Because of the visual and neighborhood importance of many of these buildings, as the older, obsolete buildings are recycled e.g., schools, they will continue to have a civic role.

*POLICIES*

UD-P-41    The City should coordinate with other public agencies in the joint siting and design of public projects.

UD-P-42    As older City buildings are recycled, new uses should continue to emulate the buildings' civic role in the neighborhood and the civic design intent will remain intact.

UD-P-43    The location of fire stations and libraries at the corner of parks should be evaluated on a case-by-case basis. Of paramount consideration should be the availability of park space for the neighborhood and the protection of the integrity of the design of the park.

UD-P-44    Private contributions to supplement public funds available for public buildings and projects are encouraged.

*STRATEGIES AND ACTIONS*

UD-A-70    Prepare design guidelines to be used in remodeling or constructing new civic buildings.
Timing: ST

UD-A-71    Develop additional funding sources including raising private funds to maintain and repair civic buildings and monuments.
Timing: ST

UD-A-72    Prepare guidelines for the joint siting of new parks and schools that ensure adequate land is available for park use and that school and park functions are integrated in the site design.
Timing: ST

138

## TASK 5.12 IDENTIFY MAJOR DESIGN CONCEPTS

This task is intended to identify the major design alternatives for the district, which will later be used as the basis for sketch planning and calculating projected growth.

### Recommended Procedure

1. Consider the major land use options that appear to be locally desirable and feasible. Consider:
- Residential areas
- Work areas
- Open space
- Community facilities
- Any other major concerns

2. Consider the options for the intensity of land uses.

3. Consider the options for circulation.

4. Keep in mind:
- Economic implications (e.g., cost of construction, market feasibility, etc.)
- Social implications (e.g., the availability of jobs in relation to the skills of the local population)
- Environmental implications
- Implications of measures needed to implement the plan (e.g., what new policies or programs would be needed?)

This Task should result in brief descriptions, accompanied by schematic diagrams, of one or more design concepts that are considered clearly desirable and probably feasible for the district.

This Task is where physical design comes into the district planning process.

If your district consists of predominantly vacant lands, you probably have many options for design, most of which are going to be strongly influenced by local market forces. If the district is already built up, and the community goal is to preserve the status quo, you probably have only one real design option. Other circumstances will lie between these two extremes.

When undertaking this Task, it is important to use staff (or volunteer committee members) who have some real skills in design. It makes no more sense to have a planner-economist attempt this job than it does to have a planner-designer attempt to make an economic feasibility study.

### Reference

See Task 3.5, Prepare Alternative Sketch Plans.

## TASK 5.13 PREPARE ALTERNATIVE SKETCH PLANS

You should prepare sketch plans so that you can examine how various development concepts would work if they were applied to the terrain in your planning area.

### Recommended Procedure

Use the general procedures outlined in Task 3.5.

This Task should produce a sketch plan for each of the design concepts identified in Task 5.12.

The specific procedures you use to prepare sketch plans will, of course, have to be adapted to the purpose of the district plan. If the district plan is to preserve an established residential area, your sketch planning process will be somewhat different than that used to plan a new community on undeveloped land, or to preserve an open space area, or to revitalize an aged central business district.

Sketch planning, in some instances, is an optional Task. If the area you are considering clearly has only one development scheme suitable to local conditions, then it might be a waste of time to concoct several "straw man" sketch plans you know will be knocked over. On the other hand, spending a little time and effort to develop imaginative solutions might be a good investment.

### Reference

See Task 3.5, Prepare Alternative Sketch Plans.

### TASK 5.14 EVALUATE THE SKETCH PLANS

This Task is intended to assist you and the participants to identify which one of the sketch plans, or which parts of several sketch plans, should be selected for further development.

### Recommended Procedure

Use the procedure described in Task 3.6, Evaluate the Sketch Plans.

    This Task should produce one evaluation of each of the sketch plans that were prepared in Task 5.13.

    The evaluations produced in this Task are to be reviewed by the participants in Task 5.15.

    When reviewing the sketch plans, identify and discuss the general qualities of each, rather than rely on a simple summary of how many pluses and minuses each received.

### Reference

See Task 3.6, Evaluate the Sketch Plans.

### TASK 5.15 MEET WITH PARTICIPANTS; SELECT PLAN FEATURES FOR FURTHER DEVELOPMENT

This Task should be undertaken so that a meeting of the minds can be arrived at con-

cerning general design concepts to be used in drafting the district plan.

### Recommended Procedure

1. Meet with the participants and review:
- Contents and general planning approaches used in the various sketch plans
- Results of the evaluations of each of the sketch plans.

2. Reach consensus (if possible) concerning which one of the sketch plans appears to be most appropriate for the district, and which features from any of the sketch plans appear to be desirable to include in future plans.

A memorandum should be prepared summarizing the conclusions reached in the meeting.

### Reference

See Task 3.7, Review Sketch Plans and Their Evaluations; Select Features for Further Development.

### TASK 5.16 PREPARE PRELIMINARY DISTRICT PLAN

We prepare district plans so those who have participated in the planning process, and others, can review and comment on them before they are recommended for formal approval.

### Recommended Procedure

1. Undertake this Task concurrently and interactively with Task 5.17, Recommend Implementation Programs, and Task 5.18, Prepare Impact Analysis of the district plan.

2. Use the selected sketch plan features (see Task 5.15, Meet With Participants; Select Plan Features for Further Develop-

ment), and comments you received on them, as a starting point for preparing the preliminary district plan.

**3.** Prepare an outline of topics to be included in the district plan. When doing this, review materials from Task 5.5, Prepare Work Program, to refresh your memory about what you have promised to produce.

While each locality has its own unique needs, consider the outline in Table 9-1 as a possible outline for your district plan.

**4.** Review the previously prepared estimates of growth that were prepared for the jurisdiction-wide general plan. Review especially those for population, employment, housing, and traffic flow.

**5.** Identify the elements that you propose to include in the plan. The Land Use and

Circulation elements are essential; they will serve as a foundation for all the other elements. Other elements to be included in the district plan will depend on the nature of the district and local issues.

It is suggested that each element include the topics listed in Table 9-2, and that consideration be given to organizing them in the manner shown in Table 9-3.

Writers of plans are faced with problems of style. Plans that are rigidly structured (as suggested in Table 9-3) make it easy for the reader to locate and identify the various parts of plans, and see their relationships, but they lack the charm and grace of good writing; they tend to be boring.

**6.** Prepare the Land Use Element, concurrently with the Circulation Element, if possible. Review the procedure for preparing the land use element of a long-range general plan in Task 3.8. Modify the procedure so it is appropriate for preparing the land use element of a short-range district plan for your specific district.

---

**Table 9-1**
**Suggested Outline for a District Plan**

Introduction
- Purpose of the plan
- Relationship of the district plan to the general plan

Background
- Brief history of the district
- Summary of present conditions in the district
- Major issues facing the district

Major Features of the Plan
- Goals, objectives, and policies
- Basic design concept for the district
- Projections of growth (summaries only; details will be in the elements)

District Plan Diagram

Elements
(Include some, but not necessarily all, of the following)
    Land Use
    Circulation
    Economic Development
    Community Facilities
    Infrastructure
    The Natural Environment
    Other Elements as Needed

---

**Table 9-2**
**Topics Suggested for Inclusion in Each Element of a District Plan**

Background
    Present conditions and trends
    (Describe with text, statistics, and graphics)
    (If appropriate, include projections for the near-term future)

Issues

Objectives

Recommended Actions
    (Actions may be: statements of policy, construction programs, regulatory programs, or some other actions)
    (For each action, indicate who is to take the action, and the time-frame for that action)

**Table 9-3**
**Suggested Structure for an Element of a District Plan**

Background
  Issue A
    Objective A-1
      Action 1
      Action 2
    Objective A-2
      Action 3
      Action 4
      Action 5
  Issue B
    Objective B-1
      Action 6
    Objective B-2
      Action 7
      Action 8

**7.** Prepare a Circulation Element, concurrently with the Land Use Element, if possible. Modify the procedure in Task 3.8 so it is appropriate for preparing the circulation element of a plan for your specific planning district. Note that for a planning district you will probably be concerned with traffic problems on arterial and collector streets, which were not considered in the jurisdiction-wide general plan.

**8.** Prepare other elements, as considered appropriate. Use information from the Land Use Element and the Circulation Element as a foundation for these.

**9.** Draft a district plan diagram. District plan diagrams often should be "parcel specific," whereas general plan diagrams usually should not.

**10.** Draft the lead-in sections for the district plan, which may include such topics as an introduction, background, and major features of the plan.

The product of this Task should be a preliminary district plan.

### References

So and Getzels, editors. *The Practice of Local Government Planning,* 2d ed. Chicago: International City Management Association, 1988.
See Chapter 4, "District Planning," by Paul H. Sedway.

### TASK 5.17 RECOMMEND IMPLEMENTATION PROGRAMS

Short-range plans, such as District Plans, imply that some actions should be taken in the short-range future. Which actions? This Task is intended to develop answers to that question.

### Recommended Procedure

**1.** Undertake this Task concurrently with Task 5.16, Prepare Preliminary District Plan, and with Task 5.18, Prepare Impact Analysis.

**2.** As the district plan is being developed, identify possible implementation measures, such as:

- Which of the jurisdiction's existing regulatory powers will be used to implement the plan? What amendments to them, if any, will be needed?
- What new regulations, if any, will be called for?
- What capital improvements in the district, or serving the district, are implied?
- What will be expected of public agencies, other than your local jurisdiction?
- What will be expected of private citizens, organizations, and investors?
- What local public policies will be recommended?

Concerning the matter of local public policies: In Task 5.10 you may have drafted some recommended public policies. At that stage of the planning process it wasn't necessary to indicate which public agencies should take what actions to implement those policies; it would be highly desirable to do so in this Task.

**3.** Prepare a text, to be made an integral part of the district plan that identifies methods proposed for implementing the plan.

This Task should produce a draft of a section of the district plan dealing with plan implementation.

It is essential to undertake this Task concurrently with Task 5.16, Prepare Preliminary District Plan. By doing this you should be able to evaluate whether existing policies, programs, and resources will be adequate to implement the district plan. If they appear to be insufficient, this will give you, and supporters of the plan, some lead time to outline new programs or policies, or to identify needed additional resources, and to muster local support.

A fundamental reason for undertaking this task concurrently with Task 5.16 is that it will substantially strengthen the effectiveness of the district plan if it is known, and generally accepted, how it is going to be implemented. Without this, substantial delays may occur, and there may even be some unpleasant surprises in store.

### References

See Task 5.16, Prepare Preliminary District Plan.
See Task 5.10, Draft Statement of Goals, Objectives, and Policies.
See Chapter 11, Methods Used to Implement Plans.

### TASK 5.18 PREPARE IMPACT ANALYSIS OF THE DISTRICT PLAN

There are three major reasons for undertaking an impact analysis of the plan.

The first is to enable you to comprehend, while you are preparing the plan, what its impacts would be. This gives you an opportunity to revise the plan while it is in draft form, to eliminate or mitigate potential adverse effects.

The second is to inform yourself and citizens of the jurisdiction you are working with about what the actual impacts of the draft plan would be, if it were to be adopted.

The third reason is a legalistic one: Some states require that impact reports be prepared before the adoption of some types of plans.

### Recommended Procedure

This Task should be undertaken concurrently with Task 5.16, Prepare Preliminary District Plan, and Task 5.17, Recommend Implementation Programs.

You should review the procedures outlined in Task 3.9, Prepare Impact Assessment of the Preliminary General Plan, and amend them to apply to the district plan.

This Task should result in the preparation of impact analyses of the preliminary district plan. These analyses may be on various topics, such as: environmental impacts, economic impacts, fiscal impacts, social impacts, traffic impacts, etc. These may be grouped together in one report, or published individually.

To repeat what was said in Task 3.9:

"This Task is an essential part of the planning process. How complex the Task should be depends upon your immediate situation.

"It would be well to note that a general plan is intended to be general. Therefore the impact assessment of a general plan should probably also be quite general in character. On the other hand, district plans are usually quite specific; therefore impact assessments of them should also be quite specific."

District plans in many cases should be parcel-specific. They should show what is planned for each (or most) of the individual parcels within the planning area.

It also means that the impact analysis of the plan can be quite specific when reporting on the amount of land devoted to each land use, the number of dwelling units projected, the area to be devoted to commercial and industrial uses, etc. This information is usually needed to estimate future fiscal and economic impacts.

It should also be possible to project traffic flows in the planning district, if you have access to a transportation planning computer model, and have collected the data required for inputs. This should make it possible to predict the future level of service (LOS) on streets in the district, and to identify problem intersections.

The district plan should, of course, be very useful in identifying planned capital improvements.

The impact analysis may also project anticipated need for various community services and facilities, if you have considered them in the district plan.

Remember, impact analyses are intended to review the effects of a plan; they are not a part of the plan. They should, therefore, not be published between the same covers as the plan itself.

### References

See Task 3.9, Prepare an Impact Assessment of the Preliminary General Plan.

Refer to the recommended sources of information cited in Task 3.6, Evaluate the Sketch Plans, and in Task 3.9, Prepare Impact Statement.

## TASK 5.19 MEET WITH PARTICIPANTS; REVIEW PRELIMINARY DISTRICT PLAN AND IMPACT ANALYSIS

This meeting gives participants a chance to review and comment on the preliminary district plan. In the process, they will become better informed about what the plan actually recommends, and what its effects might be.

### Recommended Procedure

At a meeting of participants:

1. Review the major features of the plan, such as:

- Present conditions in the district
- Projections of growth
- The basic design concept used in the plan
- Major specific recommendations in the plan
- How the plan will be implemented
- The predicted impacts of the plan

2. Call for comments on the preliminary plan.

After the meeting it may be appropriate for the staff to meet with the steering committee to determine how to accommodate the comments that were received on the preliminary district plan.

This Task should result in a memorandum that records the comments and recommendations received during the meeting.

This is an important Task. Its successful completion can add substantially to both the useability of the plan and to its acceptance by the community.

It is probably a good idea to have the preliminary district plan reviewed by key interested people before it is presented to a large group in a public meeting. If this is done, it may be possible to:

- Edit the plan to eliminate misunderstandings, and to avoid unnecessary controversies.
- Identify where to expect differences of opinion to arise.
- Identify which sections of the plan will receive support.

## TASK 5.20 PUBLISH THE DISTRICT PLAN

The purpose of this Task is to revise the preliminary district plan, and then publish it as a document that will be accepted by the community, and adopted by the planning commission, and by the local legislative body.

### Recommended Procedure

A possible course of action for this Task might include:

**1.** Review the comments received in the meeting with the participants (Task 5.19), and amend the plan as appropriate.

**2.** Review the format of the draft plan; revise it as appropriate.

**3.** If the recommendations of the plan are substantially modified, revise the impact analysis (Task 5.18) as needed.

**4.** Publish the district plan in the number of copies you believe will be needed.

This Task should produce the district plan, ready for public review and consideration.

Remember that the plan must be considered a draft until the successful conclusion of the plan review and adoption process, so it may be well to avoid substantial publication costs at this time.

### References

See Task 3.13, Publish and Distribute the General Plan.
See Task 5.16, Prepare Preliminary District Plan.

## TASK 5.21 REVIEW AND ADOPT THE DISTRICT PLAN

If the plan is to be truly effective, its contents must be known and accepted by many citizens within the sponsoring city or county, as well as by those who participated in its preparation.

The plan needs clear endorsement and official adoption by the planning commission and by the legislative body.

### Recommended Procedure

It is assumed that you have had an ongoing communitywide public information/public participation program while this project has been under way. Such a program is usually considered to be an essential part of the planning process.

With that assumption as background, the following steps are suggested:

**1.** Make sure that key people in local government have copies of the plan.

**2.** Make sure that key people outside of local government have copies of the plan.

**3.** Hold some communitywide information meetings, during which the plan and its potential impacts are reviewed.

**4.** Hold some informational meetings in the district.

**5.** Schedule and hold official public hearings on the plan.

**6.** Have the planning commission adopt the plan, with amendments, if needed.

**7.** Have the legislative body adopt the plan, with amendments, if needed.

**8.** Distribute copies of the adopted plan to appropriate people and agencies.

The completion of this Task should result in an informed citizenry and an officially adopted district plan.

**References**

See Task 3.11, Review the Preliminary General Plan and the Impact Assessment.

See Task 3.12, Formally Review and Adopt the General Plan.

See Task 3.13, Publish and Distribute the General Plan.

# 10

# Phase VI
# Implement District
# Plans

**Contents**

## INTRODUCTION

The following chapter of this book, Methods Used in Implementing Plans, provides brief descriptions of 31 programs. Most of these are suitable for implementing district plans. There are, however, five programs that are especially important to consider as a part of the district planning process. Descriptions of these programs follow.

## TASK 6.1 USE DISTRICT PLANS WHEN MAKING DAY-TO-DAY DECISIONS

Using district plans, and general plans, too, in our day-to-day work is important because:

• It keeps the content of the plans in the forefront of our minds; if this occurs there is little chance that we will forget the policies and details of the plans.

• It gives us a good basis for identifying where and when changes to district plans appear to be appropriate.

**Recommended Procedure**

1. Make sure that all those people who are expected to use the plan have up-to-date copies. This should include:
• Members of the legislative body
• Planning commissioners
• The chief administrative officer, and his/her chief deputies
• Most department heads in local government, and their chief deputies
• All the professional planners on your staff, plus others who have an interest in the plan
2. Make sure that your planning staff members use both the general plan and district plans consistently and accurately. Encour-

age others in local government to do likewise.

## TASK 6.2 REVIEW DISTRICT PLAN RECOMMENDATIONS; IDENTIFY HOW THEY CAN BE IMPLEMENTED

Making an orderly review of the recommendations included in a district plan (including policies, activity programs, and construction projects) will bring to mind what is intended to be accomplished by the plan. When this is known, specific measures may be developed to implement the plan.

**Recommended Procedure**

1. Go through the district plan, page by page, and identify what actions it recommends be taken, by whom, and when.
2. Integrate actions to be taken by the planning department into your annual work program and budget.
3. Identify actions to be taken by others, and devise a tactful procedure for reminding them of their obligations. This may be the job of the chief administrator in your local government.

## TASK 6.3 PREPARE A CAPITAL IMPROVEMENT PROGRAM BASED ON DISTRICT PLANS

Capital improvement programming is widely recognized as an effective method of getting publicly financed physical improvements built, while operating within the fiscal constraints of local government.

**Recommended Procedure**

1. If your jurisdiction does not have an established capital improvement program in-

tegrated into its annual budgeting process, recommend to your administrative supervisor that one be initiated.

**2.** Review the publicly financed construction projects that were identified in the district plan. Using a capital improvement programming procedure, prepare a schedule indicating when these projects are to be built, and identify how they are to be financed. This can be done only if the local legislative body wants it done, and if the administrator above you instructs you to undertake the program.

## TASK 6.4 REVIEW THE ZONING ORDINANCE FOR CONSISTENCY WITH DISTRICT PLANS

Regulating land use, through a zoning ordinance, is the most effective measure currently available for implementing the land use element of a district plan.

If a district plan is to be implemented as its authors and those who adopted it intended it to be, it is essential that the zoning ordinance promotes a pattern of land uses consistent with that shown in the district plan. It is also essential that the general provisions of the ordinance contain procedures that make it effective, flexible, and fair.

### Recommended Procedure

**1.** Compare the land use pattern established by the zoning ordinance with that shown in the district plan. Is the zoning pattern consistent with the planned pattern? Are the intensities of land usage consistent? If there are inconsistencies, identify where they occur, and what their characteristics are.

**2.** Review the provisions of the zoning ordinance text. Are they adequate to implement the land use element shown in the district plan? For example, are the residential zoning regulations consistent with the land uses described in the district plan? Is there enough flexibility in the ordinance to achieve the goals of the plan? Are innovative techniques, such as planned unit development regulations, performance zoning, transferable development rights, etc. needed to implement the plan?

**3.** If inconsistencies between the zoning ordinance and the district plan concerning the type or location of land uses are identified, recommend appropriate amendments to the district maps in the ordinance or, in some instance, to the land use plan.

If the text of the ordinance appears to lack suitable provisions for implementing the plan, recommend amendments to it.

## TASK 6.5 REVIEW AND REVISE DISTRICT PLANS PERIODICALLY

When we implement our plans we change local conditions. This change often warrants a look at what needs to be done next in the community.

Even if we do little to implement our plans, we find that changes occur. These changes may be in economic conditions, local priorities, opportunities open to us, etc. This usually means that we should re-examine our plans occasionally, and amend them to reflect current conditions and expectations.

### Recommended Procedure

Each year, when the planning department's work program and budget are prepared:

1. Consider which of the existing district plans appears to be in need of careful review and possible revision, and which ones still appear to be satisfactory.

2. Consider which sections of the jurisdiction not now covered by district plans should be included in a district planning program in the coming year.

3. If a review and updating of a district plan is indicated, it is suggested that the following topics be considered:

- Changes in local issues
- Changes in local objectives
- Changes in the general plan of the larger jurisdiction, or in the plans of regional or state agencies
- Changes in economic conditions
- Changes in projected growth
- Changes in the responsibilities of people or agencies who were previously expected to have a role in implementing the district plan
- Substantial changes in the pattern of local land uses
- Substantial changes in the volume or location of traffic flows

The review of a district plan need not be anywhere near as complex an undertaking as was its initial preparation and adoption. It shouldn't be necessary to repeat the data collection process, the sketch planning process, the impact analysis, etc., each time a district plan is reviewed.

It's appropriate to review and update frequently (perhaps every three to five years) plans of districts that are experiencing substantial change. But, there is probably no need to revise district plans more often than every eight to 10 years for those areas that show little change, and no evidence of deterioration.

# Methods Used in Implementing Plans

**Contents**

## INTRODUCTION

### Who Implements Plans?

Plans are implemented by:
- The planning department staff
- Staff members in other departments
- The planning commission
- The local legislative body
- Nearby cities and counties
- Regional governmental agencies
- State governmental agencies
- Land developers
- Conservation groups
- Homeowners associations
- Potential home-buyers
- Market analysts (retail store location; industrial location)
- Community residents

While governmental agencies are dominant in the list above, it should be emphasized that private citizens are important forces for implementing public plans.

### Implementation Approaches

As pointed out in an earlier, (see Steps in the Planning Process), there are many types of plan-implementation programs, such as:
- Construction of physical facilities
- Provision of services
- Regulation of land use and development
- Project review
- Fiscal policies

Most local governments today use a wide variety of programs to implement their plans; they no longer rely on a few traditional programs, such as the zoning ordinance, subdivision regulations, and official plan lines.

### Reference

Kaiser et al, in Chapter 6 of their book, *Urban Land Use Planning* 4th ed., include an excellent discussion of development management planning; that is, measures to be used to implement land-development plans. They note that plan-implementing actions should be well-coordinated, rather than adopted and administered one measure at a time on an ad hoc basis. Chapter 18 of their text includes discussion of some aspects of plan-implementation programs that are not discussed in the following program-by-program descriptions.

### Analyzing Implementation Methods

When preparing an annual work program and budget that includes new measures for implementing an adopted plan, planning agencies may choose to compile a brief analysis of each of the proposed new implementation measures, along the lines of the following outline:

1. Short title
2. Brief description
3. Program objectives
4. Criteria that may be used to measure the attainment of the program objectives
5. Estimate of resources required to start up the program (i.e., capital costs, staff time, consultant fees, etc.) Note: Cost estimates in preliminary reviews can only be approximate.
6. Annual operating costs, after a program is established
7. Proposed sources of funding
8. Preliminary impact analysis (Identify the obvious environmental, economic, social, political, and traffic impacts. Mention who would be affected by the program, and how they would be affected.)

**9.** Identification of people or agencies that would have a direct interest in the program, and who should be consulted if the program is to receive serious consideration

**10.** Discussion of alternatives to the program, including the "do nothing" option

**11.** Summary of the advantages and disadvantages of the program.

### References

(California) Office of Planning and Research. *General Plan Guidelines* Sacramento: State of California, 1990. (Available from: Office of General Services, Publications Section, Box 1015, North Highlands, CA 95660; price $16). This text provides a very good overview of the plan-making in California; it also contains a good review of the most important plan implementation programs available for use in California. Most of these programs are usable in other states.

Kaiser, Godschalk, and Chapin. *Urban Land Use Planning* 4th ed. Urbana: University of Illinois Press, 1995. See Chapter 16, "Development Management Planning," and Chapter 18, "Implementation."

Planning and Zoning Center, Inc. *Community Planning Handbook,* 2d ed. March 1992. Prepared for the Michigan Society of Planning Officials. (Available from MSPO at 414 Main Street, Suite 202, Rochester, MI 48307) (This is an extensive review of plan implementation procedures available for use in Michigan; most of them have counterparts in other states.)

## PUBLIC REGULATORY MEASURES

### ZONING

*Definition.* Zoning: *The dividing of a county or a municipality into districts and the establishment of regulations concerning the use of lands within those districts, and the placement, spacing, and size of buildings.*

All states either permit or require legislative bodies of local jurisdictions to enact zoning regulations.

### What Zoning Regulates

- Activities (described in general terms) permitted on private properties
- Minimum lot size
- The placement and spacing of structures, through establishing minimum required front, rear, and side yards, and by specifying minimum distances between buildings
- Maximum percent of the lot that may be covered by structures
- Maximum building height
- The amount and design of offstreet parking to be provided
- The amount and design of offstreet loading area to be provided (especially in commercial and industrial areas)
- The design of structures and sites (sometimes)
- The size, type, and location of signs
- The ratio of floor area within a building to the area of the building site (sometimes) (This has the effect of regulating the maximum floor area permitted.)
- The minimum floor area of single family homes (rarely)
- The number of housing units suitable for families of low or moderate income, as a share of a housing development (sometimes)
- Design review (sometimes)

### Purposes

Zoning is intended to avoid disruptive land use patterns. That is, to prevent the activities on one property from generating external effects that are detrimental to other properties.

In developed areas that are in good condition, zoning is generally perceived as a means of preserving the status quo.

In undeveloped areas, zoning is intended to preserve the status quo, or to serve as a guide for new land use patterns.

### How Zoning Ordinances are Administered

Zoning ordinances are administered primarily through the review of requests for building permits for new construction, or permits for the remodeling of existing structures. When a building permit is requested, the zoning administrator reviews the building plans to make sure the proposed use of the property complies with the zoning ordinance, and the size and the location of any buildings are also in conformance.

Some jurisdictions employ zoning inspectors to review the use of properties, and to negotiate with the owners of illegally used properties to bring about compliance with the zoning ordinance.

Some jurisdictions enforce the zoning ordinance only when a complaint is received concerning the use of some property.

### Relationship to Long-Range and Short-Range Plans

Zoning ordinances often reflect commonly held views of how lands within a jurisdiction can, or should, be used at the present time, or in the very near future. In zoning hearings, major consideration is usually given to the current structure of the community, the road system, utility systems, community facilities, and market conditions when evaluating which land uses are acceptable in which locations.

When an intensive land use is being proposed, most planning commissions are wary of approving applications that are based on hoped-for conditions that exist only in plans for the distant future. Planning commissioners want to know how the land use will fit into the community today, and when new infrastructure and community facilities will be available.

It appears to be reasonable to say that when zoning is intended to preserve the status quo for a long time (as in stable residential areas, or undeveloped natural areas) that guidance from the long-range plan is appropriate. However, if a short-range plan, which is consistent with the goals and policies of the long-range plan, has been prepared and adopted, then it should be used as a guide for zoning.

### Reference

Refer to the Zoning section of the Bibliography.

## SUBDIVISION ORDINANCES

*Definition.*  Subdivision Ordinance: *An ordinance, adopted and administered by a local government, which regulates the division of land into two or more lots, tracts, or parcels, for the purpose of sale, development, or lease.*

Subdivision ordinances usually specify administrative procedures to be followed in the division of land; design standards for subdivisions; and the identification of improvements (e.g., streets, utilities) to be installed. Some subdivision ordinances also specify fees to be paid by the subdivider to offset the impacts (financial and other) the local jurisdiction will experience if the subject land is subdivided and developed.

All states permit or require cities and counties to enact and administer subdivision regulations.

### Purposes

The purposes of subdivision regulation are to:

**1.** Ensure that clear legal records are kept of land transfers.

**2.** Permit land owners to describe properties in terms of lot and block numbers, rather than using the cumbersome metes and bounds descriptions.

**3.** Require that minimum design standards (for lots, blocks, streets, etc.) be observed.

**4.** Require that subdividers install on-site improvements (i.e., improvements on the property being subdivided), or make financial contributions for them.

**5.** Require that subdividers contribute financially for the cost of off-site improvements, (e.g., parks, sewage treatment plants, schools, etc.) that serve the property being subdivided, but are not located on the site (sometimes).

**6.** Assure that potential environmental impacts are considered in the land development process.

**7.** Prevent fraudulent practices in the sale of real estate.

**8.** Ensure that the land subdivision and development pattern is in harmony with the local general plan.

### Relationship to Long-Range and Short-Range Plans

Subdivision regulations are used to assure that the street patterns in new land developments follow the general design set forth in the long-range general plan. The long-range plan applies primarily to the location of major arterials; it does not apply to the location of local streets, because local streets are usually not shown on general plan diagrams. They are often shown on short-range district plan diagrams.

Subdivision regulations also assure that major utility lines are located in accordance with long-range plans. Local utility services (i.e., lines serving individual properties) are not generally shown in these plans.

Land uses are regulated by zoning ordinances, not by subdivision ordinances. It is important, nevertheless, that subdivision patterns be appropriate for the type and density of land uses recommended for the area in a district plan, which should be consistent with the goals and policies of the general plan. Lacking a district plan, the subdivision pattern should be consistent with the goals and policies of the long-range general plan.

Subdivision regulations are generally administered by the current planning division of a local planning office, in close cooperation with the engineer's office, and with liaison with other public and private agencies, such as the parks department, schools department, utility companies, neighborhood associations, etc.

Subdivision administration is a day-in, day-out job in growing communities, rather than an occasional happening.

The administration of a subdivision ordinance is very closely tied to short-range district plans, and to single-topic plans, such as those for circulation, utilities, housing, and conservation.

Generally speaking, subdivision ordinances are essential to have in communities that are experiencing growth or transformation.

### Reference

So and Getzels. *The Practice of Local Government Planning* 2d ed., 1988. See Chapter 8, "Land Subdivision Regulation," by Richard Ducker.

### The Official Map

*Definition.* Official map: *A map prepared and officially adopted by a city or county that shows "with reasonable accuracy" the location of existing and proposed streets, drainage easements, parks, schools, and sites for public buildings.*

After adoption of the official map, no structure may be erected within the boundaries of the site for the proposed street or other public facility. Building setback lines are often established to protect the rights-of-way of proposed future streets.

### Purpose

The purpose of the official map is to reserve lands for future streets and for other public land uses.

### Discussion

Care must be used in administering official maps. If the administration is overly rigid, the local jurisdiction can be sued for taking private property rights without giving fair compensation to the land owners. However, official maps are desirable to have, so that a jurisdiction can negotiate for the purchase of private property when and if the land owner wishes to sell or develop. There are many times when a tract is to be subdivided and developed, and the landowner can be reasonably expected to provide streets and sites for parks and other public land uses that are to be used primarily by the future residents of the new development. In this case, an official map can be useful and effective.

It is not usually considered reasonable, however, to compel a landowner to donate land to a public jurisdiction if its future use is for the benefit of the general public, many of whom may live and work in areas far from the site being considered.

### Relationship to Long-Range and Short-Range Plans

Official maps are not generally useful for implementing long-range plans because long-range general plans are prepared and presented in general terms. General plan diagrams show general locations, not specific locations of future streets and land uses. Official maps, on the other hand, must be specific when describing the location of proposed future facilities.

Official maps are potentially useful for implementing short-range plans, if they are used with discretion. Official maps can certainly show the location of future streets in a short-range jurisdiction-wide circulation plan, and they can show proposed future public lands in short-range district plans.

### Reference

Goodman and Freund. *Principles and Practice of Urban Planning.* Chicago: International City Managers Association, 1968. (See pp. 399-400).

### GROWTH MANAGEMENT PROGRAMS

*Definition.* Growth management programs: *Programs prepared, adopted, and administered by local governments which are designed to regulate urban growth.* These programs influence:

1. The amount of growth
2. The rate of growth
3. The type of growth (e.g., employment inducing, affordable housing, etc.)

**4.** The location of growth, and/or the quality of growth

Growth management programs in rapidly growing communities are generally limiting and restrictive in nature. Those in slowly growing or declining communities often attempt to stimulate and attract urban development.

### Purposes

Growth management programs are sometimes intended to discourage or severely limit unwanted urban growth, and sometimes they are intended to attract desirable new development. When growth is unwanted, these reasons are sometimes stated:

**1.** Growth would change the present character of the area.

**2.** Growth would be detrimental to the present economic base of the community (i.e., the cost of providing services to the new development would be greater than the taxes received from the area, its employees, and its residents).

**3.** Growth would generate loads that would exceed the capacity of existing schools or utility systems.

**4.** Growth would generate so much traffic that the local (or regional) street system would become excessively congested.

When growth is desired, the most frequently cited reasons are that "it will enlarge our tax base," or "it will generate new jobs for local residents."

### Relationship to Long-Range and Short-Range Plans

Growth management programs are generally used to guide development toward the attainment of long-range goals, using short-range programs and current techniques.

Most local governments already have de facto growth management programs, whether they know it or not. Often these take the form of a basketfull of semi-related programs and regulations that reflect local attitudes toward growth and development. It is probably more desirable for local planners to work with community leaders to think through local goals, which are reflected in long-range and short-range plans, and then to fashion a specific program that manages urban growth, using a variety of traditional and innovative techniques.

### DESIGN REVIEW

*Definition.* Design review: *The review and regulation of the design of buildings and their sites.*

(This program is usually included as a section of a zoning ordinance)

### Purpose

Design review often considers the physical design of:

- Individual structures
- Districts (such as historic districts or office parks)
- Sites for individual buildings or groups of buildings

Occasionally design review is exercised by planning commissioners to veto a design they do not care for.

If design controls are considered desirable in a community, it usually is more satisfactory to have the review process conducted by a board of local citizens who have qualifications in the areas of architectural design, urban design, historic preservation, building industry practices, etc. Such a design review board should establish and adhere to clearly defined design criteria.

### Relationship to Long-Range and Short-Range Plans

Buildings constructed, with or without design review, can be expected to last 30 years or more. Design review, therefore, can have significant long-range impacts, and the process may be considered important to the implementation of the long-range plan. This is especially true for those general plans that have urban design elements or historic preservation elements in them.

If a locality expects to experience considerable urban growth, through new construction on vacant lands, or through reconstruction in areas undergoing renewal, design review when conducted by a well-qualified board of reasonable people, can have a positive influence on the implementation of long-range and short-range plans.

### Reference

Solnit, Albert. *The Job of the Planning Commissioner.* Belmont, CA: Wadsworth Publishing Co., 1982. See pp. 123-125.

## HISTORIC PRESERVATION

*Definition.* Historic preservation program: *A program to identify the historic resources within a community, prepare and adopt a plan for their preservation, and to take actions to preserve them.*

These actions often include:

**1.** Official designation as a historic site, building, or area in the National Register of Historic Places (or in a similar state or county register).

**2.** Preparation, adoption, and enforcement of a special section of the local zoning ordinance, designed to protect the basic characteristics of historic sites, buildings, or areas. These zoning regulations often take the form of "overlay zones."

### Purpose

The purpose of historic preservation is to preserve the sites, buildings, or areas that contribute to the local cultural heritage.

### Relationship to Long-Range and Short-Range Plans

Historic preservation programs certainly have long-range goals and implications but, they usually call for actions to be taken in the short-term future. They are therefore relevant to both long-range and short-range planning programs.

It is desirable to have a Historic Preservation Element in the long-range general plan to serve as the foundation for a historic preservation program.

### Reference

See the Historic Preservation and Adaptive Reuse section of the Bibliography.

## IMPACT ASSESSMENT REPORTS

*Definitions.* Environmental impact assessment: *the analysis of the potential effects on the local physical environment that are attributable to some identifiable action or actions.*

Economic impact assessment: *the analysis of the potential effects on the general economic conditions within a jurisdiction that are attributable to some identifiable action or actions.*

Fiscal impact assessment: *the analysis of the potential changes to the fiscal condition of local government that are attributable to some identifiable action or actions.*

Social impact assessment: *the analysis of the potential effects on local social conditions that are attributable to some identifiable action or actions.*

## Purpose

The purpose of impact assessment is to ascertain the truth about the potential short-term and long-term effects of some proposed action, so that an informed decision can be made concerning that proposed activity.

The procedure is intended to identify the negative impacts of the project, mitigation measures that would alleviate the negative impacts, and alternatives to the project.

Impact assessment should provide a community with valid, objective data so that it can reject a project if it concludes that the negative impacts cannot be satisfactorily mitigated, or can approve a project, subject to specific mitigation measures being taken.

## Relationship to Long-Range and Short-Range Plans

It is customary to analyze the potential impacts of some proposed activity on both the short-range and the long-range future. Both analyses are important.

Impact assessment has a strong influence on short-range plans because their cost (in dollars and in time) is so great that they retard development, both good and bad.

Impact assessments are important for long-range plans because actions taken in the short-term usually have long-term effects.

## Reference

See the sources of information recommended in Task 3.6 and Task 3.9.

## EXACTIONS AND FEES

***Definitions.*** Exactions: *Contributions of land, or construction of facilities, made by a developer to a local government in order to defray some of the financial costs anticipated from land development. The land or facilities may be either on the site of the land development, or off-site.*

Fees: *Financial contributions made by a developer to a local government to defray some of the financial costs anticipated from land development. The costs to be defrayed are often for off-site utilities or streets; they may also be for off-site schools, parks, or other public facilities. Fees are often offered as alternatives to exactions.*

## Purpose

The purpose of a city or a county charging exactions and fees from land developers is to pay for the financial costs of on-site or off-site services and facilities that the new land development generates (such as the need for trunk sewers, schools, parks, additional expressway lanes, etc.).

## Discussion

Land developers, of course, pass the cost of exactions and fees on to the purchasers of the newly developed lands. The amount can be substantial. In 1993, Sonoma County, California, cities were charging fees from $7,000 to $15,000 per dwelling unit in new subdivisions. While this practice eases some of the financial burdens of local government, and alleviates some of the impacts of urban growth, it also makes it more difficult for builders to produce affordable housing.

### Relationship to Long-Range and Short-Range Plans

Exactions and fees programs are, of course, administered as land is developed. This means that the programs are closely related to short-range planning and to short-range budgeting.

The location of any new facilities contributed through exactions, or paid for by contributed fees, should, of course, be consistent with the long-range plan.

### References

So and Getzels. *The Practice of Local Government Planning* 2d ed., 1988. See pp. 215-226 in Chapter 8, "Land Subdivision Regulation."

Frank and Rhodes (editors). *Development Exactions.* Chicago: American Planning Association, 1987.

Nelson, Arthur E. (editor) *Development Impact Fees.* Chicago: APA Press, 1988.

Nicholas, Nelson, and Juergensmeyer. *The Practitioners Guide to Development Impact Fees.* Chicago: American Planning Association, 1991.

Snyder, Stegman, and Moreau. *Paying for Growth: Using Development Fees to Finance Infrastructure.* Washington: Urban Land Institute, 1986.

Urban Land Institute. *Project Infrastructure Development Handbook.* Washington: Urban Land Institute, 1989.

## PUBLIC INVESTMENT PROGRAMS
## PUBLIC CONSTRUCTION PROJECTS

*Definition.* Public construction projects: *Construction projects sponsored by a public agency. Public construction projects typically include roads, transit systems, public buildings, water supply systems, airports, etc.*

### Purpose

Public construction projects are undertaken to provide the general public with facilities that are not provided by private enterprise.

### Relationship to Long-Range and Short-Range Plans

Construction projects (both public and private) generally have a long-term usefulness (30-50 years, or more). Therefore the specific location, function, size, and character of these long-lived facilities should be compatible with the long-range plan. Note, however, since the long-range plan is general in nature, that it should not be relied on to provide specific guidelines for construction projects.

Short-range plans, either district plans or function plans, are a more appropriate setting for project design guidelines than are long-range plans.

## PUBLIC LAND ACQUISITION PROGRAMS

*Definition.* Land acquisition: *The purchase of land in fee simple (i.e., all rights in the land), or the purchase of limited rights in land (e.g., mineral rights only, or development rights only).*

### Purpose

There are two alternative purposes in public acquisition of private lands:

**1.** To make the site available for full public access and usage (e.g., as the site for a public building, an airport, a park). This usually requires acquisition in fee simple.

**2.** To acquire limited rights to the property (e.g., air rights in lands in an airport approach zone; water rights for lands that drain into a reservoir; development rights for permanent open space areas).

### Relationship to Long-Range and Short-Range Plans

Land acquisition usually implies a long-term commitment for ownership and maintenance; it is therefore usually relevant to long-range plans. Public land acquisition programs, however, may be developed and shown in considerable detail in short-range plans.

Land acquisition by public agencies is often an important part of implementation programs for these elements of general plans: Public Services and Facilities; Parks and Recreation; Open Space; and Transportation.

### ECONOMIC DEVELOPMENT PROGRAMS

*Definition.* Economic development program: *A process intended to create wealth by mobilizing human, physical, natural, and capital resources to produce marketable goods and services.* (Source: So and Getzels, The Practice of Local Government Planning, 2d ed., p. 287.)

### Purposes

(Source: So and Getzels, op cit, p. 287.)

The role of the public economic developer is to foster the growth and retention of business activity and, through a healthy local economy, provide employment opportunities and a strong tax base. Economic development programs typically are concerned with:

**1.** Retaining existing business and industry
**2.** Attracting business (manufacturing, service, or nonlocal government)
**3.** Nurturing small and start-up businesses
**4.** Developing and financing facilities that help capture business or recycle local funds

### Relationship to Long-Range and Short-Range Plans

While it is true that a long-range view of the desired future economic condition of a community should be considered, most economic development actions are undertaken within a very short-range time frame, to solve an immediate problem.

The long-range plan may appropriately contain long-range economic goals, but a short-range economic plan, containing specific objectives and strategies, is needed for an action program.

### HOUSING PROGRAMS

*Definition.* Housing programs: *Programs designed to provide shelter for residents within a specific jurisdiction.*

### Purposes

Housing programs are intended to provide housing for residents of a local jurisdiction by implementing the policies, strategies, and development proposals in long-range and short-range plans.

### Discussion

Housing programs are extremely varied. The following factors are usually considered in formulating them:

• Proposed occupancy—by type of occupant (e.g., traditional single family, migrant workers, elderly)
• Proposed occupancy—by income of occupants (e.g., high, moderate, or low income)
• Housing type (e.g., single family detached, apartment, mobile home)
• Ownership (e.g., owner-occupied or rental; also private ownership or public ownership)

• Source of financing (e.g., local savings and loan association, federally insured mortgage, local government bonds)

• Tax provisions (e.g., income tax deduction for mortgage interest, depreciation allowance for rental housing)

• Location (e.g., urban, suburban, rural)

• Cost (e.g., land cost, construction cost, taxes, utilities)

Housing programs may be either publicly sponsored or privately sponsored. In American cities and counties, privately designed, financed, and built housing is far more prevalent than is publicly sponsored housing. However, in the preparation of housing elements of city and county plans, both public and private aspects of housing must be considered.

### Relationship to Long-Range and Short-Range Plans

Housing, as a physical structure, typically has a long life (30 years, 50 years, or more). Housing construction programs have substantial implications on the long-range physical characteristics of the communities in which housing is built. This, in turn, has long-range implications on economic and social conditions.

On the other hand, the shortage of affordable housing is considered in many jurisdictions to be a social problem that requires immediate attention. It's desirable to have an officially adopted short-range housing plan; this may be a function plan that is an adjunct to the long-range general plan.

Housing program implementation strategies should be included in short-range plans, but they should be consistent with the goals of the long-range plans.

## REDEVELOPMENT

*Definition.* Redevelopment: *The replanning and rebuilding of blighted sections of American cities.* Redevelopment is sometimes known as urban renewal.

### Purposes

The purposes of redevelopment are to remove blighted sections of cities and to replace them with modern development, and, in the process, remove the causes of the urban blight.

### Discussion

The general procedure used in redevelopment is:

• Designate a project area that contains blighted properties

• Prepare a new plan for rebuilding the project area

• Provide funds for:
  —Purchasing selected properties in the project area
  —Relocating people and businesses
  —Building new infrastructure
  —Building new public facilities

• Sell properties in the project area to private parties for new construction

The federal government, which for many years was a major sponsor of redevelopment, no longer funds the program. However, the legislation that permits cities and counties to engage in the activity still exists; some local jurisdictions are using those powers today. These jurisdictions have to find their own money, which may be from federal Community Development Block Grants, tax increment financing, local general funds, etc., but they do find it worthwhile doing.

### Relationship to Long-Range and Short-Range Plans

The plan developed for a redevelopment project area is a form of a short-range district plan. This plan must be consistent with the goals and policies of the long-range general plan.

### Reference

So, Stollman, et al. *The Practice of Local Government Planning*. Chicago: International City Management Association, 1979. See Chapter 16, "Maintenance and Renewal of Central Cities," by Chester C. McGuire.

## OTHER PUBLIC PROGRAMS

## DAY-TO-DAY USE OF PLANS

Probably the most effective means of implementing plans (long-range or short-range; general or specific), is to use them in the day-to-day administration of public affairs. To have this happen, plans must have been put in the hands of all those people who will have occasion to use them. Just placing a few copies on reserve in the public library is not enough. People must be sensitized to the existence of the plan so they will reach for it, open it, and consult it whenever a relevant issue arises.

Getting the planning staff to use the plan is relatively easy. Getting planning commissioners, city councilmen, and county supervisors is more difficult, until they realize that their plan has meaningful content, that it means business, and that it is truly useful. Does your plan have meaningful content, or is it a rather bland pap that offends no one? Have you been able to get people to take the plan seriously?

Once you get your local key decision makers to start using the plan, experience shows that they will rely on it more and more—if it is a good plan. If the plan has little substance, is difficult to read and use, or contains policies readers reject, it will be ignored consistently, except when it serves the interests of the user.

Getting department heads and staff in other branches of government to use the plan is very important. This is relatively easy, if they had a voice in preparing the plan and consider it "our plan," rather than "the planning department's plan." A good way of getting this participation in plan-making is to get individual departments to assign staff to assist in preparing individual elements of the long-range and short-range plans.

If the plan is used at budget time to review requests for capital improvements and major programs, it gets the attention of department heads quickly if their pet projects are found to be not consistent with the plan.

Many private civic-improvement organizations should also be made aware of the plan; they will use it occasionally if it supports their goals and proposals, and if they believe it will build a better community. This is true of both pro-development groups, and of homeowners associations, which may be pro-development, so long as the development does not occur in their back yard.

Average citizens generally have little day-to-day use of the local plan. They may consult it on those rare occasions of buying a home or starting a business. It is still important to always keep the plan, and planning, in view of the public. This can do much to develop a public awareness, and, we hope, a pro-planning attitude that is essential for community development.

## CAPITAL IMPROVEMENT PROGRAMS (CIPS)

*Definition.* Capital improvement programming: *The multiyear scheduling of public physical improvements. The scheduling is based on studies of fiscal resources available and the choice of specific improvements to be constructed for a period of five to six years into the future.* (So and Getzels, p. 449.)

### Purposes

The purposes of capital improvement programming are to:

1. Identify present and future needs for physical improvements in a local jurisdiction
2. Identify the potential costs of requested improvements
3. Identify the possible sources of revenue to pay for the requested improvements
4. Provide decision makers with an orderly procedure for setting priorities among requested improvements
5. Promote coordination of construction programs among various public agencies and private interests
6. Provide a strong and useful tool for implementing local growth management programs
7. Provide an effective tool for implementing the local general plan; one that requires an annual review of issues, trends, and priorities

### Relationship to Long-Range and Short-Range Plans

Capital improvement programming is tied closely to short-range planning. The program is an annual event, reflecting current issues, needs, and resources. Short-range plans reflect the initial segments of growth indicated in long-range plans.

### References

So and Getzels. op cit. See Chapter 14, "Finance and Budgeting" by Frank So (pp. 447-466).

Brevard, Joseph H. *Capital Facilities Planning.* Chicago: APA Planners Press, 1985.

Management Assistance Section, Office of Local Development Programs Virginia Department of Housing and Community Development. *Capital Improvement Programming: A How-To Manual for Virginia's Local Governments.* Richmond: Virginia Department of Housing and Community Development, 1986.

## PREFERENTIAL ASSESSMENT PROGRAMS

*Definition.* Preferential assessment: *A tax policy in which lands with uses considered desirable by the local jurisdiction are assessed at relatively low values, thereby reducing the amount of property taxes due each year. In return for a lowered assessment, the property owner usually is required to agree not to substantially change or intensify the existing use of the property during a specified period of time.*

### Purpose

Preferential assessment programs are used by jurisdictions to provide incentives to owners of agricultural lands and forest lands to retain rural land uses, rather than convert their properties to suburban or urban land uses.

A form of preferential assessment can also be used to provide owners of historic buildings or sites with an incentive to retain or enhance the existing character of their property.

## Discussion

As of 1976, more than 40 states had adopted some form of preferential assessment for agricultural lands. (Council of State Governments. "State Growth Management," May, 1976.) The experience in California, with its Williamson Act, is that preferential taxation works well in agricultural areas where there is little pressure for urban development. It does not appear to be an effective long-term preservation measure in areas where there is a strong market demand for subdivision. However, the program can sometimes defer urbanization for a few years, possibly giving time to find other, more permanent measures of preserving the open character of the lands.

## Relationship to Long-Range and Short-Range Plans

Preferential assessment programs are usually intended to attain long-range goals by using short-range (year-to-year) strategies.

## Reference

Grillo and Seid. *State Laws Relating to Preferential Treatment of Farmland* (1985). Available free from Natural Resources Economics Division, ERS, USDA, 1301 New York Ave. NW, Washington, DC 20005-4788.

## URBAN SERVICE AREA DESIGNATION

*Definitions.* Planning area: *The area for which a local jurisdiction, such as a city or a county, prepares plans.*

*A planning area usually includes all lands within the local jurisdiction, plus those adjacent lands that clearly influence life or development within the jurisdiction (e.g., development of those adjacent lands would have economic, traffic, social, environmental, or other impacts).*

Planning areas are sometimes called spheres of influence.

Urban service area: *The area in or adjacent to an urban jurisdiction, such as a city, which that jurisdiction plans to provide with urban services (water supply, sewage disposal, police and fire protection) within a specified time period, after it is annexed to the jurisdiction.*

A city may have areas within its boundaries that it does not plan to provide with urban services. These non-urbanized areas may be intended to be retained as permanent open spaces, and contain land uses such as agriculture, forests, large parks, bays, lakes, rugged mountain terrain, etc.

## Purposes

Designation of urban service areas is intended to:

**1.** Promote orderly urban development. It is intended to encourage infill of bypassed lands, and to encourage the development of areas to which urban services can be logically and economically extended.

**2.** Preserve the open space character of lands planned as permanent open space. This is done by withholding urban services from these areas.

*3.* Avoid development of expensive-to-serve areas of urban sprawl and leap-frog development.

## Discussion

There are important policy implications involved with the designation of urban service areas. Designating urban service areas has great potential as a useful tool for plan implementation, if all legal hurdles can be cleared. In many states new enabling legislation must be enacted before cities may engage in the practice.

In California, the practice of designating urban service areas is incorporated in legislation that established Local Agency Formation Commissions (LAFCOs) (see citation below) These commissions are required in counties, and have the power to approve or disapprove, with or without conditions, proposals for the formation of new cities, the formation of special districts, and boundary changes by cities and special districts.

### Relationship to Long-Range and Short-Range Plans

Urban service area designation can be a major force in implementing the long-range plan. The boundaries designated should remain constant, and should not be affected by short-range considerations.

### References

Easley, Gail. "Staying Inside the Lines: Urban Growth Boundaries." Planning Advisory Service Report No. 440. Chicago: American Planning Association, 1992.

Schiffman, Irving. *Alternative Techniques for Managing Growth*. Berkeley: Institute for Governmental Studies, University of California at Berkeley, 1989. (see pp. 115-118).

Assembly Local Government Committee (of the California legislature) "Guide to the Cortese-Knox Local Government Reorganization Act of 1985." An annotated guide to the act that describes the powers and responsibilities of Local Agency Formation Commissions (LAFCO's) in California. (Available from Assembly Publications Office, State Capitol, Box 942849, Sacramento, CA 94249-0001).

## TRANSFERABLE DEVELOPMENT RIGHTS (TDRS)

*Definition.* Transferable development rights: *A concept in which some or all of the rights to develop a parcel of land in one district (the "sending district") can be transferred, by sale or barter, to a parcel of land in a different district (the "receiving district").*

It is necessary for the governing jurisdiction to agree that the increase in the level of permitted development in the receiving district is appropriate and acceptable.

The sending districts are usually those in which the local jurisdiction wishes to limit or curtail development; they are typically agricultural areas, or historic sites and buildings.

### Purpose

The concept of transferring development rights was originally developed to allow the sale of "air rights" over historic sites and buildings, as a means of preserving them. It has subsequently been used to allow the sale of development rights in rural areas where development is not wanted, and the transfer of those rights to areas where urban development is wanted.

As of 1994, relatively few states had enacted legislation that authorizes the transfer of development rights.

### Relationship to Long-Range and Short-Range Plans

The transfer of development rights, and the consequent construction of concentrated urban development, must be considered an action with long-term implications, and is therefore clearly related to long-term planning.

While zoning changes are usually responsive to current real estate market conditions (and therefore related to short-term planning), the transfer of development implies a longer-lasting effect. However, the transfer of development rights has not yet had a long history, and it may be too early to tell how permanent these transfers will be.

### References

Costonis, John. "Development Rights Transfer: An Exploratory Essay." 83 Yale Law Journal (1973).

Roddewig and Ingraham. "Transferable Development Rights Programs: TDRs and the Real Estate Market Place." Planning Advisory Service Report No. 401. Chicago: American Planning Association, 1987.

## PROJECT REVIEW

*Definition.* Project review: *Planning commission review of proposed public projects, and comment on their relationship to adopted plans. This program is also known as mandatory referral.*

In most cases the projects reviewed are those over which the local government has direct control. Projects typically considered are proposed buildings, roads, utility lines, property acquisition, and property disposition.

In some cases, the local planning commission may provide advisory comments on projects proposed by public agencies outside of local government (such as school districts, park districts, utility districts, etc.) While state and federal governmental agencies are usually exempt from local control, local governments often comment on the environmental, traffic, financial, and other impacts of proposed state and federal projects.

### Purpose

The purpose of project review is to assure that public projects support, rather than contradict, the goals and recommendations of the local general plan.

### Relationship to Long-Range and Short-Range Plans

Many proposed public projects have long-term implications, and review and comment on them, based on the local long-range general plan, is usually important and worthwhile.

As is the case with long-range plans, review of proposed public projects, based on adopted short-range plans, such as a district plan or a single-function plan, is an important job, and usually worthwhile doing.

### Reference

Goodman and Freund, op. cit. See pp. 385-387.

## TRANSPORTATION SYSTEMS MANAGEMENT (TSM)

*Definition.* Transportation Systems Management (TSM): *A short-range program to improve the efficiency of the existing transportation system by more effective use of facilities.*

### Purpose

As stated in the definition above, the purpose of TSM is to improve local transportation by using a variety of management measures, without resorting to substantial capital investment in new facilities.

### Discussion

TSM measures are many and varied. They include:

• Traffic engineering improvements (e.g., channelization, bus turnout lanes, improved signage)

- Traffic control improvements (e.g., traffic signal coordination)
- Freeway management strategies (e.g., high occupancy vehicle lanes, ramp metering)
- Ride-sharing programs
- Parking management
- Transit service improvements
- Changes in work schedules, fares, and tolls
- Providing for pedestrian and bicycle movement

### Relationship to Long-Range and Short-Range Plans

TSM is clearly related to short-range plans and planning.

### Reference

Edwards, John D., editor. *Transportation Planning Handbook*. Englewood Cliffs, NJ: Prentice-Hall (for the Institute of Transportation Engineers), 1992. See Chapter 9, "Transportation System Management," by Judycki and Berman.

## IMPLEMENTATION OF ISTEA

*Definition.* ISTEA: *The acronym for the Federal Intermodal Surface Transportation Efficiency Act of 1991. This is a transportation planning and development program for states and metropolitan areas, sponsored by the Federal Highway Administration (FHWA) and the Federal Transit Administration (FTA). Program guidelines were published October 1993.*

### Purpose

The purposes of these regulations are to:
- Carry out a continuing, comprehensive, and intermodal statewide transportation planning process, including the development of a statewide transportation plan and transportation improvement program . . . in each state.
- Implement the federal regulations that require metropolitan planning organizations (MPOs) to engage in "a continuing, cooperative, and comprehensive transportation process that results in plans and programs that consider all transportation modes and supports metropolitan community development and social goals."

### Discussion

The act is oriented toward the preparation of state and metropolitan transportation plans, and programs for their implementation.

State and metropolitan transportation planning agencies are required to prepare Transportation Improvement Plans (TIPs), which are required to be "financially constrained by year and include a financial plan that demonstrates which projects can be implemented using current revenue sources and which projects are to be implemented using proposed revenue sources."

Metropolitan areas are required to have MPOs; MPOs are required to include representation from local elected officials, among others.

Both state and metropolitan transportation improvement plans are required to have a time horizon of at least 20 years. Transportation improvement plans (TIPs) are required to cover a period of not less than three years.

Local governments are usually strongly affected by state and metropolitan transportation plans, and by their implementation programs. They are also affected by the availability of state and federal funds to support local transportation measures. Obviously, local governments should pay considerable attention to the ISTEA program, and participate in it when opportunities arise.

## Relationship to Long-Range and Short-Range Plans

Since state and metropolitan planning programs are required by ISTEA to have at least a 20 year time horizon, this indicates a clear relationship to local long-range plans.

Since the transportation improvement programs must have a time horizon of at least three years; this indicates a clear relationship to local short-range plans.

## Reference

ISTEA regulations were published on pages 58040 through 58079 of the Federal Register on October 28, 1993. The heading of the publication included: Federal Highway Administration, 23 CFR Part 450, Federal Transit Administration, 49 CFR Part 613.

## STRATEGIC PLANNING

*Definition.* Strategic planning: *A disciplined effort to produce fundamental decisions and actions that shape and guide what an organization (or other entity) is, what it does, and why it does it. (Bryson, p. xii and p. 5.)*

There appears to be no widely held definition of strategic planning, as applied to local government. This author hasn't found any widely recognized procedures for its application in local government.

## Purpose

Strategic planning in local government appears to be intended to provide a new proce-

dure for decision making in urban planning; one that is more flexible than the traditional rational model used in many long-range comprehensive planning programs.

## A Brief Description

Strategic planning identifies the key decision makers in a community, and the "stakeholders" (i.e., those individuals or groups with an interest in the outcome of decisions made in the planning process).

Strategic planning involves making a "situation assessment," sometimes identified as the analysis of Strengths, Weaknesses, Opportunities, and Threats (SWOTs), and the identification of strategic issues.

Strategic planning places major emphasis on the identification and application of strategies to resolve the identified issues, and thereby attain the desired goals.

## Comparison of Strategic Planning With Traditional Planning

Strategic planning and traditional planning have a great deal in common, despite some authors' protests.

Both programs identify decision makers and stakeholders. Strategic planning tends to narrow the range of stakeholders, while traditional planning tends to cast a wide net. This makes strategic planning more manageable, and easier to reach consensus than traditional planning. On the other hand, traditional planning may develop a broader base of citizen support. Neither program is going to be very successful in communities where there are wide differences of values and positions among citizens.

Strategic planning appears to focus its data collection and analysis on the "situation assessment" (i.e., What are the issues? What forces bear on the issues?). Traditional planning, on the other hand, often has an insatiable appetite for data and data analysis; it can be an expensive and time-consuming fetish. Traditional planners could learn from strategic planners here.

Both planning procedures use the concept of goals. Some strategic planners are quite contemptuous about them, however. (They accuse traditional planners of end-state planning, not acknowledging that life will continue after the target year of a plan)

There appears to be no consensus on the time-scale of strategic plans; some say it should be long-range (20 years), and some say short-range (three to five years). Comprehensive plans prepared by traditional methods usually have a long-range time scale, but occasionally they are short-range.

The apparent strength of strategic planning lies in its consideration of strategies that are to be used to attain the desired vision of the future (i.e., the goals of the plan). In other words, emphasis is placed on plan implementation. We traditional planners will have to admit that all too often we have enshrined the plan, and have neglected consideration of how to implement it. This text tries to show that this should not be standard practice. We need to include implementation strategies, and evaluation of their impacts, as integral parts of the planning process.

Some writers claim that strategic planning is "proactive," and that traditional planning is "reactive." They may be right, to quite a degree. Traditional planning usually deals with a broad general public, which is notoriously conservative when it comes to changing its

ways. The general public will often react strongly, and negatively, to proposed changes in the status quo; rarely will it accept a proactive position, except in times of clearly impending disaster. The lesson to be learned from strategic planning is that if you wish to effect change in a community, work with the movers and shakers, and work with them to convince the broader public to follow along.

Strategic planning appears to focus on the delivery of public services, and not on the design of the physical environment. Traditional planning, on the other hand, started life as a program to design the physical setting. In some jurisdictions, traditional planners have become involved with service-delivery systems. It has occurred where service delivery is a major issue, and design of the physical environment has a much lower priority.

Strategic planning appears to be best suited to concentrate on one, or a few topics at a time. Traditional planning attempts to consider a very broad range of topics that affect the quality of life in the urban environment, all at one time. This is the case in the preparation of the usual multitopic plan; it is not the case in the preparation of a single-function plan. Single-topic planning is far less complex than multitopic planning. It is probable, therefore, that strategic planning can be accomplished more quickly than traditional planning, and will appear to be more efficient.

Some authors of articles on strategic planning clearly state that the strategic planning procedure is not suited for the preparation of the traditional general plan. I agree, primarily for the reasons provided in the preceding paragraphs. On the other hand, strategic planning does appear to be worth trying when one is interested in implementing the recommendations concerning a single topic (or element) of a general plan.

## Relationship to Long-Range and Short-Range Plans

Strategic planning appears to be well suited for the consideration of immediate problems, and for identifying strategies to resolve them in the near future. It may therefore may be classified as short-range in nature. It does not appear to be well-suited for the contemplation of long-range issues, which often evade clear definition, and which involve a multitude of interrelated topics.

## Conclusion

Strategic planning and traditional planning appear to be quite different planning procedures, each of which is suited for a separate task. Strategic planning does not appear to be well-suited for comprehensive long-range planning, but is well-suited for developing effective strategies to resolve narrowly focused immediate problems. Conversely, the traditional planning process is not well-suited for immediate, strategic, proactive problem solving, but it is an effective procedure for comprehensive planning.

## References

Bryson, John M. *Strategic Planning for Public and Nonprofit Organizations.* San Francisco: Jossey-Bass, 1991.

Bryson and Einsweiler, editors. *Strategic Planning: Threats and Opportunities for Planners.* Chicago: American Planning Association, 1988.

Kemp, Roger L. *Strategic Planning in Local Government: A Casebook.* Chicago: American Planning Association, 1992.

## AVOIDANCE OF LITIGATION

*Definition.* Avoidance of litigation: *Preventing or eluding lawsuits.*

## Discussion

One way to stop the physical development of a city or a county is to get the jurisdiction sued for non-compliance with some local, state, or federal regulation. This can easily keep development at a standstill for years.

Lawsuits against cities and counties have been filed for a wide variety of reasons, such as:

• Having a general plan that is out of date, is internally inconsistent, or lacks the topics required by state law.

• Having a zoning ordinance which is not consistent with the general plan.

• Filing an environmental impact report that is considered by an aggrieved party to be incomplete.

• Failure to observe required legal procedures and standards, such as: failing to publish notice of public hearings in a timely manner; voting by officials with a conflict of interest; etc.

• Inverse condemnation.

The lesson is clear: If a local jurisdiction wishes to take actions to implement its general plan, it should scrupulously observe legal requirements in the process.

## Relationship to Long-Range and Short-Range Plans

This procedure applies to both long- and short-range plans.

## PRIVATE PROGRAMS

### PRIVATE CONSTRUCTION PROGRAMS

*Definitions.* Private construction: *Construction of structures, utilities, roads, or other facilities paid for by private enterprise.*

Public construction: *Construction of structures and facilities funded from government sources.*

In 1992, private sources invested $317,258 million in new construction, while public sources invested $118,785 million. ("Value of New Construction Put in Place" (June, 1993). One of the series "Current Construction Reports" published by the Bureau of the census, U.S. Department of Commerce.) The ratio of private investment to public investment in new construction in 1992 was about 2.7:1.

### Discussion:

In 1992, private construction was distributed in this manner:

| | |
|---|---|
| Residential | 59.2% |
| Non-residential | 27.5% |
| Farm non-residential | 0.7% |
| Public utilities | 11.5% |
| Other private | 1.1% |
| Total | 100.0% |

In 1992, public construction was distributed in this manner:

| | |
|---|---|
| Buildings | 43.7% |
| Highways and streets | 29.4% |
| Military facilities | 2.1% |
| Conservation and development | 5.0% |
| Sewer systems | 8.0% |
| Water supply systems | 4.0% |
| Miscellaneous public | 7.8% |
| Total | 100.0% |

From these figures, it is clear that private investment is the dominant source of funding for projects that change the physical characteristics of our urban environments.

If you are a planner concerned with implementing the physical aspects of a general plan, you must seriously consider the role of private enterprise. Yes, public agencies build a lot, but not all, of the infrastructure. Private enterprise builds most of our urban areas.

### Relationship to Long-Range and Short-Range Plans

Private construction programs are important means of implementing both short-range and long-range plans.

## NEW TOWNS

*Definition.* New town: *A new community which has these characteristics:*
*1. Is developed in accordance with a single master plan*
*2. During the crucial development stages, is under the control of a single development entity*
*3. Has reasonably balanced land uses so as to create a newly built community or major addition to an existing community, which includes most, of not all, of the basic services and facilities normally associated with a city or town.*

### Purposes

New towns have been built in the United States for a variety of reasons, including:
**1.** To provide employment for the construction industry (e.g., the Greenbelt new towns built during the 1930s)
**2.** To demonstrate the advantages of new urban patterns.

3. To provide urban development in locations adjacent to areas that have a need for a labor force, such as: military bases, mining sites, lumber mills, and large factories
4. To create an attractive and financially profitable private real estate investment
5. To provide a community where members of a religious minority can live without persecution (e.g., Salt Lake City, built by the Mormons).

It may often be difficult to draw distinctions among "new towns," "planned communities," large "planned unit developments," and very large subdivisions.

New town development, although difficult for private enterprise to make financially feasible, has a potential future role in urban planning, if there is greater cooperation among private developers and local, state and the federal government.

### Relationship to Long-Range and Short-Range Plans

New town development is very definitely a long-term undertaking. It is clearly related to long-range planning, not short-range planning.

### DEED RESTRICTIONS

*Definition.* Deed restriction: *A regulation or restriction that is made a part of the deed to a parcel of property.* Deed restrictions may be made for a specified period of time, or may "run in perpetuity" (i.e., continue indefinitely).

Deed restrictions are enforced by private parties who have legal standing to do so; government agencies usually have no power of enforcement.

### Purpose

Deed restrictions establish limits on how private properties may be used. They can have many different forms, such as: establishing easements over property for roads, trails, utility locations; restrictions on building heights; restrictions on the architectural style of buildings; etc.

Some deed restrictions are found in covenants, conditions, and restrictions (CC&Rs) which are officially recorded with a county recorder.

Condominium developments and planned unit developments (PUDs) often have covenants that:

- Require membership in a property owners' association, with payment of monthly or annual dues
- Provide for architectural control set standards for property maintenance
- Provide facilities for the use of all property owners, such as tennis courts, swimming pools, golf courses, club houses, etc.
- Require property owners to pay for the costs of constructing and maintaining the common facilities

### Relationship to Long-Range and Short-Range Plans

Deed restrictions typically have a long life, and are more relevant to long-range planning than short-range planning.

## PLAN RELATIONSHIPS AND CONSISTENCY

### Relationship of Short-Range Plans to the General Plan

A number of characteristics of short-range plans were cited earlier in this text:

**1.** Short-range plans should represent a bridge between present conditions and the planned distant future, as conceptualized in the general plan.

**2.** The short-range plan should be thought of as the first five-year increment of development of the general plan.

**3.** The short-range plan should be considerably more specific than the general plan. Short-range plans should usually make specific recommendations concerning projects and programs; general plans usually should not.

**4.** The general plan should emphasize general goals and policies. The short-range plan should contain specific objectives that show how some of the general goals of the long-range plan are to be achieved. It should contain specific policies. It should have descriptions of action programs for implementing the plan.

**5.** It is important to prepare the general plan first, so that it will provide a far-sighted vision of the desired future. The short-range plan should follow the general plan, and should be considered a major vehicle for implementing it.

### Consistency Between Plans and Plan-Implementing Programs

*Definition.* Consistency: *An action program, or project, is consistent with the general plan if, considering all its aspects, it will further the objectives and policies of the general plan and not obstruct their attainment.* (California Office of Planning and Research General Plan Guidelines, 1990.)

### Discussion

In a survey of state planning legislation made in 1993 (An unpublished survey conducted by the author), it was found that of the 29 usable responses received, 7 states require that zoning ordinances be consistent with local general plans. There may be other states that were not surveyed that also have the same requirement. The same survey indicates that several states require that plan-implementing programs in general be consistent with the local general plan. California, for example, requires that some 26 implementation programs must be consistent with the local general plan (California Office of Planning and Research, op. cit.). These programs include:

Agricultural preserves
Capital improvements
Housing authority projects
Open space acquisition
Park dedications
Parking authority projects
Redevelopment plans
Subdivisions
Power transmission line location
Zoning

The requirement of zoning ordinance consistency poses problems for those jurisdictions with long-range plans. Zoning often is enacted to reflect current or near-future market conditions. Long-range plans reflect conditions we plan to bring about sometime within the next 20 years or so.

Very often a long-range plan will indicate that some vacant land should be developed for urban purposes in the distant future. Note, however, that this future land use pattern is based on the premise that the infrastructure needed to serve it will be built, and that there is a reasonable probability that there will be a societal and a market need for the new development. Unfortunately, some courts, some state legislators, and some property owners don't see the big picture; all they see is a red dot on the map indicating a shopping center, so they jump to the conclusion that the location shown on the general plan diagram should be zoned commercial right now. Some jurisdictions, when faced with this problem, have jettisoned long-range planning, and substituted short-range planning. As we discussed earlier in this text, there is a legitimate need for short-range planning, but it is no substitute for the long-range vision. That is why this text argues that local governments should prepare both short- and long-range plans, and that zoning, and other implementing programs should be consistent with the short-range plan.

### Reference

DiMento, Joseph F. *The Consistency Doctrine and the Limits of Planning*. Cambridge: Oelgeschlager, 1980.

### Relationship Of Local Plans To Regional Plans

Regional plans come in a variety of forms. (There are many types of "regions" in the world, such as river basins, multistate areas, areas of the same ecological character, metropolitan areas, etc. We are concerned only with metropolitan areas in this discussion. We will, however, use the term "regional planning" instead of "metropolitan planning", because of the widespread use of the term.)

One form, which is not now widely used, is the "local plan writ large." It contains most of the topics found in local plans, but presented on a regionwide scale. This procedure appears to have lost favor because: local governments fought the concept of a regional agency engaging in what they considered to be a local governmental function, and because most of the

regional planning agencies had minimal powers for implementing their plans.

A second form, which appears to be in vogue, is the regional planning agency, which is a source of statistical data and other regional information, serves as a coordinating body, assisting local, regional, and state agencies to work toward common goals, and produces a regional plan consisting of generally acceptable policies.

A third form is those prepared by regional agencies that have a limited field of interest (referred to hereafter as "single-function agencies"). There are many types of these agencies. Many of them prepare single-function regional plans, have meaningful regulatory powers, and many have substantial budgets to build or manage regional infrastructure. The fields occupied by these agencies, in many regions of the United States include:

Streets and freeways
Bridges
Transit systems
Airports
Harbor facilities
Air quality
Water supply
Water quality
Solid waste management
Coastal zone management
Sewage treatment
Flood control
Regional parks
Open space preservation

Local cities and counties have a real interest in getting along with regional agencies, and vice versa. In political circles, lack of communication and cooperation usually won't do you any good, and has the potential of doing you a lot of harm. Local jurisdictions should make sure that regional agencies know of their plans and policies, and they should learn about the plans and policies of the regional agencies. Communication, accompanied by reasonable compromise and accommodation, appears to be an effective means of establishing and maintaining a good relationship between local and regional plans.

### Reference

So, Hand, and McDowell, editors. *The Practice of State and Regional Planning.* Chicago: International City Management Association, 1986.

### Relationship of Local Plans to State Plans

There are two types of state plans that planners for local jurisdictions should be aware of:

1. State development policy plans that set forth statewide goals and policies. These usually apply to state and local government agencies.

2. Plans produced by single-function or narrowly focused state agencies. These plans may contain goals and policies, as well as some specific regulations, action programs, and development proposals.

Some states have development policy plans described in the first category above. Those include: Florida, Hawaii, Maine, Maryland, Oregon, Rhode Island, Vermont, and Washington.

In states that have adopted statewide de-velopment policies any plans produced by cities and counties are required to be consistent with state policies. Procedures for state review of local plans are usually included in the legislation which sets forth the state development policies.

In the remaining states, cities and counties usually have to check with individual state agencies in order to ascertain what, if anything, is required of them. These state agencies include:

Department of Agriculture
Air Resources Board
Bureau of Economic Development
Department of Fish and Game
Department of Forestry
Department of Public Health
Department of Housing
Division of Mines and Geology
Department of Parks and Recreation
Public Utilities Commission
Department of Transportation

Again, it is to the mutual advantage of state and local agencies to keep each other well-informed concerning adopted or proposed goals, policies, programs, and development projects.

### Reference

So, Hand, and McDowell, editors. *The Practice of State and Regional Planning.* Chicago: International City Management Association, 1986.

# Appendices

Contents

# Appendix A

## Definitions of Selected Planning Terms

*Assumption: A statement of assumed present or future conditions describing the physical, social, or economic setting within which the urban general plan is to be used.*

Example: The birth-rate of the population in the planning area will continue at its present level through the year 2000.

*Criterion: A test or a means of measuring the degree to which an objective has been met, or for estimating the degree to which it may be met in the future.*

Example: If the objective is to increase the city's tax base, one criterion for measuring the degree of attainment is the dollar value of assessed value per capita.

*Data: Information concerning past or present conditions within or affecting the planning area.*

Data may be presented in many different ways, such as narrative, statistical, or graphic form. Data concerning a planning area is often summarized in an urban general plan to provide a brief description of the setting for the planning program. The data itself, however, should not be part of the plan; it may be published separately.

*Goal: A statement that describes (usually in general terms) a desired future condition.*

Goals generally express long-term rather than short-term expectations. Goals are often expressed in such general terms that it is difficult to measure the degree to which they have been attained.

Goals may be subdivided into sub-goals.

Example of a goal: To make the central business district the dominant administrative headquarters of financial institutions and governmental agencies in the region.

Examples of sub-goals: To improve access to the central business district; to keep city hall in its present downtown location.

*Issue (1) A topic for discussion.*

Example: Should we promote rapid growth in our city?

Example: Which should take precedence: the preservation of the natural environment, or new land development that will provide jobs?

*Issue (2) A problem to be considered.*

Example: The quality of air in the planning area has been below EPA standards an average of 40 days a year for the last three years.

Example: Households earning below-average incomes find it extremely difficult to find affordable housing in our city.

*Objective: A statement that describes a specific future condition to be attained within a stated period of time.*

Objectives are similar to goals, but they are substantially more specific.

The objectives of a jurisdiction should be consistent with its goals.

Objectives have these characteristics:
- They are clearly attainable.
- It is possible to measure the degree to which they have been attained.
- They are time-bound (i.e., are to be fulfilled within a stated time period).
- They require the expenditure of effort to achieve.

Example: To have at least 20 percent of the work-trips into the central business district during the morning peak-hour made by public transit by the year 2000.

*Plan diagram A graphic representation of the plan proposals, usually for a specific date.*

Although it is usually possible to illustrate in graphic form the anticipated results of future public and private construction programs, it is often difficult to use graphics to show the anticipated effects of policies, of the provision of services, or of the enforcement of regulations.

*Plan proposal An action proposed to be taken to attain the objectives of the urban general plan.*

Plan proposals are sometimes categorized as:
- Public policies to be followed.
- Public and private services to be provided.

• Public and private construction programs to be implemented.

• Public regulations to be adopted and enforced.

Plan proposals are often described in general terms in the urban general plan, but are not specific in detail. For example, while major proposals for land use regulation may be described in the urban general plan, it is inappropriate to include specific zoning regulations as part of the plan.

*Policy: A course of action or rule of conduct to be used to achieve the goals and objectives of the plan.*

Policies may be general statements that apply to the achievement of goals, or they may be specific statements that apply to the achievement of objectives.

When policies are officially adopted they commit a jurisdiction to a course of action. Principles, on the other hand, are considered to be more advisory in nature, and give the jurisdiction greater flexibility.

Example of a general policy: The city favors construction of moderate-cost apartments for middle-income families.

Example of a specific policy: The city will support a program for construction of moderate-cost apartments in the two neighborhoods that lie to the southwest of the central business district.

*Principle: A general rule of conduct that should be followed, when feasible, to achieve the objectives of the plan.*

Principles usually include "should" to denote the propriety or expediency of an action.

Example: The transportation system should be used to encourage desirable patterns of land use.

*Standard: A specification of size or performance cited as being the minimum (or maximum) to be attained.*

Example: The average density of new residential development in suburban areas of the city shall be not more than four, nor less than one, dwelling units per gross neighborhood acre.

*Strategy: A course of action incorporating a set of plan proposals, often in a specified sequence, which is devised to achieve an objective or set of objectives.*

A strategy is often a long and complex statement.

*Verbal auxiliaries:*

**Must** is mandatory and refers to a requirement, an obligation, or a command.

**Shall** is mandatory and refers to a required action which is to be taken in the future.

**May** is permissive and refers to a possible future action that is allowable but is not required.

**Should** is advisory and refers to a possible future action that is recommended but is not required.

| Column 1 | Column 2 | | | | Column 3 | | | |
|---|---|---|---|---|---|---|---|---|
| TOPIC | IS THE TOPIC AN ISSUE? | | | | SELECTION OF TOPICS TO BE INCLUDED IN A PLAN | | | |
| | Local area | | Metro area | | Local area | | Metro area | |
| | YES | NO | YES | NO | Yes | No | Yes | No |
| **URBAN FORM** | | | | | | | | |
| Metropolitan form | [ ] | [ ] | [ ] | [ ] | [ ] | [ ] | [ ] | [ ] |
| City form | [ ] | [ ] | [ ] | [ ] | [ ] | [ ] | [ ] | [ ] |
| Urban/rural definition | [ ] | [ ] | [ ] | [ ] | [ ] | [ ] | [ ] | [ ] |
| Urban sprawl | [ ] | [ ] | [ ] | [ ] | [ ] | [ ] | [ ] | [ ] |
| Preserv'n of open space | [ ] | [ ] | [ ] | [ ] | [ ] | [ ] | [ ] | [ ] |
| Historic preservation | [ ] | [ ] | [ ] | [ ] | [ ] | [ ] | [ ] | [ ] |
| Quality of design | [ ] | [ ] | [ ] | [ ] | [ ] | [ ] | [ ] | [ ] |
|   Public buildings | [ ] | [ ] | [ ] | [ ] | [ ] | [ ] | [ ] | [ ] |
|   Public spaces | [ ] | [ ] | [ ] | [ ] | [ ] | [ ] | [ ] | [ ] |
|   Institutional bldgs | [ ] | [ ] | [ ] | [ ] | [ ] | [ ] | [ ] | [ ] |
|   Housing | [ ] | [ ] | [ ] | [ ] | [ ] | [ ] | [ ] | [ ] |
|   Streets & highways | [ ] | [ ] | [ ] | [ ] | [ ] | [ ] | [ ] | [ ] |
| **THE PHYSICAL ENVIRONMENT** | | | | | | | | |
| Land - | | | | | | | | |
|   geology | [ ] | [ ] | [ ] | [ ] | [ ] | [ ] | [ ] | [ ] |
|   slope | [ ] | [ ] | [ ] | [ ] | [ ] | [ ] | [ ] | [ ] |
|   drainage | [ ] | [ ] | [ ] | [ ] | [ ] | [ ] | [ ] | [ ] |
| Vegetation | [ ] | [ ] | [ ] | [ ] | [ ] | [ ] | [ ] | [ ] |
| Wildlife | [ ] | [ ] | [ ] | [ ] | [ ] | [ ] | [ ] | [ ] |
| Pollution of environment | | | | | | | | |
|   water | [ ] | [ ] | [ ] | [ ] | [ ] | [ ] | [ ] | [ ] |
|   air | [ ] | [ ] | [ ] | [ ] | [ ] | [ ] | [ ] | [ ] |
|   noise | [ ] | [ ] | [ ] | [ ] | [ ] | [ ] | [ ] | [ ] |
| Agricultural uses | [ ] | [ ] | [ ] | [ ] | [ ] | [ ] | [ ] | [ ] |
| **POPULATION** | | | | | | | | |
| Number | [ ] | [ ] | [ ] | [ ] | [ ] | [ ] | [ ] | [ ] |
| Rate of growth | [ ] | [ ] | [ ] | [ ] | [ ] | [ ] | [ ] | [ ] |
| Distribution | | | | | | | | |
|   age | [ ] | [ ] | [ ] | [ ] | [ ] | [ ] | [ ] | [ ] |
|   race | [ ] | [ ] | [ ] | [ ] | [ ] | [ ] | [ ] | [ ] |
|   sex | [ ] | [ ] | [ ] | [ ] | [ ] | [ ] | [ ] | [ ] |
|   socio-economic group | [ ] | [ ] | [ ] | [ ] | [ ] | [ ] | [ ] | [ ] |
|   occupation | [ ] | [ ] | [ ] | [ ] | [ ] | [ ] | [ ] | [ ] |
| **EMPLOYMENT AND INCOME** | | | | | | | | |
|   qualific. of labor force | [ ] | [ ] | [ ] | [ ] | [ ] | [ ] | [ ] | [ ] |
|   number of jobs available | [ ] | [ ] | [ ] | [ ] | [ ] | [ ] | [ ] | [ ] |
|   location of employment | [ ] | [ ] | [ ] | [ ] | [ ] | [ ] | [ ] | [ ] |
|   income of workers | [ ] | [ ] | [ ] | [ ] | [ ] | [ ] | [ ] | [ ] |
|   cost of living | [ ] | [ ] | [ ] | [ ] | [ ] | [ ] | [ ] | [ ] |

| TOPIC | IS THE TOPIC AN ISSUE? | | | | SELECTION OF TOPICS | | | |
|---|---|---|---|---|---|---|---|---|
| | Local area | | Metro area | | Local area | | Metro area | |
| | Yes | No | Yes | No | Yes | No | Yes | No |
| **GOVERNMENT - GENERAL** | | | | | | | | |
| Tax rate | [ ] | [ ] | [ ] | [ ] | [ ] | [ ] | [ ] | [ ] |
| Bonding capacity | [ ] | [ ] | [ ] | [ ] | [ ] | [ ] | [ ] | [ ] |
| Honesty | [ ] | [ ] | [ ] | [ ] | [ ] | [ ] | [ ] | [ ] |
| Competence | [ ] | [ ] | [ ] | [ ] | [ ] | [ ] | [ ] | [ ] |
| Responsiveness | [ ] | [ ] | [ ] | [ ] | [ ] | [ ] | [ ] | [ ] |
| | | | | | | | | |
| **GOVERNMENT - PUBLIC SAFETY** | | | | | | | | |
| Police Dept. | [ ] | [ ] | [ ] | [ ] | [ ] | [ ] | [ ] | [ ] |
| Fire Dept. | [ ] | [ ] | [ ] | [ ] | [ ] | [ ] | [ ] | [ ] |
| Health Dept. | [ ] | [ ] | [ ] | [ ] | [ ] | [ ] | [ ] | [ ] |
| Role of the general plan | [ ] | [ ] | [ ] | [ ] | [ ] | [ ] | [ ] | [ ] |
| Effectiveness of: | | | | | | | | |
|   zoning ordinance | [ ] | [ ] | [ ] | [ ] | [ ] | [ ] | [ ] | [ ] |
|   subdivision ordinance | [ ] | [ ] | [ ] | [ ] | [ ] | [ ] | [ ] | [ ] |
|   flood plain regulation | [ ] | [ ] | [ ] | [ ] | [ ] | [ ] | [ ] | [ ] |
|   architectural control | [ ] | [ ] | [ ] | [ ] | [ ] | [ ] | [ ] | [ ] |
|   Capital Impr. Program | [ ] | [ ] | [ ] | [ ] | [ ] | [ ] | [ ] | [ ] |
| | [ ] | [ ] | [ ] | [ ] | [ ] | [ ] | [ ] | [ ] |
| **CITIZEN PARTICIPATION** | | | | | | | | |
| Amount and quality of | | | | | | | | |
| communication between | | | | | | | | |
| individual citizen and: | | | | | | | | |
|   other citizens | [ ] | [ ] | [ ] | [ ] | [ ] | [ ] | [ ] | [ ] |
|   local government | [ ] | [ ] | [ ] | [ ] | [ ] | [ ] | [ ] | [ ] |
|   county government | [ ] | [ ] | [ ] | [ ] | [ ] | [ ] | [ ] | [ ] |
|   major land owners | [ ] | [ ] | [ ] | [ ] | [ ] | [ ] | [ ] | [ ] |
|   major institutions | [ ] | [ ] | [ ] | [ ] | [ ] | [ ] | [ ] | [ ] |
| | | | | | | | | |
| **LAND USE** | | | | | | | | |
| Residential areas | | | | | | | | |
|   quality of location | [ ] | [ ] | [ ] | [ ] | [ ] | [ ] | [ ] | [ ] |
|   amount of area available | [ ] | [ ] | [ ] | [ ] | [ ] | [ ] | [ ] | [ ] |
|   variety available | [ ] | [ ] | [ ] | [ ] | [ ] | [ ] | [ ] | [ ] |
| Commercial services | | | | | | | | |
|   accessibility | [ ] | [ ] | [ ] | [ ] | [ ] | [ ] | [ ] | [ ] |
|   amount of area available | [ ] | [ ] | [ ] | [ ] | [ ] | [ ] | [ ] | [ ] |
|   variety available | [ ] | [ ] | [ ] | [ ] | [ ] | [ ] | [ ] | [ ] |
| Employment areas | | | | | | | | |
|   amount of area available | [ ] | [ ] | [ ] | [ ] | [ ] | [ ] | [ ] | [ ] |
|   accessability | [ ] | [ ] | [ ] | [ ] | [ ] | [ ] | [ ] | [ ] |
| Friction among land uses | [ ] | [ ] | [ ] | [ ] | [ ] | [ ] | [ ] | [ ] |
| Urban design quality | [ ] | [ ] | [ ] | [ ] | [ ] | [ ] | [ ] | [ ] |

| TOPIC | IS THE TOPIC AN ISSUE? | | | | SELECTION OF TOPICS | | | |
|---|---|---|---|---|---|---|---|---|
| | Local area | | Metro area | | Local area | | Metro area | |
| | Yes | No | Yes | No | Yes | No | Yes | No |
| **HOUSING** | | | | | | | | |
| quantity available | [ ] | [ ] | [ ] | [ ] | [ ] | [ ] | [ ] | [ ] |
| variety available | [ ] | [ ] | [ ] | [ ] | [ ] | [ ] | [ ] | [ ] |
| cost of land | [ ] | [ ] | [ ] | [ ] | [ ] | [ ] | [ ] | [ ] |
| cost of construction | [ ] | [ ] | [ ] | [ ] | [ ] | [ ] | [ ] | [ ] |
| cost of ownership | [ ] | [ ] | [ ] | [ ] | [ ] | [ ] | [ ] | [ ] |
| cost of renting | [ ] | [ ] | [ ] | [ ] | [ ] | [ ] | [ ] | [ ] |
| quality of maintenance | [ ] | [ ] | [ ] | [ ] | [ ] | [ ] | [ ] | [ ] |
| **CIRCULATION** | | | | | | | | |
| Traffic in resid'l areas | [ ] | [ ] | [ ] | [ ] | [ ] | [ ] | [ ] | [ ] |
| Traffic on arterials | [ ] | [ ] | [ ] | [ ] | [ ] | [ ] | [ ] | [ ] |
| Traffic on freeways | [ ] | [ ] | [ ] | [ ] | [ ] | [ ] | [ ] | [ ] |
| Parking | [ ] | [ ] | [ ] | [ ] | [ ] | [ ] | [ ] | [ ] |
| Pedestrian circulation | [ ] | [ ] | [ ] | [ ] | [ ] | [ ] | [ ] | [ ] |
| Public transit | [ ] | [ ] | [ ] | [ ] | [ ] | [ ] | [ ] | [ ] |
| Street capacities | [ ] | [ ] | [ ] | [ ] | [ ] | [ ] | [ ] | [ ] |
| Intersection capacities | [ ] | [ ] | [ ] | [ ] | [ ] | [ ] | [ ] | [ ] |
| Accident centers | [ ] | [ ] | [ ] | [ ] | [ ] | [ ] | [ ] | [ ] |
| Road maintenance | [ ] | [ ] | [ ] | [ ] | [ ] | [ ] | [ ] | [ ] |
| Bridge maintenance | [ ] | [ ] | [ ] | [ ] | [ ] | [ ] | [ ] | [ ] |
| Freight transportation | | | | | | | | |
| highway | [ ] | [ ] | [ ] | [ ] | [ ] | [ ] | [ ] | [ ] |
| rail | [ ] | [ ] | [ ] | [ ] | [ ] | [ ] | [ ] | [ ] |
| water | [ ] | [ ] | [ ] | [ ] | [ ] | [ ] | [ ] | [ ] |
| air | [ ] | [ ] | [ ] | [ ] | [ ] | [ ] | [ ] | [ ] |
| **SOCIAL PROBLEMS** | | | | | | | | |
| Crime | | | | | | | | |
| rate | [ ] | [ ] | [ ] | [ ] | [ ] | [ ] | [ ] | [ ] |
| causes | [ ] | [ ] | [ ] | [ ] | [ ] | [ ] | [ ] | [ ] |
| narcotics | [ ] | [ ] | [ ] | [ ] | [ ] | [ ] | [ ] | [ ] |
| sex-related crimes | [ ] | [ ] | [ ] | [ ] | [ ] | [ ] | [ ] | [ ] |
| juvenile crime | [ ] | [ ] | [ ] | [ ] | [ ] | [ ] | [ ] | [ ] |
| Alcoholism | [ ] | [ ] | [ ] | [ ] | [ ] | [ ] | [ ] | [ ] |
| Poverty | | | | | | | | |
| rate | [ ] | [ ] | [ ] | [ ] | [ ] | [ ] | [ ] | [ ] |
| causes | [ ] | [ ] | [ ] | [ ] | [ ] | [ ] | [ ] | [ ] |
| location | [ ] | [ ] | [ ] | [ ] | [ ] | [ ] | [ ] | [ ] |
| Homeless population | [ ] | [ ] | [ ] | [ ] | [ ] | [ ] | [ ] | [ ] |
| Education | | | | | | | | |
| quality | [ ] | [ ] | [ ] | [ ] | [ ] | [ ] | [ ] | [ ] |
| availability | [ ] | [ ] | [ ] | [ ] | [ ] | [ ] | [ ] | [ ] |
| Marital stability | [ ] | [ ] | [ ] | [ ] | [ ] | [ ] | [ ] | [ ] |
| Racial discrimination | | | | | | | | |
| residential | [ ] | [ ] | [ ] | [ ] | [ ] | [ ] | [ ] | [ ] |
| employment | [ ] | [ ] | [ ] | [ ] | [ ] | [ ] | [ ] | [ ] |
| schools | [ ] | [ ] | [ ] | [ ] | [ ] | [ ] | [ ] | [ ] |

| TOPIC | IS THE TOPIC AN ISSUE? | | | | SELECTION OF TOPICS | | | |
|---|---|---|---|---|---|---|---|---|
| | Local area | | Metro area | | Local area | | Metro area | |
| | Yes | No | Yes | No | Yes | No | Yes | No |
| **COMMUNITY FACILITIES** | | | | | | | | |
| **Schools** | | | | | | | | |
| quality | [ ] | [ ] | [ ] | [ ] | [ ] | [ ] | [ ] | [ ] |
| quantity | [ ] | [ ] | [ ] | [ ] | [ ] | [ ] | [ ] | [ ] |
| location | [ ] | [ ] | [ ] | [ ] | [ ] | [ ] | [ ] | [ ] |
| **Utilities** | | | | | | | | |
| water supply | [ ] | [ ] | [ ] | [ ] | [ ] | [ ] | [ ] | [ ] |
| sewage disposal | [ ] | [ ] | [ ] | [ ] | [ ] | [ ] | [ ] | [ ] |
| storm drainage | [ ] | [ ] | [ ] | [ ] | [ ] | [ ] | [ ] | [ ] |
| solid waste disposal | [ ] | [ ] | [ ] | [ ] | [ ] | [ ] | [ ] | [ ] |
| electric service | [ ] | [ ] | [ ] | [ ] | [ ] | [ ] | [ ] | [ ] |
| gas service | [ ] | [ ] | [ ] | [ ] | [ ] | [ ] | [ ] | [ ] |
| telephone service | [ ] | [ ] | [ ] | [ ] | [ ] | [ ] | [ ] | [ ] |
| street lighting | [ ] | [ ] | [ ] | [ ] | [ ] | [ ] | [ ] | [ ] |
| **Health** | | | | | | | | |
| preventive medicine | [ ] | [ ] | [ ] | [ ] | [ ] | [ ] | [ ] | [ ] |
| remedial care | [ ] | [ ] | [ ] | [ ] | [ ] | [ ] | [ ] | [ ] |
| emergency services | [ ] | [ ] | [ ] | [ ] | [ ] | [ ] | [ ] | [ ] |
| hospital location | [ ] | [ ] | [ ] | [ ] | [ ] | [ ] | [ ] | [ ] |
| hospital capacity | [ ] | [ ] | [ ] | [ ] | [ ] | [ ] | [ ] | [ ] |
| cost of health care | [ ] | [ ] | [ ] | [ ] | [ ] | [ ] | [ ] | [ ] |
| **Recreation and culture** | | | | | | | | |
| parks | [ ] | [ ] | [ ] | [ ] | [ ] | [ ] | [ ] | [ ] |
| recreation programs | [ ] | [ ] | [ ] | [ ] | [ ] | [ ] | [ ] | [ ] |
| library services | [ ] | [ ] | [ ] | [ ] | [ ] | [ ] | [ ] | [ ] |
| museums | [ ] | [ ] | [ ] | [ ] | [ ] | [ ] | [ ] | [ ] |
| concert facilities | [ ] | [ ] | [ ] | [ ] | [ ] | [ ] | [ ] | [ ] |
| **Churches** | [ ] | [ ] | [ ] | [ ] | [ ] | [ ] | [ ] | [ ] |
| **Private organizations** | | | | | | | | |
| services provided | [ ] | [ ] | [ ] | [ ] | [ ] | [ ] | [ ] | [ ] |
| role in community affairs | [ ] | [ ] | [ ] | [ ] | [ ] | [ ] | [ ] | [ ] |
| amount of participation | [ ] | [ ] | [ ] | [ ] | [ ] | [ ] | [ ] | [ ] |

# Appendix C

## Notes on Preparing Work Programs

A work program is a description of the scope and scheduling of work that is proposed to be undertaken to complete a specific project. Work programs usually divide the work to be undertaken into a number of individually defined tasks, describe what is to be accomplished in each task, and describe the temporal relationships among the tasks.

Work programs are used to develop answers to three simple, but often difficult, questions:

1. What are you going to do?
2. How are you going to do it?
3. What resources will you require to complete it?

Work programs are useful to planners in different ways, including the following:

• Work programming, as a discipline, forces you to think through the questions noted above. You should develop answers to these questions, for your own edification, before you make a commitment to undertake a job.

• Work programming develops estimates of the amount of labor and supplies needed to complete a job. These estimates are essential when preparing budgets for public and private agencies, and when submitting proposals to private clients.

• Work programs are often excellent documents to use when negotiating the scope of work to be done for an employer or a private client. Reviewing a work program will often clarify in the employer's or the client's mind just what he will have when the job is done. It also gives him a chance to say "I want more of this, but less of that."

• Work programs are essential when many different people or several firms are working on one project. The work program illustrates to all participants how their individual tasks fit into the overall project. This understanding is needed in order to make sure that all of the pieces fit together (e.g., use the same terminology), and that each piece is delivered when it is needed.

**General Notes and Comments on Work Programming**

Before you start preparing a work program you should have a good understanding of what work you're expected to do, when it is to be completed, what products you're expected to produce, and why the work should be done. Sometimes the person who has asked you to do some specific work has made a careful analysis of his situation, and has correctly identified problems to be overcome, and has a clear understanding of what work should be done to suit his needs and his pocketbook. Quite often he hasn't. Situation assessment, issue identification, and goal formulation are important parts of the urban and regional planning process, and should be completed before you plunge in and work on some project that your client thinks he needs.

Writing a work program for a job you've never undertaken before is never easy. You have to describe work procedures that you've never used, and make estimates of time and material requirements that you feel ill-prepared to make. Nevertheless, you still must do your best at it. You'll find that the preparation of a work program compels you to think through what you're going to produce, and what methods you're going to use. You'll find that after you've finished preparing a work program, much of your confusion and misgivings will have melted away.

Work programs have many different characters and forms. They may, for example, be:

• Programs that describe the long-term goals of an agency, and describe the strategies that will be used to attain them over the coming years.

• Short-range programs that describe a single objective to be attained, specify the procedures to be used to attain it, and estimate the resources needed.

• Mid-range programs with multiple objectives.

Work programming is most effective when a single, well-defined, concrete objective is to be attained, such as the planning and construction of a bridge. It is less useful when either the work to be done is more "process" related than it is project specific, or when the work to be done relates to the multiple, and sometimes conflicting goals of a community.

Sometimes the work to be done is a tremendously

large project, consisting of thousands of individual tasks. If this is the case, divide the large project into a number of smaller interrelated sub-projects, each of which can be conceptualized individually. A separate work program is then written for each of the sub-projects.

It is usually desirable to prepare a work program in outline form before you start in on your detailed work program. This will help you to see the big picture that can easily be obscured by minutia. And the preliminary trial run will tell you the approximate size of the project you are dealing with. When you know that you may wish to reduce the scope of some tasks, and enlarge the size of others.

Sometimes it is desirable to start the outline form of a work program at the conclusion, and work backward toward the initiation. This is an especially useful technique when you have a specific deadline to meet. It is also applicable when you have a clearly defined product to produce, and you need to trace back to find out what data, manpower, and materials you will need to produce it.

In many cases it will be worthwhile to prepare alternative work programs in outline form before you start detailing one specific work procedure. The detailed work program that you finally produce should include the best features of the alternative programs you have examined.

The work programming process combines text that describes individual tasks, graphics to illustrate the temporal relationships among the tasks, and statistics that specify the resources needed to complete each task. All of these should be used concurrently as the work program is being prepared. Don't do all of your writing before you diagram how the tasks relate to each other, or before you add up the numbers to see if the project is feasible.

There are a variety of forms of diagrams appropriate to use in the work programming process. Four of these, illustrated in Figure A-1, are:

- The box diagram
- The bar chart
- The who-does-what diagram
- The critical path diagram

The box diagram usually shows the title of each task in a work program in a box. The boxes are connected by arrows, so that it is evident which tasks provide output that is used as input to following tasks. The box diagram is usually easy to prepare and easy to understand. It lends itself well to summarizing the major phases of a work program, especially for laymen.

The bar chart, sometimes known as a Gantt diagram, is a display in which a series of boxes are plotted on a chart on which the horizontal dimension represents time. The boxes are labeled with the names of the tasks in the work program. Usually vertical lines are drawn on the chart to indicate units of time, such as days, weeks, or months. The bar chart is especially useful in work programming when the completion date of each task is of crucial importance. The bar chart is usually easy to prepare and is fairly easy for many people to understand.

In the who-does-what diagram the horizontal dimension represents approximate time. The vertical dimension is divided to identify the individuals or work groups that will participate in the work. The individual tasks, which are represented by lines on the diagram labeled with the task name, indicate their time relationships (horizontal dimension), and who is assigned to complete them (vertical dimension). The horizontal axis of the diagram is marked with a number of nodes that indicate when individual tasks start and finish. The who-does-what diagram requires more work to prepare than the box diagram or the bar chart, but it really is not difficult. It is an excellent tool for coordinating the work of many different work groups; it is very good for manpower planning; and it is well suited for coordinating the work-review process. It is easily understood by most technically trained people, but not by most laymen.

The critical path diagram is used in both the critical path method (CPM), and in the program evaluation and review technique (PERT) of work scheduling. Critical path diagrams consist of a number of arrows that connect a number of nodes. Each arrow represents one task in the work program. Each node represents a point in time known as an event. The diagram indicates in graphic form which tasks must be completed before other tasks can be started. Information is made available from the work program concerning how much time and manpower is required to complete each task. Through an analysis of the network of arrows and nodes, and of the manpower requirements for each task,

**Figure A-1** Four Commonly Used Types of Work Program Diagrams

## BOX DIAGRAM

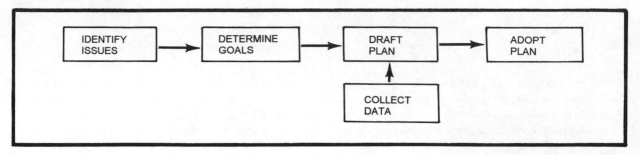

## BAR CHART

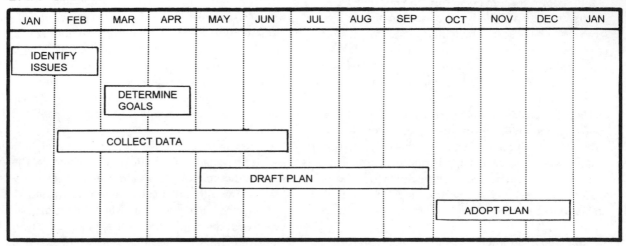

## WHO-DOES-WHAT DIAGRAM

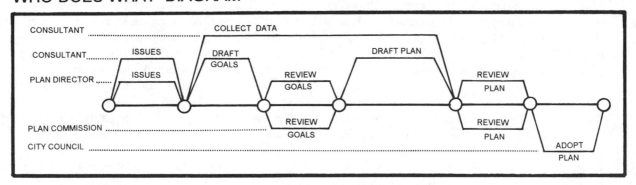

## CRITICAL PATH DIAGRAM

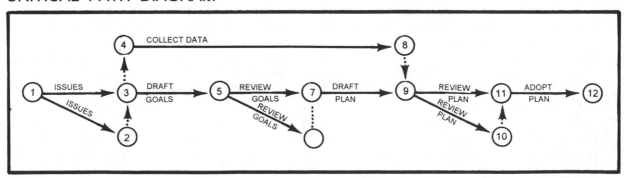

conclusions can be reached concerning how long it will take to complete the entire project, which tasks must be completed as scheduled if the project is to be completed on time, and which tasks have some latitude in their timing. The critical path method diagram is almost indispensable for planning complex projects. Fortunately, computer programs are readily available to do all the required computations. CPM diagrams are not difficult to prepare, but their analysis requires some computer time.

Work programs must usually be tailored to fit within the constraints that limit every work project. The most common of these constraints are:

• Time limits (i.e., by which calendar date must the project be completed?)

• Manpower limits (i.e., how many of your staff members can be assigned to the project, and for how long?)

• Limited skills of available manpower (i.e., does your presently available staff have the skills to undertake the type of work that is called for in the work program?)

• Financial limits (i.e., what is the a dollar limit on the amount that can be spent on the project? How much can be spent for presently employed staff, for added staff, for outside consultants, for materials and supplies, etc.?)

It is usually very desirable to involve the people who will be doing the work in the preparation to the work program. This will improve their understanding of the process, will probably increase their motivation, and may bring about an improvement in the quality of the work program itself. (One has to use judgment as to how far this participation can be carried. Often people at the lower end of the skills level cannot contribute much to the conceptualization of an intricate program, but key supervisory personnel certainly can.)

The scheduling of work in work programs must be carefully reviewed to make sure that the available manpower is to be used in an effective and reasonable way. You don't want to drive your workforce at overtime rates part of the time, and then have them sitting around with little or nothing to do shortly thereafter.

After work has been started in accordance with a work program, all sorts of unforeseen (and unforeseeable) things can happen. National events (wars, recessions, etc.) can bring substantial changes in the work environment; some of the tasks will take substantially more time (rarely less) than was anticipated; promised data fails to materialize, etc. So, you should review the progress being made in the accomplishment of the work on a regular basis, and make changes in the content and the scheduling of work as is appropriate. For example, for a project that will take a year to complete, it is a good idea to have monthly or even weekly "howgozit" reports, which indicate how closely the work is conforming to the original schedule and budget, and alert those who need to know of impending crises. Changes in a work program are inevitable and often desirable if new conditions are to be met as they arise.

# Appendix D

## Four Levels of Land Use Codes

The following four land use codes were developed from the two land use codes presented by Anderson, Hardy, Roach, and Witmer in their report, A Land Use and Land Cover Classification System for Use with Remote Sensor Data (U.S. Geological Survey Professional Paper 964, published in 1976).

### Level I

The land use code at Level I listed below was presented in USGS Professional Paper 964. It is appropriate for interpretation of terrestrial features using remotely sensed data from satellites. (Modern satellites are reported to have far greater image definition than the satellites of 1976, but their imagery is not yet widely available to civilians.)

Level I land uses are appropriate to mapping land uses in very large geographic regions, and at map scales such as 1:1,000,000 to 1:100,000. This mapping is generally of little or no use for the analysis of individual communities or metropolitan areas.

*Level I Land Use Code*

1  Urban or built-up land
2  Agricultural land
3  Range land
4  Forest land
5  Water
6  Wetland
7  Barren land
8  Tundra
9  Perennial snow or ice

### Level II

The Level II land use code is appropriate for land use analysis at the metropolitan scale, or for large rural counties. Mapping at scales between 1:24,000 and 1:125,000 is appropriate here.

The land use codes in categories 21 through 92 listed below are the same as those presented in USGS Professional Paper 964. Land use codes 10 through 19 were modified to reflect land use analysis problems frequently found in urban areas.

The primary source of data for land use analysis at the Level II scale is conventional medium altitude aerial photography, preferably at a scale of 1:24,000 or larger. (The USGS paper says that high altitude photography, at a scale of 1:80,000 or less can be used. While this is so, more detailed photography is far easier for urban planners to work with.) Some information on land ownership (not usually available from aerial photography) is needed to define the boundaries of large parks, large institutions, and large military bases.

*Level II Land Use Code*

10  Low density residential, predominantly single family
11  Medium density residential
12  Commercial and commercial services
13  Industrial
14  Transportation facilities
15  Utilities and communications facilities
16  Large institutions
17  Large parks
18  Large military bases
19  Vacant urban lands and mixed urban uses
20  Unassigned
21  Cropland and pasture
22  Orchards, groves, vineyards, etc.
23  Confined feeding operations
24  Other agricultural land
31  Herbaceous range land
32  Shrub and brush range land
33  Mixed range land
41  Deciduous forest land
42  Evergreen forest land
43  Mixed forest land
51  Streams and canals
52  Lakes
53  Reservoirs
54  Bays and estuaries
61  Forested wetland
62  Nonforested wetland
71  Dry salt flats
72  Beaches

73   Sandy areas other than beaches
74   Bare exposed rock
75   Strip mines, quarries, and gravel pits
76   Transitional areas
77   Mixed barren land
81   Shrub and brush tundra
82   Herbaceous tundra
83   Bare ground tundra
84   Wet tundra
85   Mixed tundra
91   Perennial snowfields
92   Glaciers

## Level III

The land use code at Level III is appropriate for use in facility, utility, land use, and transportation planning at the community scale. Mapping at scales of 1:2,400 (1"=200') to 1:24,000 (1"=2,000') is appropriate here.

It is recommended that you consider using data inputs in the form of uniformly sized grids which have been defined by one of the three major map coordinate systems (latitude and longitude; Universal Transverse Mercator; or a state coordinate system), rather than by parcels, census tracts, or other irregularly shaped areas. Land use data should be used as part of a computerized data base (a geographic information system [GIS]). In this medium it can be easily combined with data on physical, social, or economic topics if that data is input using the same data format.

Measurements of land use areas at Level III are generally made of gross areas. That is, the major land use assigned to each grid may include local streets, and may also include small areas of land use anomalies.

The land use categories in Level III for uses numbered from 100 through 199 were developed from land use categories 10 through 19 in the Level II code, and are intended for urban land uses. Land use categories 20 through 92 are the same as the USGS Level II code. (It should be noted that if one wished to make an analysis of rural land uses at the Level III scale, land use categories in the 20, 30, and 40 series could be expanded to define more detailed agricultural, range, and forest uses.)

The primary source of data for land use analysis at Level III is usually conventional aerial photography, taken from medium to low altitudes. Photographic prints at scales between 1:2,400 and 1:24,000 are appropriate here. A limited amount of on-the-ground field inspection (and perhaps interviews) will be needed to determine some commercial and industrial uses, residential densities, and employment densities.

### Level III Land Use Code

10   Single Family Residential
100   Vacant land in areas dominated by single family homes
101   Very low density
102   Low density
103   Low medium density
104   Medium density
105   High medium density
106   High density
107   Mobile homes
108   Unassigned
109   Other single family homes

Note: The various classifications of density have to be determined locally. What is considered "low density" in one area may be considered high density in another. This same remark also applies to the levels of labor intensity set forth in the industrial categories.

11   Multifamily Residential and Group Quarters
110   Vacant land in areas dominated by multifamily residential
111   Very low density
112   Low density
113   Low medium density
114   Medium density
115   High medium density
116   High density
117   Very high density
118   Group quarters
119   Other multiple family quarters

12   Commercial and Service
120   Vacant land in areas dominated by commercial land uses
121   Individual, isolated commercial or service operations
122   Central business districts
123   Strip commercial
124   Shopping centers
125   Service commercial (repairs, personal services, etc.) Includes outdoor storage of materials

related to retail or wholesale sales, such as lumberyards.

126   Hotels and motels

127   Offices

128   Commercial recreation (outdoor theaters, amusement parks, etc.)

129   Other commercial and service uses

13   Industrial

130   Vacant land in areas dominated by industrial land uses

131   Light industry—low labor intensity

132   Light industry—medium labor intensity

133   Light industry—high labor intensity

134   Heavy industry—low labor intensity

135   Heavy industry—medium labor intensity

136   Heavy industry—high labor intensity

137   Outdoor storage of materials for industrial use (includes tank farms)

138   Unassigned

139   Other

Note: light industry generally involves the assembly, packaging, or finishing of products. Heavy industry generally involves the transformation of raw materials, as in smelters, oil refineries, or manufacturing of heavy machinery.

14   Transportation

140   Vacant land committed as a future transportation right-of-way

141   Unassigned

142   Freeways, interchanges, bridges

143   Off street parking (other than areas dedicated to serve specific adjacent land uses)

144   Rail lines, rail terminals, rail yards

145   Airports

146   Harbor facilities (other than recreational marinas)

147   Unassigned

148   Unassigned

149   Other transportation facilities

15   Utilities and Communications

150   Vacant land committed for future utility use

151   Water supply and distribution facilities

152   Sewage treatment facilities

153   Solid waste facilities

154   Storm drainage facilities

155   Electric power generation, transmission, distribution

156   Natural gas storage or transmission facilities

157   Communications facilities

158   Unassigned

159   Other

16   Institutions

160   Vacant land committed for future institutional use

161   Primary schools

162   Secondary schools (high schools)

163   Colleges and universities

164   Private for-profit vocational schools

165   Health institutions (excluding doctors' offices)

166   Religious institutions

167   Cemeteries

168   Cultural institutions

169   Governmental services (other than health, recreation, education)

17   Park and Recreation Facilities

170   Undeveloped park or recreation lands

171   Urban parks and playgrounds

172   Large regional parks and open spaces

173   Marinas

174   Golf courses

175   Sports arenas, field houses, stadiums, etc.

176   Unassigned

177   Unassigned

178   Unassigned

179   Other

18   Military Bases

180   Vacant land owned by armed forces, but not utilized

181   Military bases

182   Unassigned

19   Vacant Land and Mixed Urban Uses

190   Vacant urban land (general category)

191   Mixed uses—predominantly residential

192   Mixed uses—predominantly commercial

193   Mixed uses—predominantly industrial

194   Mixed uses—predominantly institutional

195   Unassigned

196   Unassigned

197 Unassigned

198 Unassigned

199 Unassigned

21 through 92   Non-Urbanized Areas

(Same as the Level II code, unless expanded to meet local needs.)

## Level IV

The land use code at Level IV is intended to record data that reflects the use of individual sites or parcels, or uses within buildings. Land uses are measured in terms of net area; they do not include the adjacent streets or land use anomalies.

The Level III land use code provided can be expanded to a Level IV code by subdividing the three-digit codes where needed into four-digit codes.

This type of data is used in neighborhood planning studies, district planning, zoning studies, and detailed studies of specific urban activities, such as manufacturing or retailing.

Because each application of the data at Level IV is specialized, it is impossible to provide a single land use code that will apply to all situations. Each Level IV code must be tailored to meet the specific need at hand.

The scale of mapping Level IV land uses is generally between 1"=50′ (1:600) and 1"=200′ (1:2400). The sources of data may include:

1. Sanborn insurance maps
2. Assessor's maps and property records
3. Large scale aerial photographs
4. City directories
5. Address-indexed telephone directories
6. Extensive field investigation.

Two illustrations of Level IV land use codes follow.

## For a Study of Retail Sales Within a Jurisdiction

The following land use information is to be correlated with data on floor area, and data on the dollar volume of retail sales.

1211   Building materials, hardware, and garden supplies

  1211.1   Lumber

  1211.2   Hardware

  1211.3   Garden supplies

  1211.4   other

1212   General merchandise group stores

  1212.1   Department stores

  1212.2   Variety stores

  1212.3   Miscellaneous general merchandise

1213   Food stores

1214   Automotive dealers

  1214.1   New cars

  1214.2   Used cars

1215   Gasoline service stations

1216   Apparel and accessory stores

  1216.1   Women's clothing

  1216.2   Men's and boy's clothing

  1216.3   Family clothing

  1216.4   Shoe stores

  1216.5   Other apparel or accessory stores

1217   Furniture, home furnishings, and appliances

  1217.1   Furniture stores

  1217.2   Home furnishings

  1217.3   Household appliances

  1217.4   Other

1218   Eating and drinking places

  1218.1   Eating places

  1218.2   Drinking places

1219   Drug stores and proprietary stores

1210   Miscellaneous retail stores

  1210.1   Liquor stores

  1210.2   Florists

  1210.3   Other

## For a Study That Compares Existing Land Uses With Existing Zoning Regulations

101   Single family homes

  1011   SF homes complying with R-1-A regulations

  1012   SF homes complying with R-1-B regulations

  1013   SF homes complying with R-1-C regulations

103   Townhouses and rowhouses

  1031   Complying with R-2-A regulations

  1032   Complying with R-2-B regulations

104   Duplexes and triplexes

  1041   Complying with R-3-A regulations

  1042   Complying with R-3-B regulations

121   Retail uses

## References

Anderson, Hardy, Roach, and Witmer. *A Land Use and Land Cover Classification System for Use With Remote*

*Sensor Data* (U.S. Geological Survey Professional Paper 964). Washington: U.S. Government Printing Office, 1976.

Campbell, James B. *Mapping the Land*. Washington: Association of American Geographers, 1983.

Kaiser, Godschalk, and Chapin. *Urban Land Use Planning*, 4th ed. Urbana: University of Illinois Press, 1995.

U.S. Urban Renewal Administration and U.S. Bureau of Public Roads. *Standard Land Use Coding Manual*. Washington: U.S. Government Printing Office, 1965.

# Appendix E

## Notes on Land Use Mapping

The degree of detail required in a land use map depends on the use intended for the map.

Land use maps may be general if they are intended to serve as a basis for preparing a general plan in which only general land use locations are to be shown.

Land use maps should be specific and accurate if they are to be used as the basis for designating proposed zoning for an area, on a parcel by parcel basis.

See Appendix D for a discussion of alternative levels of detail for use in land use mapping and analysis.

One of the frequently overlooked uses of a land use map is the analysis of the amount of land per capita found in cities and counties. It is desirable that land use maps be reasonably measurable, so that they can be the source of this information.

The colors used in land use maps should follow the generally accepted convention:

- Yellows—single family homes
- Browns—multiple family housing
- Reds—commercial development
- Blues—institutions (and water)
- Greens—open spaces, recreation areas
- Grays—industrial uses

The colors on land use maps should be coordinated with the colors used on general plan diagrams and on zoning maps. A given color should imply the same type and intensity of use on all three types of maps.

The intensity of color should be related to the intensity of land use. Low intensity uses should be represented by low intensity colors; high intensity uses should be represented by high intensity colors.

When planning the collection of data for a land use map thought should be given to what information can be derived from the map when it is competed. Very often a land use map will be planned for a single purpose (such as recommending zoning for an area), but a number of secondary uses could be made of the map if just a little more data were to be collected, at perhaps little more effort and expense. It is wise to consider what information may be available, and whether or not the compilation of that information would be worth the added effort. For example, should information on the condition of housing be included? How about the amount of parking in relation to each land use? How about the density of employment in some areas?

However, one of the most common errors made in making land use surveys is collecting data that never will be used. Land use data collection and analysis is a time-consuming and expensive process. Land use data should not be collected unless you know that you are going to use it in the future.

Land use maps should be designed to give information on residential densities. This means the number of dwelling units in a given area must be recorded. A land use map that just shows a large brown blob identified as "apartments" is not very informative. We need to know how many apartments, and at what residential density they were built. When inventorying land uses some means must be provided for recording the number of dwelling units on each parcel, when making a detailed land use survey, or on an acre or hectare, when making a generalized land use survey.

Densities of residential development and employment should be clearly identified as net or gross measurements. That is, does the land area of each use measured include parcel area only (a net measurement), or does the area include some street or vacant areas (a gross measurement)?

Land use maps should provide a means for ascertaining employment densities, especially in retail, office, institutional, and industrial areas. This information is essential input for transportation studies.

In some areas, such as central business districts, a procedure should be developed to display the difference between ground floor uses and upper floor uses.

In some jurisdictions it may be appropriate to devise a procedure for mapping land uses within mixed use developments.

The basic source of data for land use mapping and analysis is the aerial photograph. Field inspection of land uses should be used only as a secondary source.

Field inspections should be used to confirm the interpretation of aerial photography, not the other way around. Field inspections are time consuming and expensive in comparison with aerial photo interpretation.

If field inspections are necessary, do them on the first days of good weather that come along. Don't gamble that "next Thursday will be OK."

The scale of aerial photographs to be used for land use interpretation should be appropriate to the scale of land use map being prepared.

• Aerial photos at a scale of 1"=200' are often suitable for work in urban areas.

• A scale of 1"=100' is often useful for detailed analysis.

• If an individual site is being examined, a scale of 1"=50' is to be preferred.

• Photos at a scale of 1"=2000' are often usable for countywide or regional land use mapping, although 1"=1000' is usually preferable. The 2000' scale photos are desirable because they are the same scale as U.S. Geological Survey topographic maps. The 1000' scale maps are desirable because they show more detail.

• LANDSAT satellite images, which have a resolution of 30 meters (i.e., only objects that are 100 feet or more in size are distinguishable) are useful for natural resource identification in very large geographic regions, but are virtually worthless for land use mapping in urban settings.

It is essential to compile a written list of land uses and their definitions before the data-collection phase of a project is started. General procedures to be used should also be documented. All personnel involved with the land use mapping project should become familiar with these documents.

Anticipate that both the general procedures and the list of land uses will have to be amended as the land use study proceeds. This is completely acceptable, providing that any changes made are well-documented, rather than left to the memories of temporary workers, or scribbled in the margins of field sheets.

While professional planners should be used to structure land use surveys, they are not required to do all the inventorying and mapping. Intelligent and motivated temporary helpers from many backgrounds can be trained quite quickly to do the work.

An essential part of any land use survey is checking for accuracy and consistency. Don't just hope your crew is doing a good job; have crew members help you check for errors and omissions, and find ways of improving the reliability of the survey.

## Notes on Maps and Base Maps

Each diagram, graph, table, or map MUST BE SELF EXPLANATORY. Never rely on accompanying text to provide a title, a legend, or the source of data for these materials; the text is used to interpret mapped features, not to present them.

Maps are usually made by starting with a base map (an outline map with basic information on it, such as streets, rivers), to which is added detailed information on a special topic (traffic flow, land use, location of poverty areas, etc.). The base map usually can be reproduced in many copies, and used as needed. The original of the base map is always kept "clean," and secondary data is never added to it. Secondary data is added to a print made from the base map, or on a reproducible duplicate copy of the base map, so new information can be added later.

The map's scale depends on need, space available, and accuracy required.

- Small scale objects appear small on small scale maps
- Large scale objects appear large on large scale maps
- Small scale maps can show the general picture without a plethora of detail and they take less space
- Large scale maps can show greater detail, they can provide greater precision, and they take more space
  - Each base map must have:
    —Scale
    —North point
    —Appropriate line quality

When information is added to a print or a reproducible copy of a base map in order to illustrate some specific topic, the following must also be added:
- Map title
- Legend
- Source of data
- Date

Each base map usually should have:
- Date of base map
- Source of base map
- Draftsman's name or initials
- A distinct border

Sources of information for making base maps include:
- City engineer
- Utility companies
- County engineer
- State highway department
- Contract with air photo/mapping firm
- Assembly of many large scale maps from assessor's office, or subdivision plat files
- Sanborn maps
- Enlargement of USGS topographic maps
- Tracings of aerial photos

(Note: Tracing aerial photos produces maps with built-in distortions, and should be used only as a last resort.)

When compiling a base map, decide on largest scale required, and on the degree of precision required. Decide if a planimetric map will be satisfactory, or whether topographic features are needed. If a topographic map is needed, what is the required contour interval?

Decide which of the following you need:
- Major streets
- All streets and alleys
- All property lines
- All building outlines

Remember that you can always edit out unwanted detail later on, but you can never "invent" additional detail to add to a generalized map.

Remember that inclusion of detail in maps is expensive when measured in dollar outlay or in time. Don't invest in detail you will never need.

How you will use your map determines its form (that is: scale, sheet size, degree of detail, and specific content). Is the map to be used:
- As a study map
- For in-office records
- For wall displays
- To be photographed and projected from the resulting slide
- In a publication

The line widths on your base map will depend upon the distance from which the viewer will see the map. As a rough rule of thumb, lines are visible at distances (measured in feet) which are 1,000 times the line width (measured in inches). For example, a line of width 1/50 inch will be visible at 1,000 x 1/50=20 feet.

The size of lettering on your map will depend upon the function of the lettering, and on the distance from which the viewer will see the map. Some lettering, such as street names on a map, need be legible only upon close examination, and may therefore be quite small. Titles, on the other hand, which are an essential ingredient of the map, must be legible from normal viewing distances. As a rough rule of thumb, good clear lettering is legible at distances (measured in feet) which are 50 times the letter height (measured in inches). For example, a printed title 1/2" high will be readable at 50 x 1/2=25 feet.

These rules-of-thumb are meant to be starting points in your design, not definitive rules. Always test line weight and lettering size in draft form before you make a firm design decision. Test line quality and the legibility of lettering by drawing lines and some lettering on paper, and looking at them from the same distance from which the finished map will be viewed.

Reproduction processes often used for maps:
• Diazo print from a Mylar positive (or from tracing paper)
• Offset printing—in black and white or in color
• Photocopy (Xerox, etc.)
• Print-out from a computer file, using a plotter. This may be in black and white, or it may be in color.

When preparing maps for publication, you should plan on some photographic reduction for the final map, if your printing process permits this. Reduction to two-thirds or one-half of original size "tidies up" the map appearance nicely; it hides ragged drafting, and minimizes the effects of irregular lettering. It won't work miracles on sloppy work. Generally speaking, reduction

in size by one-third or one-half is helpful; reduction to less than one-half size is dangerous to attempt because you run the risk of losing too much detail. Remember, if you reduce your map to half its original size, your lettering height will be half its original size, and a line which was originally 1/100 of an inch wide will be about 1/200 of an inch wide. (Hairlines in the original will usually be lost entirely in the final print).

When preparing base maps for publication, determine the final page size, establish the margins required, locate the area for the title and legend, and decide on an attractive and effective format.
• Use standard paper sizes whenever possible.
• "Gatefold" inserts can be used in publications, but they are troublesome and expensive.
• The size of your margins will depend upon your publication binding process, on your printing method, and on your text page layout.
• The "gutter" (i.e., the margin adjacent to the binding) must be large enough so your map is legible when the publication is opened.
• Most printing methods require a "gripper edge" (a space for the paper-feed mechanism of a printing press to grab onto each sheet of paper, enabling it to move the sheet through the press); usually this must be at least one-fourth inch from some edge
• You can "bleed" your map off the edge of the page, but this usually requires trimming the edges of the publication after binding. If you plan on bleeding and trimming, be sure that no important information is located in the outside one-fourth inch of the page; it may be trimmed off. Remember that if you plan on trimming one page in a bound volume, you will be trimming all pages.

The preceding notes apply to maps and diagrams produced by Computer Aided Drafting (CAD), as well as to traditionally drawn materials.

# Appendix G

## Summary of a Visual Resource Analysis of Blacksburg, Virginia

From a June 30, 1981, report prepared by C. David Loeks

*Generalized Description.* A map was prepared showing areas of Blacksburg that are visually sensitive by virtue of observation (i.e., primary movement corridors), providing a pleasing foreground to a major landform (i.e., intermediate viewshed), or being major landforms

*Specific Information Shown on Map.*

1. Items shown on map legend
   - Primary movement corridors
   - Intermediate viewsheds
   - Major landforms
2. Map scale: 1"=1,000'
3. Areas included: Blacksburg and vicinity
   - Media used to prepare map: pastel and felt-tip marker pens
   - Mapping methodology developed by: C. David Loeks

*Summary of Methodology Used to Develop the Map.* The purpose was to indicate areas that are visually sensitive by virtue of frequency of observation by the public, and therefore tend to establish the dominant visual character of the community. Two categories of such areas were identified on the basis of available data and from field inspections:

- Primary movement corridors, where concern is for what is seen on the edges of travel corridors (signs, landscaping, facades, utility lines, lighting, parking areas, etc.)
- Intermediate viewsheds, defined as areas adjacent to primary movement corridors that serve as the foreground for views of distant ridges and valleys (major landforms).

*Summary of Findings Made from Analysis of the Map.* The map shows that significant areas of the community are visually sensitive, by virtue of their relationship to corridors, viewsheds, and landforms. Since the development of such areas affects the visual character of Blacksburg in fundamental ways, they should be the focus of detailed study to identify opportunities for enhancing the appearance of existing development and guiding the future development of undeveloped land that is visually sensitive.

The concept of corridors-viewsheds and distant landforms affords an opportunity to focus on those areas that are most frequently seen by a majority of the population. However, the cumulative visual impact of the design and use of public and private lands which are not frequently seen by the majority of the population can also be a significant determinant of community appearance. The assessment of such lands was considered to be beyond the scope of the resources available for this study.

# Appendix H

## Typical Residential Densities

### Definitions

*Net residential density.* The number of dwelling units per unit area (such as acres) of land devoted to a residential building site.

*Gross residential density.* The number of dwelling units per unit area (such as acres) of land devoted to residential building sites plus the area of streets serving those building sites (measured to the centerline of the perimeter streets).

*Neighborhood density.* The number of dwelling units per unit area (such as acres) of land devoted to residential building sites, local streets, and facilities serving the local population (such as local schools, local parks, local shopping facilities, etc.). Usually includes vacant lands.

**Table A-1**
**Typical Residential Densities:**

| Residential use | Lot Area Per du sq.ft/du | Net Residential Density du/ac | Gross Residential Density du/ac | Neighborhood Density du/ac |
|---|---|---|---|---|
| Rural estates | 20 ac | .05 | .05 | .05 |
| Rural residential | 5 ac | .20 | .16 | .15 |
| Low density SF | 20,000 | 2.2 | 1.7 | 1.5 |
| Medium density SF | 8,000 | 5.5 | 4.0 | 3.5 |
| High density SF | 5,000 | 8.7 | 6.5 | 5.2 |
| Duplexes | 4,000 | 11 | 8 | 6 |
| Low density TH | varies | 8 | 6 | 5 |
| High density TH | varies | 10 | 8 | 7 |
| 1 story apartments | 2,400 | 18 | 13 | 10 |
| 3 story apartments | 1,200 | 36 | 25 | 20 |
| 6 story apartments | 600 | 72 | 50 | 35 |
| 12 story apartments | 300 | 145 | 100 | 60 |

# Appendix I

## Notes on General Plan Diagrams

### Anderson's 2-Percent Rule

*The specific details included in a general plan (in text or in map form) should be relevant to at least 2 percent of the people who will live or work in the area affected by the plan.*

### The Amount of Detail in Relation to the Time Span of a Plan

The further into the future a plan is for, the less specific it can be about its details.

Short range plans can (and should) be quite specific, because we can be quite sure about the short-term future. Long range plans should be quite general, because we are quite unsure about the specifics about the long-term future. While we may be quite confident about the general trends that will (or should) occur in the coming 20 years, we cannot say with great assurance how the details of the development will occur.

### The Use of Base Maps in General Plan Diagrams

If you print your plan diagram on a base map that is very detailed (for example, showing all streets, or perhaps all individual property lines) the reader will be led to believe that the plan is very specific, and will be able to make a very specific interpretation from it. See example: Mountain View, California, general plan.

If you print your plan diagram on a base map that shows only major landmarks, then the reader will not be as tempted to make a parcel-specific interpretation from it. See example: Santa Rosa, California, general plan.

The best way to avoid specific interpretation of the details of the plan probably is to present your plans in a schematic manner. See example: Redwood City, California, general plan of Redwood Peninsula.

**Figure A-2** Section of the Land Use Map from the Mountain View (Calif.) General Plan

Scale 1″ = 1500′ (Legend omitted here)
NOTE: All streets are shown on the base map

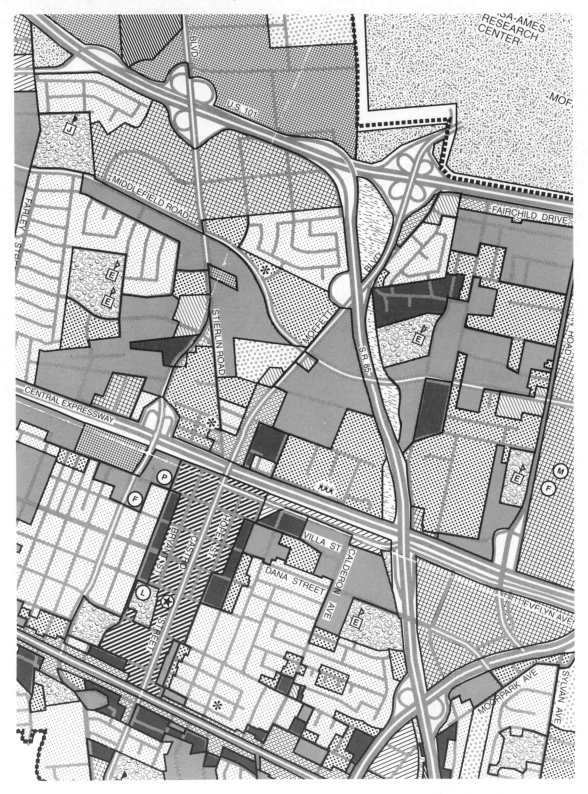

**Figure A-3** Section of the General Plan Land Use Diagram from the Santa Rosa (Calif.) General Plan

Scale 1″ = 2000′   (Legend omitted here)
NOTE:   Only major streets are shown

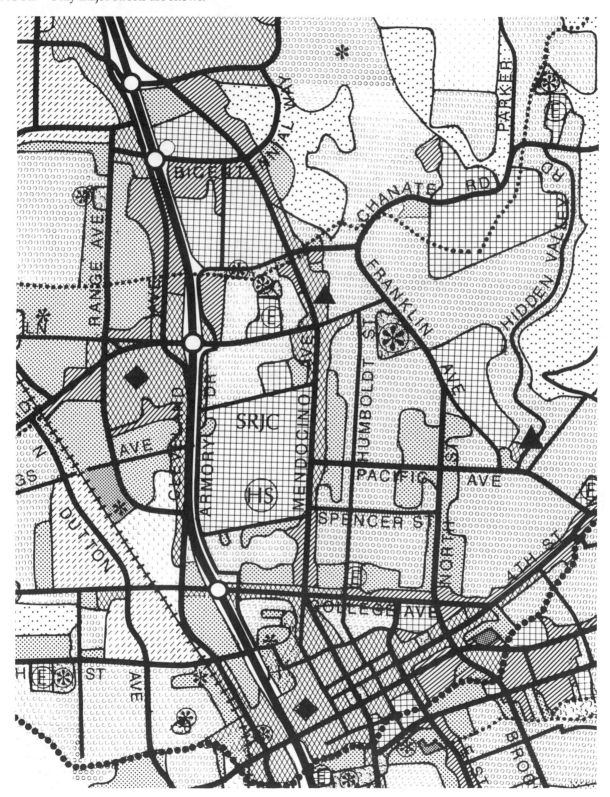

**Figure A-4**   General Plan of the Redwood Peninsula City of Redwood City (Calif.)

Source: The SWA Group
Scale 1″ = 2000′   (Legend omitted here)
NOTE:   Only major arterial streets are shown

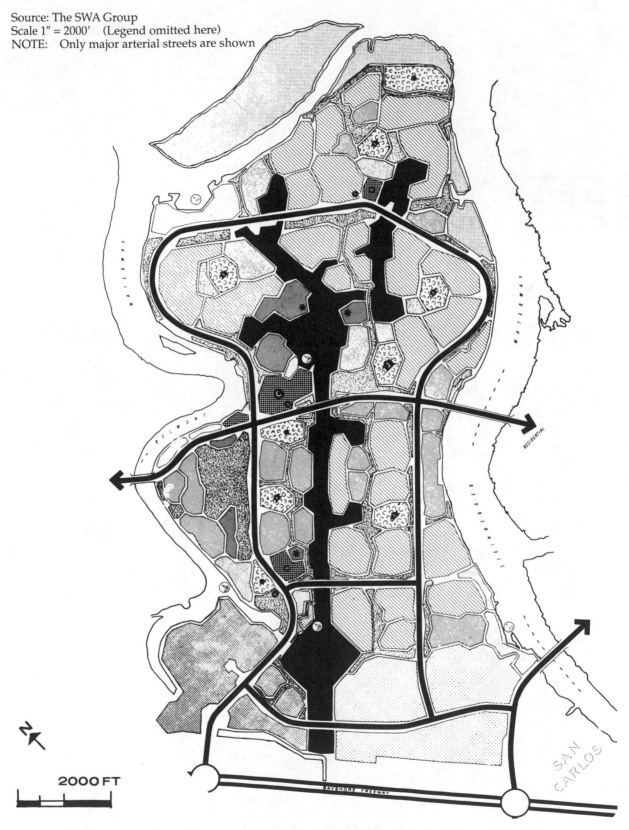

2000 FT

# REDWOOD PENINSULA

# Appendix J

## Skills Professional Planners Need

The following list was compiled to identify what skills an urban planner should acquire to become an effective professional. It is intended for use in graduate schools of urban and regional planning.

Professional planners who consider themselves generalists should know about most of the topics in the list, and should also be able to undertake most of them. Planners who consider themselves specialists should know about most of them, and have expert skills in subject-area clusters of them.

### Identifying Issues and Priorities.
- Opinion surveys
- Interviews
- Content analysis of budgets, reports
- Needs assessment
- Situation assessment
- Use of the Delphi process

### Formulating Goals, Objectives, and Criteria.
- Goals programs
- Specifying objectives implied by goals
- Defining criteria to be used to measure attainment of objectives

### Identifying Policies, Principles, and Standards.
- Review of locally accepted practices
- Review of policies, principles, and standards accepted by other areas
- Public policy analysis

### Collecting And Analyzing Data.
- Data banks
- General analysis of the constraints of the natural environment on land use patterns and circulation
- Structured land capability analyses
- Acquisition and analysis of remote sensing data
- Land use mapping
- Quantitative analysis of land use inventories
- Running inventory and life-cycle analysis of the capital assets of the community
  —Housing
  —Infrastructure
  —Publicly owned structures
- Needs assessment

- Monitoring indicators of social, economic, and physical change
- Monitoring indicators of the quality of life

### Making Projections.
- Drafting alternative futures scenarios
- Extrapolation of trends
- Cohort survival population projections
- Projections of economic activity
- Projections of land use requirements based on population and economic projections
- Trip generation and traffic assignment Land use simulation models
- Transportation models

### Making Plans.
- The issue paper
- Planning the natural and built environment
  —Diagramming spatial relationships among future land uses
  —Quantifying future land use requirements
  —Relating individual land uses to the environmental setting, utility infrastructure, trip generation and travel patterns, and other land uses
  —Sketch planning
  —Urban design
- Planning the local and regional economy
  —Assembling and analyzing data on economic conditions
  —Planning economic development programs
- Planning the social environment
  —Identifying services needed by the local population
  —Identifying and measuring the adequacy of services presently provided to the local population
  —Identifying unmet social service needs
  —Devising strategies for providing the unmet social service needs
- Planning governmental structure and activities
  —Identifying needed governmental services
  —Identifying and evaluating the present governmental service delivery system
  —Recommending changes to the type and amount

of governmental services to be provided

—Identifying methods of monitoring the fairness and efficiency of the provision of governmental services

—Identifying methods of monitoring the fairness and efficiency of existing tax policies

—Identifying methods of monitoring the efficiency of governmental entrepreneurial activities

*Designing Plan Implementation Programs.*

• Formulating basic strategies to implement plans for the:

—Built environment

—Natural environment

—Economic environment

—Social environment

—Governmental/political environment

• Formulating basic strategies to be used in:

—Public programs

—Provision of services

—Entrepreneurial activities

—Provision of subsidies and grants

—Regulatory measures

—Construction and maintenance of facilities

—Tax policies

—Private programs

• Drafting Specific Implementation Programs.

—Operating budgets

—Capital improvement programs

—Capital facility management programs

—Tax generating programs

—Tax abatement programs

—Seeking subventions and grants

—Distributing subsidies

—Regulatory measures

—Land use regulations

—Subdivision regulations

—Construction programs

—Public construction programs

—Private construction programs

—Development impact fees

—Provision of services

—Provision of services by public agencies

—Provision of services by private agencies

—Public entrepreneurship

—Public/private partnership programs

—Stimulating private development

*Administering Plan Implementation Programs*

*Making Impact Analyses.*

• Environmental impact analysis

• Economic impact analysis

• Fiscal impact analysis

• Social impact analysis

• Input/output analysis

• Benefit/cost analysis

• Cost/effectiveness analysis

• Goals achievement matrix analysis

• Program evaluation

*Engaging Public Participation.*

• The Delphi process

• Informing the public

• Developing effective public participation

*Communicating.*

• Using the spoken word

• Using the written word

• Using numbers

• Using graphics

—Maps

—Drawing

—Photography

—Display graphics

—Publication graphics

• Press relationships

—Print

—Radio

—Television

• Other media

—Audio tapes

—Video cameras

• Negotiation and mediation

*Using Other Techniques.*

• Work programming

• Preparing and responding to requests for proposals

• Effective use of consultants

• Application of statistical techniques

• Application of decision theory

• Analysis of the efficiency of the urban system

• Analysis of the efficiency of public programs

• Application of Computers in Planning.

—Word processing

—Desktop publishing

—Databases

—Graphics (general)

—Presentation graphics

—Computer mapping

—Spreadsheets

—Management information systems (MIS)

—Geographic information systems (GIS)

—Tailor-made programs

# Appendix K

## Subject Areas Considered in Urban and Regional Planning

The listing of separate topics in this table is not intended to imply that work in any single subject area constitutes planning. To the contrary, to be a city and regional planner a person must know of or about most of the topics listed below, must have basic skills in many of them, and may have expert skills in one or several.

### Physical Planning

- Land use
- The built environment
  - Buildings
  - Infrastructure
  - Transportation
- The natural environment
  - Natural resources
    - Land
    - Air
    - Water
    - Fauna
    - Flora
  - Natural hazards
    - Geologic
    - Weather
    - Water
- Energy

Topics within the realm of physical planning that are sometimes the subjects of specialization by planners include, but are not limited to:

Land use planning
Transportation planning
Infrastructure planning
Urban design
Zoning administration
Community facility planning
Site planning
Subdivision design
Park and recreation planning
Rural planning
Preservation of agricultural areas
Historic preservation
Urban renewal
Shopping center location and design

Central business district planning
Campus planning
Growth management
Housing
Air quality planning
Water quality planning
Environmental impact analysis
Open space preservation
Seismic safety planning
Natural resource management
Energy planning
Solid waste management planning

### Social Planning

- Social policy planning
  - Public policies concerning the provision of social services
  - Taxation policies
  - Redistribution of resources (wealth, housing, etc.)
  - Regulatory measures
- Social impact analysis
- Delivery of social services
  - Income
  - Education
  - Health
  - Criminal justice
  - Vocational training
  - Housing
  - Transportation
  - Public safety

Advocacy planning

### Economic Planning

- Economic policy planning
  - Policies concerning urban growth and development
  - Taxation policies
  - Collection of financial resources from federal, state, local sources, and redistribution of them to federal, state, and local levels
  - Policies concerning development of new employment opportunities

- Economic development planning
  —Retention of existing jobs, and development of new jobs
  —Tax base retention and development
  —Local economic development
  —Regional economic development
- Economic impact analysis
  —Economic impacts of metropolitan or local community growth
  —Economic impacts of individual projects
  —Fiscal impact analysis

*Management Planning*
- Public policy development
- Goal setting
- Policy analysis
- Management and budgeting
- Strategic planning
- Governmental structure

- Citizen participation
- Political processes
- Program evaluation
- Information systems
- Operating budgets
- Capital improvement programs

*Comprehensive Planning*
- Regional planning
- Metropolitan planning
- City planning
- County planning
- Neighborhood planning
- New towns

*Other Subjects*
- The history of human settlements
- The study of alternative futures
- Demography

# Appendix L

## Notes on Public Presentations

*C. David Loeks and Larz Anderson*

***Know Your Audience.*** How much do they already know about the topic under discussion? What importance do they attach to it? Gear the presentation's content to their level of understanding.

***Decide in Specific Terms What You Want to Achieve.*** Is it for consciousness raising concerning issues and options? Comment and feedback? General approval and support in principle? Approval of specific recommendations? Design the presentation to achieve its stated purpose.

***Know Your Subject.*** Prepare, organize, rehearse, evaluate and fine tune the presentation. Your credibility as a professional is on the line every time you address an audience.

***Inspect the Site for Your Presentation Well in Advance.*** Note the size of the room, the seating arrangement, the availability of space to display maps, etc. Check the speaker's podium. Note where and how to turn the lights on and off.

***Prepare Your Audio-Visual Equipment.*** Check your projector. Make sure there will be a projection screen. Consider taking along an extension cord, a spare projector bulb, and a pointer.

***Prepare Your Graphics.*** Make sure your displays are prepared at an appropriate scale, so that they will be clearly legible by a seated audience. (Displays that are to be viewed from a distance of 30 feet should have a very different character than those designed to be viewed from 3 feet). If you are going to use slides, get them in slide carriers right-side-up, and in the proper sequence. Rehearse your presentation, using the slides, so that you won't be surprised when you see them on the screen later on.

***Give Your Audience a Break.*** Let them know at the outset the who, what, why, when, and how of the topic. Tell them in advance the organization and sequence of the presentation and where it will take them. Let them know where you are going, take them there and conclude by telling them where they are

***Be Upbeat and, Where Appropriate, Enthusiastic About the Subject.*** Don't spend too much time trying to warm up the audience. This will be perceived as beating around the bush and turn them off. They will warm to the consideration you show them by how well organized you are and by your integrity of purpose.

***Use Graphics When Possible.*** Use charts, maps, diagrams, outlines, photos, cartoons, topical headings, etc. Brief handouts outlining the presentation or selected aspects of the topic help. Carefully consider how you will balance the oral and the graphic—generally, one or the other should dominate. Use slides, overhead projectors, maps pinned to walls, etc. as appropriate.

***When Presenting Quantitative Data Slow Down for Emphasis.*** When feasible, interpret its significance. Don't drown your audience with more numbers then they can assimilate. Focus on information that highlights the strategic issues, conclusions, and considerations.

When referring to a graphic display, slow down and carefully explain what it shows. Remember you've been staring at this for quite a while. Take some time to get your victims up to speed. Explain legends, orient the viewer in space-time-scale relationships, and authenticate your data by identifying primary sources.

Communicate qualifications and limitations on reliability and application of the data presented. Don't pretend to be the chief expert if someone who is involved knows more. Spread the glory (and the blame).

***Be Prepared That Someone in the Audience Will Be Uptight About Planning, Planners, and the Issue at Hand.*** Never allow the audience to fluster you or make you angry or defensive or aggressive. If you don't know something, say so, with dignity and generally without apology. If it's a conflict situation, acknowledge and clarify the difference of opinion, why you feel as you do, and the legitimacy of the contrary views. Remember, there's plenty of ignorance to go around for everyone.

***Start And Finish on Time.*** Thank the audience for their attendance and attention. Go in peace, secure in the knowledge that you have given it your best shot.

208

Then evaluate the event. Ask yourself and ask others, how it went. Incorporate what you've learned in the next presentation.

Even if you are reasonably confident in your ability to handle yourself in front of an audience, it's not a bad idea to periodically consult a good public speaking text to brush up.

**Reference**

Dandekar, Hemalata, editor. *The Planner's Use of Information.* Stroudsberg, PA: Hutchinson Ross, 1982. (Republished in 1988 by APA's Planners Press). See Chapter 8, "Considerations for Verbal Presentations," by Alfred W. Story.

# Appendix M

## Notes on Planning Consultants

### Reasons for Retaining Planning Consultants

1. To supply specialized technical skills that the in-house staff does not possess, such as: transportation planning, economic planning, urban design, seismic safety planning, etc.
2. To supplement staff services for a short term, when a buildup of in-house staff is considered to be undesirable (for example, preparing plans or special studies, because the local staff is fully occupied with other work).
3. To provide part-time staff services to a community that does not wish to employ a full-time planner.
4. To produce an objective study and recommendation concerning a controversial subject.
5. To undertake a politically unpopular job
6. To lend prestige to a project (regardless of whether the in-house staff is able to perform the work just as well as the well-known consultant).
7. To provide needed staffing while waiting for the civil service procedure to clear the way for hiring permanent local staff members.
8. To provide expert witness testimony in court cases.
9. To speak as an advocate in a zoning case.
10. To advise on the most effective and desirable organization for the local planning/decision making process.
11. To prepare work programs for the in-house staff to undertake.
12. To draft requests for proposals (RFPs) to be used by the local agency as a basis for employing other consultants.

### Recommended Procedures for Selecting a Consultant

1. Define the scope of the work to be done.
2. Make a ball-park estimate of the cost of doing the proposed work.
3. Check on the availability of funds.
4. Send copies of the request for qualifications (RFQs) to:
   - All consultants who have been asked to be notified of this or similar projects
   - Consultants that you have reason to believe may be well qualified to do the work
5. Sort through the qualifications of those consultants who respond to the RFQ. (It is usually appropriate to have a committee to do this. It is often desirable to have a variety of people on the committee, not just technical experts. Consider legislators, planning commissioners, residents of affected areas, etc.)

Select the three or four best qualified consultants for further consideration.

6. Send to the three or four consultants a request for proposal (RFP) (A more detailed discussion of the RFP follows).

Invite the consultants who submit proposals to make presentations in which they outline the scope of the work they propose to do, and give some evidence of why they believe they are qualified for the job. Usually it is desirable to have a carefully selected committee review the proposals and listen to the presentations. Committee members should often have people with a variety of backgrounds, but must include some members who are well qualified to judge the professional skills of the consultants.

7. Select the consulting firm that appears to be best qualified to do the work that is anticipated. Negotiate with them on the specific scope of the work to be done, and, following that, the fees to be paid for services and materials.

If a mutually satisfactory agreement can be reached with the first choice consultant, sign a firm contract.

8. If a mutually satisfactory arrangement for services cannot be reached with the first-choice consultant, break off negotiations, and start negotiations with the second-choice consultant. Be sure that you have a clear understanding of where things stand with the first consultant before you start negotiating with the second.

### What The Request For Qualifications (RFQ) Should Contain

1. General goals of the program
2. Specific objectives of the program (if known)

3. General work procedures thought to be appropriate (if known)

4. Proposed time schedule

5. Approximate amount of funds to be allocated for the project (if known)

6. Deadline for submitting statement of qualifications

7. Whom to contact for more information

8. What is requested from prospective consultants:
   - Name and qualifications of the person who would be in charge of the project
   - Names and qualifications of all persons who would have substantial roles in the project
   - Examples of work similar to that being proposed in the project, with the names of who was in charge of each
   - A listing of the last five assignments of similar budget range that were completed by the firm, with the names of the primary client representative, and of the firm's lead person

## What the Request for Proposal (RFP) Should Contain

Most RFPs are written by in-house staffs. However, if the proposed project is large, complex, controversial, or deals with an area the in-house staff is not familiar with, it is often considered desirable to employ a consultant to prepare the RFP. If such a consultant is employed, his/her firm should not be considered to undertake the work that is described in the RFP.

The RFP should usually contain:

1. A clear, concise description of the product or services desired

2. An indication of what work procedures are thought to be appropriate

3. An indication of the desired, or required, time schedule

4. Anticipated approximate budget (optional)

5. Description of data to be furnished by the client

6. Description of supplies, materials, or facilities to be furnished by the client

7. Statement of the amount and general qualifications of staff assistance to be furnished by the client

8. Time and place of a "briefing session for prospective bidders," if one is planned

9. Deadline for submitting the RFP

10. Whom to contact for more information

## How Consultants Estimate Fees for Proposed Services

When private firms estimate the financial costs that are implied by a work program they usually estimate the costs of labor, other direct costs, and indirect costs.

The cost of labor consists of the wages paid directly to the workers, plus the employer's costs (where applicable) for Social Security contributions, unemployment insurance, retirement programs, health plan contributions, life insurance, and other fringe benefits. Labor cost is calculated to be the wages paid plus 7 percent for hourly workers who receive few benefits, up to wages plus 50 percent for professional workers who receive substantial benefits.

When estimating the cost per hour of labor it should be remembered that many employees are paid for 10 days of vacation, 10 days of sick leave, and about seven holidays per year. In a year of 52 five-day work weeks the number of days actually worked is 233.

Other direct costs usually include those items that can be separately identified, other than labor or general overhead. Items in this category often include costs for: travel, printing, outside consultants, special equipment, etc.

Indirect costs usually refer to the general overhead that is required of a firm (or of a public office), and may include: general office administration, support staff costs, rent, telephone, photocopying, computer services, local travel, promotion of the firm, participation in professional organizations, amortization of office equipment, library costs, and profit.

Indirect costs vary from job to job, depending upon what is agreed upon as appropriate direct cost charges. For example, travel costs, printing costs, and computer costs are sometimes considered as direct costs and sometimes as indirect costs. Indirect costs usually amount to a low of about 50 percent of the total of labor costs plus direct costs, to a high of about 150 percent of those costs.

Private planning consultants often make approximations of the cost of a job by multiplying the estimated direct labor costs by a multiplier. This multiplier usually ranges from 2.0 for uncomplicated jobs that use little professional labor, through an average of 2.5, up to a high of 3.5 for jobs that require specialized professional skills and involve considerable uncertainty. The use of this rule of thumb is not a substitute for the preparation of a good work program, and the careful calculation of anticipated labor costs, direct costs, and indirect costs.

**Alternative Methods of Payment for Consultant Services**

1. Lump-sum payment, upon satisfactory completion of the contract
2. Progress payments, upon satisfactory completion of specified tasks within the contract, usually with a specified percent withheld until satisfactory completion of the entire contract
3. Payment for expenses incurred, on a month-by-month basis, with a "not-to-exceed" figure for the total contract
4. Payment on a per diem basis for labor, plus expenses

**Potential Problems**

Clients may find that:

1. Consultants in their presentations may describe the skills of the senior members of the firms, and then, if they receive the contract, assign the work to junior members, with minimal participation by the senior members.

To avoid this problem, the contract should identify by name those persons who will be in charge of the project, and those senior staff members who will be participating in the work.

2. The members of the consulting firm who were described as being available to work on a project become unavailable, because of assignment to other jobs, transfer, or resignation.

This problem is quite prevalent when it takes an agency a long time to find the money for a project, negotiate a contract, and authorize initiation of the work. The apparent solution is to shorten the time period between the issuance of the RFP and the authorization to start work.

3. Some consultants will start a job and do most of the work, but then fail to finish up the last part of the work in a timely manner. This sometimes happens when a consultant has run through the authorized budget, and has concluded that it will cost him more money to complete the job than he will be paid. The consultant probably will finish the job, but only when he has time available to do so.

A suggested solution is to write the contract so that it is clear that a substantial sum will be withheld until satisfactory completion of the job. Another suggestion is to talk with the consultant, and determine if there is any justification for the agency to amend the contract to provide additional funds for work that the consultant has done that was over and above the work specified in the original contract. Be reasonable; pay for the work you receive, but do not pay for the consultant's mismanagement.

Consultants may find that:

1. Some agencies will request proposals from an excessive number of consultants. This means that a great many consultants will be wasting their time and money responding.

2. Some agencies interview an excessive number of consultants for a prospective job, and as a result the interviews are too brief, and the interviewers' memories become hazy.

3. Some agencies take too long between issuing an RFP and awarding a contract. During this time the consultant's staff may be assigned to other projects.

4. Sometimes clients are not clear on what criteria will be used to select a consultant. (Will it be on the basis of quality of work, timeliness, price, or what?)

5. Sometimes an agency already knows which consultant it wants to employ, even before the proposal request is issued (sometimes for valid reasons, sometimes for improper reasons), and the selection process is used to make it look as if a legal process was followed.

6. Some agencies don't assign qualified local staff people to serve as liaison people with the consultant, and to carry on after the consultant's work is completed. If this happens, the effectiveness of the consultant's work is greatly diminished, and the client does not get full value for his money.

7. Some agencies promise, during contract negotiations, to provide staff assistance, and data. Later on, it may turn out that the staff assistance does not materialize, and that the data is incomplete or inaccurate.

8. Some clients will use proposal requests as a means of getting good ideas for free, and then turning the work over to a favored consultant, or to the in-house staff.

9. Some clients don't take the trouble to get even a

ball park estimate of cost before issuing an RFP, and are shocked by prices suggested by consultants. They may then decide to not undertake the project at all. This results in a complete waste of time for all consultants who submitted proposals.

**10.** Some clients ask for work that they want, but which was not provided for in the contract; sometimes they become quite disgruntled if the consultant declines to provide it free.

**References**

American Planning Association. "Working With Consultants" (Planning Advisory Service Report No. 378) Chicago: American Planning Association, 1983.

American Planning Association. "Selecting and Retaining a Planning Consultant." (Planning Advisory Service Report No. 443) Chicago: American Planning Association, 1993.

# Bibliography

Contents

**Introduction**

The purpose of this bibliography is to provide practitioners and students of urban planning with a list of those works considered basic to their professional field in the United States.

The publications listed here are generally those that a planner might turn to first when investigating a topic in urban planning.

A conscious attempt has been made to limit the number of references on each topic to the 10 or 12 best known works, preferably those that are readily available.

Those who desire more extensive listings should consult Additional Sources of Information at the end of this bibliography.

**History of Cities and City Planning**

Coke, James G. "The Antecedents of Local Planning." In Goodman, William I. and Eric C. Freund, eds. *Principles and Practice of Urban Planning.* Washington: International City Managers Association, 1968.

Cooper-Hewitt Museum of Design. *Cities and the Forces Which Shape Them.* New York: Rizzoli International Publications, 1982.

Gerckens, Lawrence C. "Historical Development of City Planning." In So, Frank S. and Judith Getzels, eds. *The Practice of Local Government Planning* 2d ed. Washington: International City Management Association, 1988.

Hall, Peter. *Cities of Tomorrow: An Intellectual History of Urban Planning and Design.* Cambridge, Mass.: Basil Blackwell, 1988.

Krueckeberg, Donald A., ed. *Introduction to Planning History in the United States.* Piscataway, N.J.: Center for Urban Policy Research, 1983. (An interesting collection of articles representative of the various eras in the history of planning.)

Mumford, Lewis. *The City in History.* New York: Harcourt, Brace and World, 1961. (A classic work.)

Reps, John. *The Making of Urban America.* Princeton, N.J.: Princeton University Press, 1965.

Scott, Mel. *American City Planning Since 1890.* Berkeley, Ca.: University of California Press, 1969. (The definitive text in the field.)

**Urban Planning—General Overview**

Branch, Melville C. *Comprehensive City Planning.* Washington: American Planning Association, 1985.

Catanese, Anthony and W. Paul Farmer. *Personality, Politics, and Planning.* Beverly Hills, Ca.: Sage Publications, 1978.

Jacobs, Allan. *Making City Planning Work.* Chicago: American Society of Planning Officials, 1978.

Kaiser, Godschalk, and Chapin. *Urban Land Use Planning,* 4th ed. Urbana: University of Illinois Press, 1995.

Knox, Naphtali and Charles E. Knox, eds. *The California General Plan Glossary.* Palo Alto, Ca.: California Planning Roundtable, 1990. (Although some of the terms described relate to California law, most of them are in nationwide use.)

Levy, John M. *Contemporary Urban Planning* 2d ed. Englewood Cliffs, N.J.: Prentice Hall, 1990.

Smith, Herbert H. *Planning America's Communities.* Chicago: American Planning Association, 1991.

So, Frank S. and Judith Getzels, eds. *The Practice of Local Government Planning* (Second Edition). Washington, DC: International City Management Association, 1988.

Solnit, Albert with Charles Reed, Peggy Glasford, and Duncan Erley. *The Job of the Practicing Planner.* Washington: American Planning Association, 1988.

Stein, Jay M., *Classic Readings in Urban Planning.* New York: McGraw-Hill, 1995.

**Urban Planning—Methods**
(See also Strategic Planning)

Bair, Frederick H. Jr. *Planning Cities.* Chicago: American Society of Planning Officials, 1970. (Although this book was written many years ago, most of the planning issues and procedures discussed are still relevant.)

Kaiser, Godschalk, and Chapin. *Urban Land Use Planning,* 4th ed. Urbana: University of Illinois Press, 1995.

Dandekar, Hemalata C. *The Planner's Use of Information.* Chicago: American Planning Association, 1988. (A reprint of the 1982 edition.)

Dickey, John W., and Thomas M. Watts. *Analytical Techniques in Urban and Regional Planning.* New York: McGraw Hill, 1978.

Goodman, William I. and Eric C. Freund. *Principles and Practice of Urban Planning.* Washington: International City Managers Association, 1968. (Note: This edition of "the green book" deals much more extensively with planning methodology than does the 1979 edition by So, Stollman, Beal, and Arnold, or the 1988 edition by So and Getzels.)

Kreuckeberg, Donald A. and Arthur Silvers. *Urban Planning Analysis: Methods and Models.* New York: John Wiley & Sons, 1974.

Lynch, Kevin and Gary Hauck. *Site Planning,* 3d ed. Cambridge, Mass.: MIT Press, 1984.

Perloff, Harvey. *Planning the Post-Industrial City.* Washington: American Planning Association, 1980.

Roberts, Margaret. *An Introduction to Town Planning Techniques.* London: Hutchinson, 1974. (Although written primarily for British readers, 95 percent of this text is directly applicable to U.S. practice.)

So, Hand, and McDowell, eds. *The Practice of State and Regional Planning.* Chicago: American Planning Association, 1986. (See Chapter 9, "Policy Analysis," by Carl V. Patten, and Chapter 11, "Basic Studies for State and Regional Planning," by Hughes and Kruekeberg.)

**Urban Planning—Theory**

Branch, Melville C. *Urban Planning Theory.* Stroudsburg, Pa: Dowden, Hutchinson, and Ross, Inc., 1975.

Bolan, Richard S. "Emerging Views of Planning." *Journal of the American Institute of Planners* 33 (July 1967): 233-245.

Burchell, Robert W. and George Sternlieb. *Planning Theory in the 1980's: A Search for Future Directions.* Rutgers, N.J.: Center for Urban Policy Research, 1979.

Faludi, Andreas. *A Reader in Planning Theory.* Oxford, England: Pergamon Press, 1973.

Friedman, John. *Retracking America: A Theory of Transactive Planning.* Garden City, N.Y.: Anchor Press/Doubleday, 1973.

Hudson, Barclay M. "Comparison of Current Planning Theories: Counterparts and Contradictions." *Journal of the American Planning Association.* Vol. 33, No. 4 (October 1979): 387-406.

Kent, T. J., Jr. *The Urban General Plan.* Chicago: American Planning Association, 1990. (A reprint of the 1964 edition. A very basic work in urban planning.)

McDowell, Bruce. "Approaches to Planning." In So, Hand, and McDowell, eds. *The Practice of State and Regional Planning.* Chicago: American Planning Association, 1986.

Meyerson, Martin. "Building the Middle Range Bridge for Comprehensive Planning." Journal of the American Institute of Planners 22 (Spring 1956), 58-64.

Perloff, Harvey. *Planning the Post-Industrial City.* Washington: American Planning Association, 1980.

**Administrative Aspects of Planning**

American Planning Association. "Planning Advisory Service Reports," published monthly. (Some of these reports deal with the administrative aspects of planning.)

Banovetz, James M., ed. *Managing the Modern City.* Washington: International City Management Association, 1971. (See especially Chapter 12, "City Planning.")

Goodman, William I. and Eric C. Freund. *Principles and Practice of Urban Planning.* Washington: International City Managers Association, 1968. (See Chapter 18, "The Local Planning Agency: Organization and Structure," by James H. Pickford, and Chapter 19, "The Local Planning Agency: Internal Administration," by John T. Howard.)

Jones, Warren W. and Albert Solnit. *What Do I Do Next?* Chicago: American Planning Association, 1982.

Slater, David C. *Management of Local Planning.* Washington: International City Management Association, 1984.

So, Frank S. and Judith Getzels, eds. *The Practice of Local Government Planning* 2d ed. Washington: International City Management Association, 1988. (See Chapter 13, "Planning Agency Management," by Frank So.)

Solnit, Albert. *The Job of the Planning Commissioner.* 4th ed. Belmont, Ca: Wadsworth Publishing Co., 1987.

Zucker, Paul C. *The Management Idea Book.* San Diego, Ca: West Coast Publishers, 1983. (A management book specifically for planners.)

**Citizen Participation in Planning**

(Note: Most of the entries below are ancient. There appear to be few significant recent works on the subject.)

Arnstein, Sherry R. "A Ladder of Citizen Participation." *Journal of the American Institute of Planners.* 35 (July 1969): 216-224.

Burke, Edmund M. *A Participatory Approach to Urban Planning.* New York: Human Sciences Press, 1979.

Creighton, James L. *The Public Involvement Manual.* Cambridge, Mass.: Abt Books, 1981.

Langton, Stuart, ed. *Citizen Participation in America.* Lexington, Mass.: Lexington Books, 1978.

Rosenbaum, N. *Citizen Involvement in Land Use Governance: Issues and Methods.* Washington: The Urban Institute, 1974.

So, Hand, and McDowell, eds. *The Practice of State and Regional Planning.* Chicago: American Planning Association, 1986. (See Chapter 12, "Citizen Participation," by Cogan, Sharpe, and Hertzberg.)

The topic of "visioning" is of current interest. There appear to be few publications on the subject, but the following ones should be considered:

*Planning* magazine, May 1993 issue (published by American Planning Association). See pp. 10-16 for a series of short articles under the title "Visions of Things to Come."

Department of Community Development, State of Washington. *Towards Managing Growth in Washington: A Guide to Community Visioning.* (A 32 page brochure, published in 1991. From: Growth Management Division, Department of Community Development, P.O. Box 48300, Olympia, Wash. 98504.)

Oregon Chapter, American Planning Association. "Oregon Vision Trilogy," 1993.

**Commercial Area Planning**

Berk, Emanuel. *Downtown Improvement Manual.* Chicago: American Planning Association, 1976.

Black, J. Thomas, Lilly Howland, and Stuart L. Rogel. *Downtown Retail Development: Conditions for Success and Project Profiles.* Washington: Urban Land Institute, 1983.

Casazza, John A. and Frank H. Spink. *Shopping Center Development Handbook* 2d ed. Washington: Urban Land Institute, 1985.

Lion, Edgar. *Shopping Centers: Planning, Development and Administration.* New York: John Wiley & Sons, 1976.

Lynch, Kevin, and Gary Hauck. *Site Planning,* 3d ed. Cambridge, Mass.: MIT Press, 1984. (See pp. 313-325.)

McBee, Susanna, with Ralph J. Basile, Robert T. Dunphy, John M. Keeling, Ben C. Lin, David C. Peterson, Patrick L. Phillips, and Richard D. Wagner. *Downtown Development Handbook,* 2d ed. Washington: Urban Land Institute, 1992.

Nelson, Richard L. *The Selection of Retail Locations.* New York: McGraw Hill, 1966. (The principles of retail location set forth in this historic book are still valid.)

O'Mara, W. Paul and John A. Casazza. *Office Development Handbook*. Washington: Urban Land Institute, 1982.

Roca, Rueben A. *Market Research for Shopping Centers*. New York: International Council of Shopping Centers, 1980.

Sales and Marketing Management. *Survey of Buying Power—Data Service*. New York: Sales and Marketing Management (issued annually).

So, Frank, Israel Stollman, et al. *The Practice of Local Government Planning*. Washington: International City Management Association, 1979. (See pp. 246-262.)

Sternlieb, George, and James W. Hughes. *Shopping Centers: USA*. Piscataway, N.J.: Center for Urban Policy Research, 1981.

**The Comprehensive Plan**

American Law Institute. *A Model Land Development Code*. (Complete text adopted by ALI 5/21/75 with Reporter's Commentary.) Philadelphia: American Law Institute, 1976.

Bolan, Richard. "Emerging Views of Planning." *Journal of the American Institute of Planners* No. 33 (July 1967): 233-245.

Fishman, Richard P., ed. *Housing for All Under Law*. (A report of the American Bar Association Advisory Commission on Housing and Urban Growth.) Cambridge, Mass.: Ballinger, 1978. (See Appendix to Chapter 5, "The State of the Art in Local Planning.")

Haar, Charles. "The Content of the General Plan: A Glance at History." *Journal of the American Institute of Planners* 16 (Spring-Summer 1955): 85-86.

Kaiser, Godschalk, and Chapin. *Urban Land Use Planning*, 4th ed. Urbana: University of Illinois Press, 1995.

Kent, T. Jack. *The Urban General Plan*. Chicago: American Planning Association, 1990. (A reprint of the 1964 edition. This is the definitive work on the subject.)

Meyerson, Martin. "Building the Middle-Range Bridge for Comprehensive Planning." *Journal of the American Institute of Planners* 22 (Spring 1956): 58-64.

Perloff, Harvey. *Planning the Post-Industrial City*. Washington: American Planning Association, 1980.

So, Frank S. and Judith Getzels, eds. *The Practice of Local Government Planning* 2d ed. Washington: International City Management Association, 1988. (See Chapter 3, "General Development Plans," by Hollander, Pollock, Reckinger, and Beal. See also Chapter 4, "District Planning," by Paul Sedway.)

**Computers in Planning**

American Planning Association. "Planning Software Survey 1990." Planning Advisory Service Report No. 427/428. Chicago: American Planning Association.

Brail, Richard K. *Microcomputers in Urban Planning and Management*. New Brunswick, N.J.: Center for Urban Policy Research, 1987.

Gordon, Steven I., and Richard Anderson. *Microcomputer Applications in City Planning and Management*. New York: Praeger, 1989.

International City Management Association. "Micro-Software News." Monthly newsletter on microcomputer applications in local government. Published by International City Management Association, Washington.

_____. *Software Reference Guide* 1993. Washington: ICMA, 1993.

Kaiser, Godschalk, and Chapin. *Urban Land Use Planning*, 4th ed. Urbana: University of Illinois Press, 1995.

Klosterman, Richard E., ed. "A Planners Review of PC Software and Technology." Planning Advisory Service Report No. 414/415. Chicago: American Planning Association, 1989.

Klosterman, Richard E. and Earl G. Brossard, eds. *Spreadsheet Models for Urban and Regional Analysis*. New Brunswick, N.J.: Rutgers Center for Urban Policy Analysis, 1993.

Ottensman, John R. *BASIC Microcomputer Programs for Urban Analysis and Planning*. New York: Chapman and Hall, 1985.

Sipe, Neil G., and Robert W. Hopkins. *Microcomputers and Economic Analysis: Spreadsheet Templates for Local Government*. Gainesville, Fl.: Bureau of Economic and Business Research, University of Florida. Revised and expanded by McKay and Burrows in 1987. (Contains spreadsheet templates for economic base analysis, population projections, fiscal impact analysis, revenue projections, etc.)

Wiggins, Lyna L. and Steven P. French. "GIS: Assessing Your Needs and Choosing a System." (Planning Advisory Service, Report No. 433), Chicago: American Planning Association, 1991.

### Economic Development Planning

(See also Commercial Area Planning, Computers in Planning)

Bendavid-Val, Avrom. "Local Economic Development Planning: From Goals to Policies." (Planning Advisory Service Report No. 353). Chicago: American Planning Association, 1980.

Beyard, Michael D. *Business and Industrial Park Development Handbook.* Washington: Urban Land Institute, 1988.

California Office of Planning and Research. *Economic Practices Manual: A Handbook for Preparing an Economic Impact Assessment.* Sacramento, Ca.: Office of Planning and Research, 1984 (out of print).

Conroy, Michael. *The Challenge of Urban Economic Development.* Lexington, Mass.: DC Heath & Co., 1975.

Hopkins, Robert W., Anne H. Shermyer, and Neil G. Sipe. *Preparing the Economic Element of the Comprehensive Plan.* Gainesville, Fl.: Bureau of Economic and Business Research, University of Florida, 1989. (While this report is intended for use in Florida, the procedures described are readily transferable to other places.)

Levy, John M. *Economic Development Programs for Cities, Counties, and Towns.* 2d ed. New York: Praeger, 1990.

So, Frank S. and Judith Getzels, eds. *The Practice of Local Government Planning* 2d ed. Washington: International City Management Association, 1988. (See Chapter 10, "Economic Development," by Stephen Friedman and Alexander Darragh.)

U. S. Conference of Mayors, National Community Development Association, and Urban Land Institute. *Local Economic Development Tools and Techniques: A Guidebook for Local Government.* Washington: U.S. Government Printing Office, 1979.

### Energy Planning

(Note: Most of the entries below are ancient. There appear to be few significant recent works on the subject.)

Burchell, Robert W. and David Listokin. *Energy and Land Use.* New Brunswick, N.J.: Center for Urban Policy Research, 1982.

Jaffe, Martin, and Duncan Erley. *Protecting Solar Access for Residential Development.* Washington: U.S. Government Printing Office, 1979.

Lovins, Amory B. *Soft Energy Paths: Toward a Durable Peace.* New York: Harper & Row, 1979.

Morris, David. *Self-Reliant Cities, Energy and the Transformation of Urban America.* San Francisco: Sierra Club Books, 1982.

National Association of Counties, National Association of Cities. *Community Energy Strategies.* Washington: NACO, 1982.

Schurr, Sam H., et al. *Energy in America's Future.* Baltimore: The Johns Hopkins University Press, 1979.

Solar Energy Research Institute. *A New Prosperity: Building a Sustainable Energy Future.* Andover, Mass.: Brick House Publishing, 1981.

_____. *Solar Law Reporter.* (Published bimonthly between 1979-82. Contains articles on solar energy developments, examples of programs, review of new legislation, etc. Back issues available from the American Solar Energy Society, Boulder, Colo.)

Stern, P., and E. Aronson. *Energy Use: The Human Dimension.* New York: W. F. Freeman, 1984.

Stobaugh, Robert, and Daniel Yergin. *Energy Future: The Report of the Harvard Business School Energy Project.* New York: Random House, 1979.

### Environmental Planning

Dunne, Thomas, and Luna Leopold. *Water in Environmental Planning.* San Francisco: W. H. Freeman & Co., 1978.

Griggs, G., and J. Gilchrist. *Geologic Hazards, Resources, and Environmental Planning.* Belmont, Ca: Wadsworth, 1983.

Marsh, William. *Landscape Planning—Environmental Applications.* Reading, Mass.: Addison-Wesley, 1983.

McHarg, Ian. *Design with Nature.* New York: John Wiley & Sons (reissued 1991).

Moran, Joseph M., Michael D. Morgan, and James H. Wiersama. *Introduction to Environmental Science.* San Francisco: W. H. Freeman and Co., 1980.

Peavy, H., D. R.. Rowe, and G. Tchobanoglous. *Environmental Engineering.* New York: McGraw Hill, 1985.

Simonds, John O. *Earthscape: A Manual of Environmental Planning.* New York: Van Nostrand Reinhold, 1978.

So, Frank S. and Judith Getzels, eds. *The Practice of Local Governmental Planning* 2d ed. Washington: International City Management Association, 1988. (See Chapter 5, "Environmental Land Use Planning," by William Toner.)

So, Hand, and McDowell, eds. *The Practice of State and Regional Planning*. Chicago: American Planning Association, 1986. (See Chapter 19, "Environmental Protection," by Daniel R. Mandelker.)

Westman, W.E. *Ecology, Impact Assessment, and Environmental Planning*. New York: Wiley, 1985.

Way, Douglas. *Terrain Analysis*, 2d ed. Stroudsburg, PA: Dowden, Hutchinson & Ross, 1978.

### Growth Management
(See also Legal Aspects of Planning)

Brower, Godschalk, and Porter, eds. *Understanding Growth Management*. Washington: Urban Land Institute, 1989.

Burrows, Lawrence B. *Growth Management: Issues, Techniques, and Policy Implications*. New Brunswick, N.J.: Center for Urban Policy Research, 1978.

DeGrove, John M. *Land, Growth, & Politics*. Washington: American Planning Association, 1984.

Finkler, Earl, et al. "Urban Growth Management Systems: An Evaluation of Policy Related Research." Planning Advisory Service Report 309/310. Chicago: American Society of Planning Officials, 1975.

Godschalk, David R. et al. *Constitutional Issues of Growth Management* rev ed. Chicago: American Planning Association, 1979.

Kelly, Eric. *Managing Community Growth: Policies, Techniques, and Impacts*. New York: Praeger, 1993.

Porter, Douglas R. *Growth Management: Keeping on Target*. Washington: Urban Land Institute, 1986.

Schiffman, Irving. *Alternative Techniques for Managing Growth*. Berkeley, Ca.: Institute of Governmental Studies, 1989. (102 Moses Hall, University of California, Berkeley, CA 94720)

Scott, Randall W. et al. *Management and Control of Growth: Issues, Techniques, Problems, Trends*. Washington: Urban Land Institute, 1975.

### Historic Preservation and Adaptive Re-Use

Austin, Richard L. *Adaptive Reuse: Issues and Case Studies in Building Preservation*. New York: Van Nostrand Reinhold, 1988.

Derry, Anne, et al. *Guidelines for Local Surveys: A Basis for Preservation Planning*. Washington: U.S. Government Printing Office, 1977.

Lester Thomas Associates. *Historic Preservation in California*. Sacramento, Ca: Office of Historic Preservation, California Department of Parks and Recreation, 1986. (A guide to setting up a local historic preservation program.)

Morris, Marya. "Innovative Tools for Historic Preservation." Planning Advisory Service Report No. 438. Chicago: American Planning Association, 1992.

National Trust for Historic Preservation in the United States. *A Report on Principles and Guidelines for Historic Preservation in the United States*. Washington: National Trust for Historic Preservation, 1964.

Office of Planning and Research, State of California. *Historic Preservation Element Guidelines*. Sacramento, Ca.: Office of Planning and Research, 1976.

Roddewig, Richard J. "Preparing a Historic Preservation Ordinance." Planning Advisory Service Report No. 374. Chicago: American Planning Association, 1983.

"Preservation News." A periodical published by The National Trust for Historic Preservation. Washington.

Williams, Norman, Edmund Kellogg, and Frank B. Gilbert. *Readings in Historic Preservation*. Rutgers, N.J.: Center for Urban Policy Research, 1983.

### Housing

Fishman, Richard, ed. *Housing for All Under Law*. Report of the American Bar Association Advisory Commission on Housing and Urban Growth. Cambridge, Mass.: Ballinger, 1978.

Hughes, James W., and George Sternlieb. *Dynamics of America's Housing*. New Brunswick, N.J.: Center for Urban Policy Research, 1987.

Listokin, David. *Housing Rehabilitation: Economic, Social, and Policy Perspectives*. New Brunswick, N.J.: Center for Urban Policy Research, 1983.

Nenno, Mary K. and Paul C. Brophy. *Housing and Local Government*. Washington: International City Management Association, 1982.

Bookout et al. *Residential Development Handbook*. 2d ed. Washington: Urban Land Institute, 1990.

So, Hand, and McDowell, eds. *The Practice of State and Regional Planning*. Chicago: American Planning Association, 1986. (See Chapter 16, "Housing Planning," by Stegman and O'Connor.)

So, Frank S. and Judith Getzels, eds. *The Practice of Local Government Planning* 2d ed. Washington: International City Management Association, 1988. (See Chapter 12, "Planning for Housing," by Constance Lieder.)

Struyk, Marshall, and Ozanne. *Housing Policies for the Urban Poor.* Washington: Urban Institute, 1978.

U.S. Conference of Mayors, National Community Development Association, and Urban Land Institute. *The Development Process.* Washington: U. S. Government Printing Office, 1979. (A brief but excellent overview of how private housing developers make investment decisions.)

**Impact Assessment**

In 1976 The Urban Institute, Washington, D.C., published five excellent reports on impact analysis:

*Social Impacts of Land Development* by Kathleen Christensen

*Land Development and the Natural Environment* by Dale L. Keyes

*Fiscal Impacts of Land Development* by Thomas Muller

*Economic Impacts of Land Development* by Thomas Muller

*Using an Impact Measurement System to Evaluate Land Development* by Philip Schaenman

The Schaenman report gathers information from the other four reports, and recommends a procedure for measuring the probable impacts of land development; this has great potential for use in estimating the probable effects of general plans.

Burchell, Robert W. *Development Impact Analysis: Feasibility, Design, Traffic, Fiscal, Environment.* Piscataway, N.J.: Center for Urban Policy Research, Rutgers University, 1988.

J H K & Associates (principal authors: William R. Riley, James H. Kell, and Iris J. Fullerton). *Design of Urban Streets.* Prepared for the U.S. Department of Transportation, Federal Highway Administration. Washington: Superintendent of Documents, U.S. Government Printing Office, 1980. (See Chapter 18, "Social and Economic Impacts of Design," and Chapter 19, "Environmental Factors." While these chapters were primarily written to consider the impacts of streets, they are excellent overviews of impact analysis in general.)

So and Getzels. *The Practice of Local Government Planning* 2d ed. 1988. See Chapter 5, "Environmental Land Use Planning," especially pp. 127-138. (Note that this chapter deals only with *environmental* impacts, and does not discuss economic, social, or other non-environmental impacts.)

Westman, W. E. *Ecology, Impact Assessment, and Environmental Planning.* New York: Wiley, 1985.

**Legal Aspects of Planning**
(See also Growth Management, Zoning)

American Law Institute. *A Model Land Development Code.* Philadelphia: The American Law Institute, 1975.

Anderson, Robert C. *American Law of Zoning.* Rochester, N.Y.: Lawyers Co-operative Publishing Co., 1972.

Babcock, Richard F. and Charles L. Siemon. *The Zoning Game—Revisited.* Boston: Oelgeschlager, Gunn and Hain, 1985.

Blaesser, Brian W., and Alan C. Weinstein, eds. *Land Use and the Constitution.* Chicago: American Planning Association, 1989.

Bosselman, Fred P. et al. *The Quiet Revolution in Land Use Control.* Washington: U.S. Government Printing Office, 1971.

Hagman, Donald G. and Dean J. Miscynski, eds. *Windfalls for Wipeouts.* Chicago: American Society of Planning Officials, 1978.

Mandelker, Daniel. *Land Use Law.* 2d ed. Charlottesville, Va.: Michie Company, 1988.

Meck, Stuart, and Edith Netter eds. *A Planner's Guide to Land Use Law.* Chicago: American Planning Association, 1983.

**Neighborhood Planning**

American Public Health Association, Committee on the Hygiene of Housing. *Planning the Neighborhood.* Chicago: Public Administration Service, 1948. (This text discusses the rationale of neighborhood planning in considerable depth, and has a lot of interesting computations in it. It is one of the "classics" in the field, although severely out-of-date.)

Corbett, Michael N. *A Better Place to Live.* Emmaus, Pa.: Rodale Press, 1981.

Downs, Anthony. *Neighborhoods and Urban Development.* Washington: The Brookings Institution, 1981.

Jones, Bernie. *Neighborhood Planning.* Chicago: American Planning Association, 1990.

Keller, Suzanne. *The Urban Neighborhood: A Sociological Perspective.* New York: Random House, 1968.

Bookout, Lloyd W., Jr. et al. *Residential Development Handbook* 2d ed. Washington: Urban Land Institute, 1990.

Sterling, Raymond, John Carmody, and Gail Elnicky. *Earth Sheltered Community Design.* New York: Van Nostrand Reinhold, 1981. (This book covers a much broader range of physical development topics than its title implies.)

Werth, Joel T., and David Bryant. "A Guide to Neighborhood Planning." Planning Advisory Service Report No. 342. Chicago: American Planning Association, 1979.

## New Town Planning

(Note: Most of the entries below are ancient. There appear to be few significant recent works on the subject.)

*Architectural Record.* December 1973. (Entire issue of the magazine is devoted to the topic of new towns.)

Bailey, James, ed. *New Towns in America: The Design and Development Process.* New York: John Wiley & Sons, 1973.

Burby, Raymond J. et al. *New Communities, USA.* Lexington, Mass.: Lexington Books, 1976.

Downs, Anthony. "Alternative Forms of Future Urban Growth in the U.S.," *Journal of the American Institute of Planners* 36 (January 1970): 3-11.

Ewing, Reid. *Developing Successful New Communities.* Washington: Urban Land Institute, 1991.

Golany, Gideon. *New Town Planning: Principles and Practice.* Somerset, N.J.: John Wiley & Sons, 1977.

Howard, Ebenezer. *Garden Cities of Tomorrow.* New York: Transatlantic, 1951. (reprint of 1898 text).

Osborn, Frederick. *Greenbelt Cities.* New York: Schocken Books, 1969 (reprint of 1946 text).

Stein, Clarence. *Toward New Towns for America.* New York: Reinhold, 1957.

U.S./U.S.S.R. New Towns Working Group. *Planning New Towns: National Reports of the U.S. and the U.S.S.R.* Washington: U.S. Department of Housing and Urban Development, Office of International Affairs, March 1981. (Provides an excellent summary of new town planning in the United States in the late 1970s.)

## Open Space Planning

(See also Rural Planning)

(Note: Most of the entries below are ancient. There appear to be few significant recent works on the subject.)

American Farmlands Trust. *Planning and Zoning for Farmland Protection: A Community Based Approach.* East Lansing, Mich.: American Farmlands Trust, 1987.

Cooper-Hewitt Museum of Design. *Urban Open Spaces.* New York: Rizzoli International Publications, 1981.

Coughlin, Keene, et al. *The Protection of Farmland: A Reference Guidebook for State and Local Governments.* Washington: U.S. Government Printing Office, 1981.

McHarg, Ian. *Design With Nature.* Garden City, N.Y.: The Natural History Press, 1969.

Steiner, Frederick. *Ecological Planning for Farmlands Preservation.* Chicago: American Planning Association, 1981.

Strong, Ann Louise. *Open Space for Urban America.* Washington: U.S. Government Printing Office, 1965.

Whyte, William H. *The Last Landscape.* Garden City, N.Y.: Doubleday & Co., 1968. (Probably the most important book on the subject.)

Zisman, Samuel B. *Where Not to Build,* Technical Bulletin No. 1. Washington: U.S. Department of the Interior, Bureau of Land Management, 1968.

## Park And Recreation Planning

(Note: Most of the entries below are ancient. There appear to be few significant recent works on the subject.)

Bannon, Joseph J. *Leisure Resources: Its Comprehensive Planning.* Englewood Cliffs, N.J.: Prentice Hall, 1976.

Clawson, Marion and Jack L. Knetsch, *Economics of Outdoor Recreation.* Baltimore, Md.: Johns Hopkins University Press, 1966.

Gold, Seymour. *Recreation Planning and Design.* New York: McGraw-Hill, 1980.

_____. *Urban Recreation Planning.* Philadelphia: Lea & Febiger, 1973.

National Recreation and Park Association. *Recreation, Park and Open Space Standards and Guidelines.* Alexandria, Va.: National Recreation and Park Association, 1983.

Outdoor Recreation Resources Review Commission. *Outdoor Recreation for America.* Washington: U.S. Government Printing Office, 1962. (A series of 27 basic research reports; old, but important.)

U.S. Department of the Interior. *National Urban Recreation Study,* Executive Report. Washington: U.S. Department of the Interior, 1978.

**Physical Development Planning**
(See also Commercial Area Planning, Transportation Planning)

Kaiser, Godschalk, and Chapin. *Urban Land Use Planning*, 4th ed. Urbana: University of Illinois Press, 1995.

Corbett, Michael N. *A Better Place to Live*. Emmaus, Pa.: Rodale Press, 1981.

Beyard, Michael D. *Business and Industrial Park Development Handbook*. Washington: Urban Land Institute, 1988.

Lynch, Kevin and Gary Hauck *Site Planning* 3d ed. Cambridge, Mass.: MIT Press, 1984.

Casazza, John A. and Frank H. Spink. *Shopping Center Development Handbook* 2d ed. Washington: Urban Land Institute, 1985.

National Association of Home Builders. *Land Development*. Washington: National Association of Home Builders, 1987.

Bookout et al. *Residential Development Handbook* 2d ed. Washington: Urban Land Institute, 1990.

Tabors, Richard D., Michael H. Shapiro, and Peter P. Rogers. *Land Use and the Pipe*. Lexington, Mass.: Lexington Books, 1976.

**The Political Context of Planning**

Benveniste, Guy. *The Politics of Expertise* 2d ed. San Francisco: Boyd & Fraser, 1977.

Bolan, Richard and Robert L. Nuttall. *Urban Planning & Politics*. Lexington, Mass.: DC Heath Co., 1975.

Catanese, Anthony. *Planners and Local Politics*. Beverly Hills, Ca.: Sage Publications, 1974.

Catanese, Anthony, and W. Paul Farmer. *Personality, Politics, and Planning*. Beverly Hills, Ca.,: Sage Publications, 1978.

Harrigan, John J. and William C. Johnson. *Governing the Twin Cities Region: The Metropolitan Council in Comparative Perspective*. Minneapolis: University of Minnesota Press, 1978.

Jacobs, Allan B. *Making City Planning Work*. Chicago: American Society of Planning Officials, 1978.

Johnson, William C. *The Politics of Planning*. New York: Paragon House, 1989.

Lucy, William. *Close to People*. Chicago: American Planning Association, 1988.

Myerson, Martin, and Edward C. Banfield. *Politics,*

*Planning, and the Public Interest*. New York: Free Press, 1964.

**Rural Planning**

Brower, David J., et al. *Managing Development in Small Towns*. Chicago: American Planning Association, 1984.

Bryce, Herrington J. *Planning Smaller Cities*. Lexington, Mass.: Lexington Books, 1979.

Daniels, Thomas L., and John W. Keller. *The Small Town Planning Handbook*. Washington: American Planning Association, 1988.

Ford, Kristina, James Lopach, and Dennis O'Donnell. *Planning Small Town America*. Chicago: American Planning Association, 1990.

Getzels, Judith, and Charles Thurow, eds. *Rural and Small Town Planning*. Chicago: American Planning Association, 1980.

Heyer, Fred. "Preserving Rural Character." Planning Advisory Service Report No. 429. Chicago: American Planning Association, 1990.

Lapping, Mark B. *Rural Planning and Development in the U.S.* New York: Guilford Press, 1989.

Sargent, Frederic O. et al. *Rural Environmental Planning for Sustainable Communities*. Covelo, Ca.: Island Press, 1991.

So, Hand, and McDowell. *The Practice of State and Regional Planning*. Chicago: American Planning Association, 1988. (See Chapter 14, "Rural Development," by William S. Bonner.

**Social Planning**
(Note: Most of the entries below are ancient. There appear to be few significant recent works on the subject.)

Brooks, Michael. "Social Planning and City Planning," Planning Advisory Service Report No. 261. Chicago: American Society of Planning Officials, 1970.

Carter, L. W., S. F. Atkinson, and F. L. Liebowitz. *Impact of Growth: A Guide to Socio-Economic Assessment and Planning*. Chelsea, Mich.: Lewis Publishers, 1985.

Christensen, Kathleen. *Social Impacts of Land Development*. Washington: The Urban Institute, 1976.

Frieden, Bernard, Wayne F. Anderson, and Michael Murphy. *Managing Human Services*. Washington: International City Management Association, 1977.

Gans, Herbert. *People and Plans: Essays on Urban Problems and Solutions*. New York: Basic Books, 1968.

Kahn, Alfred J. *Theory and Practice of Social Planning.* New York: Russell Sage Foundation, 1969.

League of California Cities. *Social Element Planning in California.* Los Angeles: League of California Cities, 1977.

Perloff, Harvey S. "New Directions in Social Planning," *Journal of the American Institute of Planners* 31 (November 1965): 297-304.

So, Frank S. and Judith Getzels, eds. *The Practice of Local Government Planning* 2d ed. Washington: International City Management Association, 1988. (See Chapter 11, "Social Aspects of Physical Planning," by Elizabeth Howe).

So, Frank, Hand, and McDowell, eds. *The Practice of State and Regional Planning.* Chicago: American Planning Association, 1986. (See Chapter 22, "Social Services and Education," by Margaret L. Lotspeich and Linda Donelly.

**Strategic Planning**

Bryson, John M. *Strategic Planning for Public and Nonprofit Organizations.* San Fransisco, Ca.: Jossey-Bass, 1988.

Bryson, John M. and Robert C. Einsweiler, editors. *Strategic Planning: Threats and Opportunities for Planners.* Chicago: American Planning Association, 1988. (A reprint of 13 papers prepared for the May 1986 APA symposium on strategic planning. Includes all of the papers that were printed in the Winter 1987, Vol 53, No. 1, issue of the Journal of the American Planning Association.)

Kemp, Roger L., ed. *Strategic Planning in Local Government.* (17 Case Studies in the Application of Strategic Planning.) Chicago: American Planning Association, 1992.

**Transportation Planning**

American Society of Civil Engineers, National Association of Home Builders, and Urban Land Institute. *Residential Streets* 2d ed. Washington: (published by the authors), 1990.

Carter, Everett C., and Wolfgang S. Homburger. *Introduction to Transportation Engineering.* Reston, Va.: Reston Publishing Co., 1978.

Edwards, John D., ed. *Transportation Planning Handbook.* Englewood Cliffs, N.J.: Prentice Hall, 1992. (Published for the Institute of Transportation Engineers.) Institute of Transportation Engineers. Parking Generation 2d ed. Washington: Institute of Transportation Engineers, 1987.

_____. *Trip Generation* 5th ed. Washington: Institute of Transportation Engineers, 1991.

So, Frank S. and Judith Getzels, eds. *The Practice of Local Government Planning* 2d ed. Washington: International City Management Association, 1988. (See Chapter 6, "Transportation Planning," by Sandra Rosenblum.)

Stover, Vergil A., and Frank J. Koepke. *Transportation and Land Development.* Englewood Cliffs, N.J.: Prentice Hall, 1988. (Published for the Institute of Transportation Engineers. While this text was written for professional traffic engineers, there is much in it that land use planners should be aware of.)

Urban Land Institute and the National Parking Association. *The Dimensions of Parking* 3d ed. Washington: Urban Land Institute, 1993.

Weant, Robert A. *Parking.* Westport, Conn.: Eno Foundation for Transportation, 1990.

**Urban Design**

Alexander, Christopher, et al. *A Pattern Language.* New York: Oxford University Press, 1977.

Bacon, Edmund. *Design of Cities.* rev. ed. New York: Viking Press, 1974.

Barnett, Jonathan. *An Introduction to Urban Design.* New York: Harper and Row, 1982.

Habe, Reike, et al. *Design Guidelines and Community Compatibility.* Los Angeles: School of Urban and Regional Planning, University of Southern California, 1988. (A study of design guidelines from 147 communities across the nation.)

Hedman, Richard, and Andrew Jaszewski. *Fundamentals of Urban Design.* Washington: American Planning Association, 1984.

San Francisco Department of City Planning. *Urban Design Plan.* San Francisco: San Francisco Department of City Planning, 1969. (An excellent example of the application of the urban design process.)

Sitte, Camillo. *The Art of Building Cities* (English tran). New York: Reinhold, 1945.

So, Frank S. and Judith Getzels, eds. *The Practice of Local Government Planning* 2d ed. Washington: International City Management Association, 1988. (See Chapter 7, "Urban Design," by Jonathan Barnett.)

Spreiregen, Paul. *Urban Design: The Architecture of Towns and Cities*. New York: McGraw-Hill, 1965.

Woolfe, Myer R., and Richard D. Shinn. *Urban Design Within the Comprehensive Planning Process*. Seattle: Department of Urban Planning, University of Washington, 1970.

## Zoning
(see also Legal Aspects of Planning)

Babcock, Richard F. and Charles L. Siemon. *The Zoning Game Revisited*. Boston: Oegeschlager, Gunn and Hain, 1985.

Bair, Frederick H., Jr. *Planning Cities*. Chicago: American Society of Planning Officials, 1970.

_____. *Zoning Board Manual*. Washington: American Planning Association, 1984.

*Land Use Law and Zoning Digest*. Chicago: American Planning Association (periodical).

Goodman, William I., and Eric C. Freund. *Principles and Practice of Urban Planning*. Washington: International City Managers Association, 1968. (See Chapter 15, "Zoning," by Robert M. Leary.)

Smith, Herbert H. *The Citizen's Guide to Zoning*. Chicago: American Planning Association, 1983.

So, Frank S. and Judith Getzels, eds. *The Practice of Local Government Planning* 2d ed. Washington: International City Management Association, 1988. (See Chapter 9, "Zoning," by Eric D. Kelly.)

Weaver, Clifford L. and Richard F. Babcock. *City Zoning*. Chicago: American Planning Association, 1979.

*Zoning Bulletin*. Boston: Quinlan Publishing Co. (periodical).

## Additional Sources Of Information
*Serially Issued Bibliographies:*

**Art Index.** Indexes articles on planning and design published in a selected list of periodicals.

**Council of Planning Librarians.** A series of bibliographies, each on an individual topic. Some bibliographies are annotated.

**Information Sources in Urban and Regional Planning.** Piscataway, N.J.: Center for Urban Policy Research, 1994.

**Impact.** A compilation from 1976 of the *Monthly Catalog of U.S. Government Publications*. On CD-ROM, searchable by title, author, subject, keyword, SuDocs, and report number. (CD-ROM stands for "compact disc, read-only memory.") These compact discs can be used with microcomputers to store and retrieve a great deal of information. Updated monthly.

**Index to Current Urban Documents.** Provides bibliographic descriptions of reports and documents produced by many local governments in the U.S. Published quarterly, cumulated annually in May issue. Microfiches of the referenced documents are usually available in the libraries that have the index.

**InfoTrac.** A CD-ROM index, comparable to *Reader's Guide to Periodical Literature*. Indexes more than 800 periodicals.

**Journal of Planning Literature.** Published quarterly since 1985 by the Department of City and Regional Planning, The Ohio State University. Contains bibliographies of books and journal articles, and a number of book reviews and abstracts.

**Merriam Center Library.** *Recent Publications on Governmental Problems*. A serial published 24 times a year by the Charles E. Merriam Center for Public Administration, 1313 E. 60th St., Chicago.

**National Technical Information Service.** *Weekly Government Abstracts*. A compendium of abstracts of government sponsored research; issued weekly, with quarterly and annual compilations. Abstracts are compiled by subject area; most planners will wish to review the series: "Urban and Regional Technology and Development." A bi-weekly index and an annual index of NTIS reports, for the full range of subjects, is published under the title, "Government Reports Annual Index."

**NewsBank Index.** New Canaan, Conn.: NewsBank, Inc.

# Index